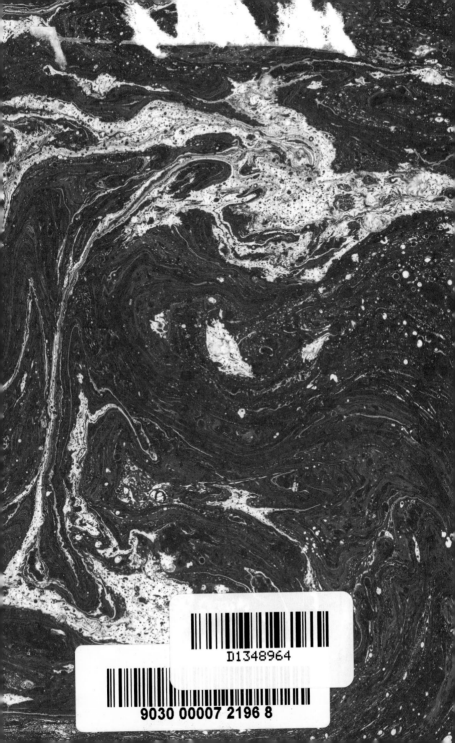

This Too Shall Pass

Praise for *Grief Works*:

'A profoundly moving book by an extraordinary storyteller – Samuel describes her patients' stories of loss with great sensitivity and fascinating psychological insight . . . Essential' Helen Fielding, bestselling author of *Bridget Jones's Diary*

'A wonderfully important and transforming book – lucid, consoling and wise' William Boyd, bestselling author of *Sweet Caress*

'Brilliant' Mariella Frostrup

'What an amazing book! Intelligent, empathetic, modest, funny, and learned – an amazing feat' Rabbi Julia Neuberger

'Samuel turns out to be a remarkable writer. What is impressive is that such harrowing material should result in such a readable book' *Oldie*

'Fascinating. A wise and compassionate book full of insight and understanding . . . I am so glad this book exists' Cathy Rentzenbrink, author of *The Last Act of Love*

'Through the inspirational stories of those many people she has helped . . . Julia Samuel dissipates fear and demonstrates the extraordinary resilience of humankind' Juliet Nicolson, author of *A House Full of Daughters*

'The stories of Julia's clients are set out with such eloquence, sensitivity and insight and I learned something from each one of them . . . I don't often read a book which offers such direct and generous support' Helen Dunmore, author of *Birdcage Walk*

'This book is self-help at its most philosophical, practical and profound . . . Anyone who has every struggled with the obscure, muddled, vulnerable, uncertain, fearful, elemental process of bereavement, or facing their own mortality, should find this book of help' Helen Davies, *Sunday Times*

This Too Shall Pass

Stories of Change, Crisis and Hopeful Beginnings

JULIA SAMUEL

PENGUIN LIFE

AN IMPRINT OF

PENGUIN BOOKS

PENGUIN LIFE

UK | USA | Canada | Ireland | Australia
India | New Zealand | South Africa

Penguin Life is part of the Penguin Random House group of companies
whose addresses can be found at global.penguinrandomhouse.com.

First published 2020
003

Set in 11/13 pt Bembo Book MT Std
Typeset by Jouve (UK), Milton Keynes
Printed and bound in Great Britain by Clays Ltd, Elcograf S.p.A.

A CIP catalogue record for this book is available from the British Library

ISBN: 978–0–241–34886–4

www.greenpenguin.co.uk

MIX
Paper from
responsible sources
FSC® C018179

Penguin Random House is committed to a
sustainable future for our business, our readers
and our planet. This book is made from Forest
Stewardship Council® certified paper.

This book is dedicated to Michael, Natasha, Emily,
Sophie and Benjamin with all my love, always

'Everything flows and nothing abides, everything gives
way and nothing stays fixed.'
Heraclitus

An early English citation of 'this too shall pass' appears in 1848:

When an Eastern sage was desired by his sultan to inscribe on a
ring the sentiment which, amidst the perpetual change of human
affairs, was most descriptive of their real tendency, he engraved
on it the words: — 'And this, too, shall pass away.'

Contents

Introduction

I remember lying in bed on my tenth birthday when, having reached the inexorable heights of double digits, adulthood seemed tantalizingly close. I imagined that my life would be exactly as my mother's: I would meet a man, fall in love, marry, have children and instantly be grown up. It seemed straightforward. It would just happen. On the face of it, that is how my life has unfolded. I have been unusually lucky. But it doesn't account for the losses, the living losses that forced me to change internally to adapt to them, the consequent transitions I have made: the five different marriages I've had (all with the same man), the multiple relationships I have had with each of my children, the distress and powerlessness in the face of ill-health, for me and those I love, all the endings and beginnings, my unsuccessful enterprises with their striving and failing. Even the wins were never quite what I imagined and required adjustment. There is no perfect way to live a life. Life is change. We know this in theory, but the experience of it is often more complex than we expect, and we are left fearful, even paralysed. Then we assume we must be doing it wrong.

Change is an active process that demands commitment and endurance, and requires us to look at uncomfortable truths. We underestimate how *much* we will change over even the next ten years, let alone our lifetime. If we truly thought about the impact of some of the choices we made, would we still make them? Probably not. Unfortunately, change is for the bad as well as the good. When life sucks, we say, 'This too shall pass,' and hopefully it does – but here's the hitch: when life is good, it, too, inevitably, will pass. The difficult truth we must face is that only death stops life changing.

One thing is certain: we need to adapt in order to grow through that change. The research is robust: those who try to remain rigidly the same are more likely to suffer when change is forced on them; it will limit their capacity for joy in life and even success. This calls for courage. Everybody wants to avoid discomfort and nobody welcomes the heartache change can bring. Time and again, I have witnessed the limitless creative ways in which we anaesthetize pain, but trying to avoid unhappiness means it will last longer. Pain is the agent of change: if we build walls around it, it remains untouched and alive inside us, slowly contaminating our other feelings. It is in the movement between the poles of the past and the future that we adapt. Our innate drive to get on is profoundly powerful, yet we need to slow down, to give ourselves space between our old and new selves. In therapy, we call this a 'fertile void', a time of not knowing, a neutral zone of uncertainty that is uncomfortable or even crazy-making. When we block it, the same problems may reoccur in every phase of life. If we accept the pain of change, and learn how to adapt, we will have the energy and confidence to take the next step.

Since Darwin developed his theory of natural selection, we have understood that we are wired to adapt. At its most extreme this means we change or we die. I have written this book to examine that process of change for people through the course of a life. The phases of life that we usually find most difficult are those that bring with them fear and uncertainty: emerging into adulthood from university, settling down and having children, entering the menopause in middle age, retiring and facing old age with its accompanying health issues. I have explored the particular experiences of individuals who are going through those transitions while in therapy with me. The stories of my clients show that even the most robust people can find change difficult. The thread that connects them, whatever their age or circumstance, is that each person had to work on themselves actively to understand their unique response to change, and develop the necessary coping mechanisms. But if change is part of the natural order of things, why do so many of us feel ill-equipped to deal with it?

I would like *This Too Shall Pass* to help answer that question and give you an insight into your own experience. I believe we learn best through understanding each other, and the unvarnished stories of those in therapy are a particularly powerful resource. Perhaps a young person who is struggling to find a job will be inspired by how Caz, aged twenty-four, overcame his self-doubt, even crisis, when he left university. Wande's tale of becoming the mother she wanted to be shows how small steps can have transformational outcomes. These are not tidy stories of perfectly curated lives. I want to tell the truth of how difficult life is, to highlight the distress and sadness as well as the glorious moments of joy, and for you to see how different people found ways of navigating the tough times, surviving and even thriving through the simple act of talking and being heard.

Societal changes have had profound implications for our own experience. In the last fifty years there have been seismic shifts in the West in every aspect of life, and now people have to cope with more change than ever before. The past is no longer a reliable predictor of the future, and the twenty-first century is more fluid: all of the old certainties – age, gender, sexuality – are being questioned and boundaries broken. It seems we live in a culture of limitless choice. Most of these changes may be positive, but life is now infinitely more complex. These factors, and the overwhelming number of choices we face, have heightened the possibility of more existential crises.

Among other things, social change means the institutions of religion and marriage are not fixed norms. This raises big questions about fidelity. We may still believe in marriage as an ideal, but the prospect of a hundred-year life raises fundamental questions about how a single relationship can last many decades. Marriage was, after all, an institution created when the average life span was forty years. Medicine has extended our life expectancy, which is positive if we remain healthy, but a longer life costs more and, with technology, this has wrought huge changes in the work environment.

The predictable three-stage life – education, career, retirement – has been dismantled. Our career is likely to have many stages and phases, which bring both thrilling possibilities and opportunities – but also potentially frightening uncertainties.

In this book I have chosen five different themes, Family, Love, Work, Health and Identity, because they represent to me the five central aspects that make up our lives. We cannot dismiss or let one aspect fail long term without it being detrimental to the whole. Happiness comes when there is harmony overall. There are overlapping themes within every section (for example, KT's main focus was identity, but their first-love relationship was central to our work together). But the most important theme throughout the whole book is Relationships.

'A good life is built with good relationships.'* How we construct them is the foundation of everything else. Again and again, through my research and work with my clients, I see we cannot do it alone, whatever life stage we have reached. People need people, and the quality of those relationships is what matters most to us when we look back at our lives. Ultimately our wellbeing and health are predicated on being connected and close to the people we love most, and that they stay healthy and alive for as long as possible – which includes ourselves.

I hope this book will help inform and normalize what is often frightening about the different phases of life. If we have the courage to face our difficulties with self-compassion, learn to know ourselves rather than distract ourselves, then change will bring growth. With it comes the liberating humility of being grateful in the present while having hope for a positive future. We keep growing throughout our lives. We are in a process of becoming: it is not a place at which we arrive, although if we know the direction in which we are headed, we are more likely to thrive. To live a life that has meaning, a reason for being and a sense of belonging. A life in which we love and are loved.

* Waldinger, R. (2017), *75-year Harvard Study of Happiness*, https://harvard.edu

The Process of Change in Life

'Life is a series of natural and spontaneous changes. Don't resist
them – that only creates sorrow. Let reality be reality. Let things
flow naturally forward in whatever way they like.'

Lao Tzu

In popular culture, change we choose has a positive reputation. It
brings with it the sheen of newness and excitement. Big life events,
such as the birth of a child, usually conjure picture-perfect images
and gasps of delight. Even retirement is seen as freedom: a permanent
holiday. Ageing, on the other hand, has a bad reputation. Every other
phase of life is seen as a development but ageing comes with the
image of the slippery slope to death. Naturally we do what we can to
avoid it, anti-ageing being the operative word. The truth is that
change on all fronts requires work. We need to work at actively
adapting, which can be straightforward but also challenging.
Although we want it to be quick, it can take time to catch up emotionally with an external event: we cannot force our feelings to go at
the same speed as our removal van, new job, new role, new status.

We are brought up thinking life is an upward journey, a stair-
way to a better place, each step higher than the last. But the reality
is far less certain: there are ups and downs, and the only certainty
that exists is that there will be change.

Life is a set of alternating phases, a period of change followed
by a period of stability, then another change. Research shows we
tend to take stock and think about change every seven to ten years
(yes, the seven-year itch is a thing), and the process of change can
take up to a year to be integrated into our life. Sometimes the
changes feel like success, at others failure, but the key is to learn

from them. It is well researched that the more we allow ourselves to learn and expand in response to life changes the more likely we are to thrive. It is worth noting that, as much as the change we face may be unknown, we will carry all of the important aspects of the past with us. As my client Maria said, 'I've folded a lot of my past pain into my heart.' We never lose where or who we've been, which can be a source of potency and growth.

Change isn't linear, and we all carry invisible baggage, but we also go through a cycle when we make the decision for change.

Thinking about Change

Any change begins with an assessment. We start with thinking about it: we have a vision of what it might be like, then seek out information to help us evaluate how it will affect us. This can be a quick process or it can take a long time. It can halt before the cycle is complete because the next step requires action. We need to make the decision, which in itself requires a level of trust and self-belief.

Even change we choose, like committing to a partner, requires an emotional adjustment. We may know we want to marry the person we love, but our commitment to them inevitably means saying no to other fabulous imagined partners, which can feel difficult. Sometimes this process will happen without disturbing us, but change rarely sneaks through that easily. Anxiety often accompanies new beginnings: the not-knowing can scare us. Anxiety is a form of energy that forces us to adjust, informing us we have to shift our role, behaviour or view. We need to shed the old way of being, like reptiles shed their skin, for a new way of being to grow.

Resisting Change

Inevitably change we don't want is harder to deal with, such as divorce or losing our job. Dramatic external events can trigger a psychological crisis, but a breakdown can ultimately be a break-through. Humans crave safety, and we are reluctant to give up the familiarity of the past: it feels less scary than the unknown. When a new experience happens, such as losing a job, it can reignite old – but powerful – feelings. One of my clients, Cindy, lost her job and found that she had never examined her beliefs about herself, such as 'I'm a loser', which might have led her to sabotage the change that was needed. The most common ways we resist change are by being too busy or too terrified to engage.

Change tests our beliefs and forces us to question what we once took for granted. It is important to allow these beliefs to evolve while holding on to our core beliefs, to let ourselves learn from our new experience. And sometimes we have to fail so that we can move forward. Some of us will choose unhappiness over the pain of uncertainty. But when facing disruption, it can also be liberating to remind ourselves that we have no control over the key things in life that matter most to us: birth and death, the behaviour and feelings of the people around us. We can influence them, but mentally fighting to have absolute control is futile.

What Disruption Feels Like

The external event that may have prompted the change is often easy to describe, but it may be harder to make sense of how it feels. Our initial reaction may be a sensation, but over time we tend to become aware that the sensation transforms into distinct thoughts. Sometimes they remain unclear, but as we come to understand our thoughts, it can feel like growth.

We all have a natural coping mechanism when change hits us, which we learn in childhood. It is a habitual response – perhaps we switch off, become overwhelmed or, if we're among the fortunate few, immediately absorb and deal with change. We need to understand what our response is so that we can learn to be more flexible.

In most of my clients I see, as Carl Rogers observed, who was an American psychologist and one of the founders of the humanistic approach, a paradoxical facet to change: the more we can accept the aspects of change we find unacceptable, the more likely it is that the change will occur. So, when we stop fighting against it, the more likely it is that we can embrace it.

Accepting change takes time, often much longer than anyone wants or allows. In the movement between where we were and where we're heading, we need to allow space, time to just be, a time for not knowing: the 'fertile void'. As human beings, not machines, we can't switch ourselves off and on. We need time to withdraw, reflect and restore before we jump in again. We move forward with trepidation, exploring and testing, perhaps taking action, doing things differently, and then a natural stepping back and evaluating. Over time, the new landscape becomes familiar and is less scary.

Often we adapt to change by making tiny adjustments. As in all psychological theories, nothing is certain, in some cases a sudden shift can liberate and transform someone. The different types of change will have different degrees of impact, depending on how big the change is. Aspects that support a successful change vary, and will depend on economic security, emotional resilience and health. Our relationship with family, friends and colleagues, allowing them to support us, is fundamental to how we manage the discomfort of this process. The love of family and friends can help hold us steady when we're shaken.

Hope

A key factor in how we manage change. If we have no hope of light at the end of this tunnel, it is extremely difficult to bear the pain and distress of the process. We are more likely to have hope if, in our experience, our hopes have been realized. If, however, our hopes have been regularly dashed, it is likely the story we tell ourselves is negative, often using absolutes like 'never' and 'always'.

Then we will find it hard to trust that this time we will get through it. We need hope to sustain us, and without it we are unlikely even to attempt the change.

We would like to give ourselves the amount of hope that will be matched by the outcome of our dream. Unfortunately we can't control hope, and we can't protect ourselves from the pain of loss, should our dreams fail by having less hope in the beginning.

From the research of the American psychologist Charles Snyder in understanding how hope operates, it is helpful to recognize it is not just an emotion, although emotions support it. Hope is about how we think. It has three parts: the capacity to set realistic goals, the ability to work out how to achieve them, including the adaptability for a backup plan, and finally self-belief.

Integration and Meaning

The final phase of the process of change is tentative acceptance, which comes with a greater sense of calm. Over time we may realize, often with a start, that we are no longer thinking about the change: it doesn't preoccupy us as it did. This augurs true acceptance – our new normal. An important addendum is to explore what this change means to us, learning from the experience and making sense of our life now. Through discussion and reflection the final piece of the puzzle, integration into our post-transition world, falls into place. Now we start to let go of the past, without forgetting it remains part of us but remembering that it no longer holds such power. It is an ending that marks a beginning: the moment at which we confront the true nature of change. It brings with it a new energy, at times even a sense of being reborn, as we step into our renewed life.

The image for the transition cycle on the next page shows the shift in our feelings in the process of change. The initial excitement is often followed by confusion and depression. It takes time to explore and understand this change to build up to new confidence and recovery.

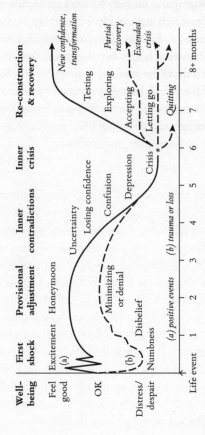

The transition cycle – a template for human responses to change (Williams, 1999)

Reflections

In the reflections at the end of each theme, I have given relevant statistics and research. Statistics give a broader perspective, letting us know that, as abnormal as we may feel, we are by no means alone. I have focused the research and guidance in response to my particular clients' experiences to expand our knowledge from the personal to the universal. Shelves of books have been written on each topic, but I have chosen to show the wisdom of specialists in the field who reflect my view of the world. Inevitably it is a subjective and limited view, which has been shaped by my experiences as an imperfect woman, wife, mother and daughter. For further exploration it might be useful to go to Sources, pages 303–21.

Family Relationships

'What you leave behind is not what is engraved in stone monuments,
but what is woven into the lives of others.'

Pericles

Leena

Mother of the Bride

Leena was angry. She knew she should be happy that her daughter, Anita, was engaged to be married. She liked her prospective son-in-law well enough, but she was fighting with her daughter. As she spoke she twisted her watch distractedly, anger written on her face. Her eyes looked as if they were searching for a target; I suspected it would be me. I guessed beneath her anger was a pulsating hurt, which I would need to understand, and keep in mind now, to maintain my empathy for her.

I acknowledged the differences between us, particularly with regard to our contrasting attitude to family. I was a white, non-practising Christian, who held Western beliefs – we tend to be more individualistic, valuing self-reliance and independence. An Indian Hindu, Leena had a collectivistic view, valuing community dependence and authority. I'd understood duty was her abiding attitude. It wasn't for her to question; it was her duty as a daughter, wife and mother to follow the code set by generations. Naturally I was biased: she might at times have to set me right. From the authoritarian manner in which Leena spoke to me, I was left in no doubt that she was used to getting her own way and was not interested in a different viewpoint.

She would happily put me right. I asked her to tell me a little about herself.

She had come to England from India thirty-five years ago to marry Devang, a member of a wealthy, property-owning family. As it was an arranged marriage, Leena had not met him prior to her engagement, which she stated with weight, as if it demonstrated her obedience at that age, tipping her chin forward as she spoke, her perfectly coiffed hair bouncing in agreement. Leena had built a good life in the UK: she was proud of her family, and happily married, with one son and two daughters. Anita was their younger daughter, a solicitor, and their last child to marry. Leena now worked in the family business, in charge of the interiors, and oversaw their philanthropic work.

Devang had suggested she see me because he didn't know how to resolve her dispute with Anita. As Leena spoke, the heat of her anger reverberated in her body, a shield of rage that pushed everyone away: the filter through which each thought was processed and influenced. I felt it was burning her inside, shutting down every other feeling, blocking tenderness and warmth. As she described her conflict with Anita, it was as if she was obsessively building the case against her in her mind to knock her out. Like building a battalion with which to attack her. Her rage sought action, which she couldn't take: it was stuck in her body. I needed to let her express it fully.

I didn't want to stoke her anger by colluding with her and adding outrage I didn't feel to hers. I wanted to let her know I had heard her feelings, reflecting her view and her fury, as accurately as I could, and that I could see how distressed she was. Anger cannot be argued away: that increases it. It needs to be listened to, and understood, to reduce its force.

At the heart of Leena and Anita's argument was love, separation and power. It played out over the kind of wedding they each envisaged. Leena wanted a full-length traditional Hindu wedding, with all their family and friends present. Anita wanted a simpler wedding, with fewer ornate ceremonies, and only the friends and family she knew. The further question as to whether they have a

ceremony in India, too, as was traditional, hadn't been addressed
by either woman: they knew it would cause further conflict.

Over a number of weeks, in many different ways, Leena said
the same thing. She believed her daughter's selfishness, arrogance
and single-mindedness were abhorrent. Leena felt she had learned
to adapt to a more Western culture, but she held core beliefs that
were central to her, particularly in line with the more traditional
idea of the Indian mother. I questioned Leena: did she feel guilty
that at some level her daughter was diluting their Indian heritage
or being disloyal to their Indian identity?

I caught a glimpse of the scared child doing wrong as she nodded
and spoke of her own mother's pride and trust in her, which she did
not want to betray. Anita's fight for her wishes, against the family
view, not only felt wrong but disturbed her. It threatened her sense
of unity as a family. For Leena, criticizing her daughter, telling her
what was right and wrong, was a way of loving her: 'Who else is
going to care?' Leena added. 'In India there is no sense of personal
space, personal decisions, personal views. We hold close together
to survive. Everybody knows what everybody is doing, and their
opinion is included. We don't have separate views, or closed doors.'
I could see the disturbance in her eyes as she described the look of
contempt Anita had given her at their last meeting, following
Leena's vehement argument for a traditional wedding. It had stung.
How dare her daughter disrespect her in that way? Leena had
woken up ruminating and, throughout the day, she had fights and
confrontations with her daughter in her mind. When I commented
gently that it must be isolating and exhausting, she nodded.

I felt warmth towards Leena as I stepped inside her world, feeling
that her love for Anita was matched by the pain of Anita's rejection.
I began to wonder whether Leena's forcefulness covered up earlier
versions of herself that were more vulnerable. I described to her the
different sources of her rage that were informed by her experiences,
and how they were profoundly challenged by Anita. There was the
memory of herself as a child, having been dominated by a strong
mother and grandmother, whom she had loved deeply but had been

afraid of, receiving sharp slaps if she wasn't totally obedient. Leena came from a long line of strong women, but those women had for centuries been subservient to men and the requirements of duty. There was herself as the fearful young woman coming to a strange country, entering the life of a family she'd never met, and remembering her respect for their rules. Neither of her other two children had brought up these feelings in her. Their weddings had been as she wanted – uncomplicated. Two families joining together was everyone's business, not only the couple's choice.

I could see she felt shocked that Anita, who had been the child she was closest to, given a life of privilege, was adamantly refusing to do as she was asked. It felt such a small request in comparison to her own upbringing. Anita's stubbornness baffled her. Leena believed that as Anita's mother she had earned her daughter's compliance, from a position of absolute authority. But vulnerability, too, lay beneath this, the question of her own failure as a mother: what had she done, what had she missed, that meant she had such a daughter?

Leena's relationship with Anita was deteriorating. They'd had a fight in the kitchen, when Leena had commented on her new haircut. I could tell by the tone she used when repeating the incident that her seemingly innocuous words – 'I see you have a new haircut' – had been loaded with criticism. Anita had banged down her mug, looked at her with cold disgust, said, 'How dare you?' and stormed out. Leena felt that look had conveyed many unspoken words: 'Who are you? I don't even know you. I certainly don't like you.'

Anita had refused to speak to her mother since, not replying to texts or calls. This had shaken Leena. As she told me, I could see more of the wound that lay beneath her anger and confusion. I felt the hit of Anita's verbal punch in my stomach. Over the next weeks of therapy sessions it felt as if a battle was taking place inside Leena – she woke in tears most mornings, but then would attack the day, keeping frantically busy with endless meetings and site visits, numbing her pain with activity.

I sensed, although Leena didn't voice it, the longing she felt to be close to her daughter. Yet the pain she felt, which was expressed as righteous fury, came from the fear that she might have lost Anita. I could feel her worrying about the future and worked hard to find out what she imagined. I came up against subtle resistance: whatever I said, there was a nod but no emotional movement. I realized she didn't want to feel the pain of the void left by the loss of her youngest child: she wanted to skip to the 'next' thing, where she was right and happy again. But she had no emotional energy to do that, because she was invested in holding on tight.

I wondered whether the more Western approach, with the child becoming an adult, finally leaving home and being independent, would help her understand. As I spoke, Leena turned away. I wished I could reach her – I felt for her as a woman and a mother, and wanted to show I knew how hard it is to let go of our children. A new beginning cannot start without an ending: we have to go through the phase between, to experience the chaos and turbulence of not knowing. My strongly held Western perspective is that, as parents, we must learn to shift our position, take a back seat, let our children make their decisions for their lives, let them actively leave us, which frees them to choose to come back. If only she could change how she looked at Anita, it would enable Anita to change. The relationships would recalibrate, yes, but remain loving.

Over the next weeks, I felt we needed to bring into focus the broader relationship Leena had with Anita. It had been lost in the polarization of their wedding battle. I suggested Leena show me photographs of Anita as a child. She lit up at the idea – she loved those photographs. When she brought them in, I could see Anita tucked into her shoulder as a newborn baby, that new-mother bliss in Leena's face, luxuriating in loving her last child, pouring time and attention into her, enjoying her in a way she hadn't been able to with her first two children. As she spoke, slowly sifting through the photos, I could almost smell the deep bond of a mother and her newborn, her skin pressed to soft baby skin. Other photographs of holidays and birthdays showed a happy child, funny and outgoing, who looked very like her mother – making faces, dancing. Even her adolescence had been relatively calm. This meant, to me, that they had not worked through many of the conflicts that allow the necessary separation between adult child and parent. I also wondered how much Anita had hidden from her mother to be, as Leena had voiced, 'the traditional perfect daughter' of her mother's dreams, while living life as a Westernized young woman.

I looked up from the photographs and clarified what I saw: Leena's intense love for Anita. I found a way to say that love was interchangeable in Leena's mind with control. Anita had opposed her, not to hurt her but with the intention of being an adult, soon-to-be wife. Anita's identity as a wife and adult was as much shaped by her Western upbringing as her Indian roots. She wanted to hold both. It seemed to me that, unconsciously, Leena viewed Anita's marriage as a threat to their bond, and was trying to regain control of their close connection through taking charge of the wedding. She had conflated love with obedience: if Anita didn't obey her, she didn't love her.

As I spoke, Leena froze. She looked very young and stricken. I described to her what I could see, and commented that she wasn't breathing. Leena took a big breath, then short shallow ones, as she held tight. She couldn't quite bear to let herself know her greatest fear. Her silence conveyed her uncertainty, a shift away from her position of being right. She moved around in her chair, crossing and uncrossing her legs, as if part of her could take in the push and pull of holding on and letting go, and another part couldn't . . . quite. I told her that I wasn't trying to force her in a particular direction: I understood the complexity of her dilemma. I hoped that, by bringing their whole relationship into her awareness, perhaps Leena had a clearer insight into what was going on. Leena nodded. The process of change, as uncomfortable as it was, had begun.

At a family dinner to celebrate Leena's son's birthday, Anita had not said a word to her but had been affectionate and warm with the rest of the family, in particular her father. Their closeness versus Leena's distance from Anita had created an atmosphere that pervaded the room. I felt Leena's jealousy and her rage. I asked

Leena what she felt in her body. She put a hand to her chest: it felt tight. As she breathed into it, she made a sound, animal-like, quiet but distressed. I asked her to stay with it. Tears came down her face, tears that signalled a loosening of her rigid grip.

Over the next weeks Leena's body was in revolt. She had headaches and tummy aches, and her back hurt. I talked to her about listening to her body, asking her what she thought it might be telling her. I suggested she take up exercise to release the tension, and develop habits to help calm herself. This was not natural to Leena, who knew how to overcome difficulty with grit and determination but had no idea about self-care. Duty was her abiding rule, not meeting or even knowing her own needs. Reluctantly she began to go to a yoga class, and significantly she started to write, which became an outlet for her whirring furious mind. She surprised herself with what came out of her pen, quoting her journal: 'I was never asked what I needed, felt, thought or wanted. I never argued or made demands on my mother.'

This led us to explore her silence as a child and a young woman. It had been passed down for perhaps twenty generations from mother to daughter, and to a great extent from her to Anita. It might have gone unchallenged if she hadn't come to the UK, but now Anita had different expectations. It was at the heart of their difficulty: Leena had no way to understand the emotional cost to herself of that silence. Yet again she was not being listened to, or being allowed to make a decision. Even when it was her time as a mother to influence her daughter, she was not being heard. She felt as if she had been oppressed and now she was still being oppressed, but by the younger generation. Our work was to help her develop a fuller picture of the different emotions, often conflicting, that were going on inside her.

I asked her to tell me what her husband and other family members thought. She sighed, twisted her watch. They wanted the disagreement to end. Her husband looked at her as if she was a mad woman. She felt alienated from them all. Being 'right', I said, could be lonely and make you angry. Finally, I felt I could tell her that I suspected a primitive physical yowling lay beneath her anger. It overrode her thinking. She didn't want to let her daughter go – her last child. Her baby. It was as if she was mourning the ideal daughter she wanted and couldn't quite come to terms with the daughter she had, who wanted to be allowed to shift the centre of her world from her mother to her husband. I empathized with the strength of her feelings and how they must scare her. How she wanted to punish, almost crush, the child she had loved and protected most in the world through the hurt of losing her. Yet acting out her anger was harming them both.

Leena pulled her tailored jacket across her chest, as if armouring herself against my words, but she was silent, taking them in. Or at least some of them.

After a long five minutes, she asked me quietly what she should do. I responded equally quietly. It wasn't so much what she should do but what she could allow in herself. Could she allow herself to want to hold on to her daughter, and allow her daughter some independence? Could she let Anita be the child she was rather than the child Leena had imagined she should be? I acknowledged how confusing it was, since Anita was bi-cultural, and was, in her own way, negotiating how she could live an Indian and a British life.

Leena stamped her foot, with childlike frustration. She pressed her hands against her ears, as if her head was about to burst. I asked her to close her eyes, and breathe, then to hold her body very tight, squeezing every muscle for a few minutes, then release and let go. I followed with a relaxation exercise and could see the calm wash through her body. Now wasn't the time for words: it was time to let her system unwind. She left silently, allowing me to give her a hug, her large frame shaky as I held her.

I learned the following week that Leena had gone from our session and called Devang out of a meeting. She had asked him to come home early to her. A first. She needed him to hold her. She breathed in the scent of his peppery hair, felt the warmth of his arms. The pressure in her chest eased and she felt safety running through her veins. He listened as her tirade of loss and sadness, rage and hurt flowed out of her into his increasingly damp shoulder. She'd cried for a long time, sobbing noisily. He had been kind, and he had held her. He had made her a cup of tea. She was surprised by how much calmer she felt. They agreed they needed to see Anita together: they needed to find a way forward.

Leena looked at me with a pride and warmth in her eyes that I hadn't seen before. The process between one phase of life and another can be achingly long, and sometimes it is wonderfully simple. In this case there was a real shift in Leena: her husband's support and love enabled her to picture a future where they were a close family, but she didn't have to maintain such a tight grip. They had met with Anita and agreed a compromise for the wedding. Anita was still wary of her mother, there was tension between them, but they had leaped the largest hurdle and had a plan to go forward. Leena loved a plan.

I felt the release of tension in my body. I told Leena that the power parents have to influence the wellbeing of their adult children is often underestimated. The relationship needs to be reconfigured, for sure, and the power balance recalibrated, but fundamentally the child is always a child with their parents. I wanted Leena to know that she could use her power collaboratively with Anita. She didn't have to have power over her. I talked about the importance of argument, which, when voiced, can be better than simmering disagreements. There are ways to have arguments that do battle over views but don't attack those engaged in them. Closeness can follow an honest disagreement, maybe allowing time for each party to feel less raw. It is never the argument that truly matters but the capacity to repair.

I touched on the symbolic meaning of her daughter's marriage. It was psychologically for Leena the symbol of her own physical decline, when she had to relinquish her unconscious youthful dream of immortality – her repair came through recognizing the healing power of generational continuity, perhaps even her future grandchildren, in whom the youth and beauty would reside.

Leena didn't need to see me any more: she had allowed herself to change and felt our work was done. I very much hoped it was and wished her well.

Lucas

Newborn, New Dad

Lucas contacted me through an online search, asking me if I would see him to help him adjust to the birth, six months previously, of his son Lee. He told me in the email that life was calming down after the initial stress of a newborn. He wanted to take time to focus on how he felt, and on his central question: 'What kind of father am I?'

A few weeks later, when he walked into my room, he grinned broadly, his green eyes twinkling as he sat down. He was small but strong. He looked around the room, checked it out and nodded, not necessarily approvingly but getting his bearings as to where he was. I could feel him centring himself. On hearing his accent, I made the infuriating mistake of assuming he was American, and was told firmly that, no, he was Canadian, from Toronto.

Lucas lived in London as a freelance artist working for media campaigns, but that wasn't his choice. His voice dropped, he frowned and pushed his hand up against his jaw, against the discomfort of his words. He was selling his creative soul to the commercial sector because he hadn't as yet (the 'as yet' was very important) been able to establish himself securely as an artist to earn a decent living. His wife, Heather, a Chinese Canadian, was seven years older than Lucas. Aged forty-six, she worked as an executive in the pharmaceutical industry. It meant long hours and a lot of travel. She earned considerably more than her husband.

I soon realized how different this process would be from my usual therapy work. Lucas had high energy and a curiosity that drove the sessions. In adapting to being a father, he wanted to raise his awareness of all aspects of himself; he was distressed, maybe 'shaken' is a better word, but he wasn't in pain. Pain isn't the only agent of change. Lucas seemed confident. This was going to be a robust exchange, which was interesting for me.

Lucas told me his story to give me context. He had already had therapy, and he wanted to use his childhood as the reverse map of how he'd bring up Lee but didn't want to delve too deeply – he'd done that. His starting position was, and this was said with emphatic certainty, that life was a constant flux of change. 'Change happens, but rarely in a straight line.' He said he was quoting Barack Obama, perhaps not the exact words the President spoke. I nodded vigorously.

Lucas had been brought up with what he felt was a deluded view, that the world worked by a fixed set of rules, and if they were followed – doing the prescribed job, dressing in a particular way, going to the right school – success would follow. As a child he'd been confused by this narrative, but now saw it as an attitude that had brought him real unhappiness. When he told me, 'It was gaslighting,' I sat up. That is a strong term: I understood it to mean that because his parents hadn't told him the truth, he felt as if they had been psychologically manipulating him, which was crazy-making.

I could see humour was his default response, but beneath it I sensed the embers of anger, which had been slowly scorching him for years. The biggest lie was more significant: his mother was a lesbian. She had known it for a long time, but it terrified her, and she'd sublimated her sexuality until Lucas was nineteen, when she finally came out and divorced his father. As he spoke his voice faltered. He had some sympathy for her difficulty – to be a lesbian had been unacceptable then – but he was hurt: he hadn't been able to trust the people he loved and needed most. The lies he'd been told, the mask his parents had put on, to paint a picture of a 'happy family' had caused it to collapse in on itself. In the process it robbed Lucas of his childhood story, and left a void in him: he couldn't be sure of what was real and what was fake.

Understandably, Lucas felt enormously protective of his son and this pulsated through him. He feared his story or, even worse, his pain would unconsciously transfer to Lee. He knew they were separate beings, but he had seen history repeat itself too often. I felt touched by his energy to be the parent he hadn't had and warmed by thinking how fortunate Lee was to have a dad like him. I also felt a little old: I knew that as part of the process he would have to forgive himself when he failed to be the perfect parent, as he inevitably would. We need to be, as Donald Winnicott, the British pioneer of child development, said, 'a good enough parent'. But at least he would fail differently from his parents.

Lucas had described his wife as 'clever, beautiful and really, really fun'. Heather came from a family of business people who had moved to Toronto from Hong Kong in the early 1990s. A mutual friend had often talked about her, and tried to introduce them, but Heather's work had got in the way. When he had finally met her, briefly at a gallery, he had felt a spark – 'She was kind of wonderful.' He rang her the next day and left a voice message saying how much he liked her, how incredibly pretty and smart she was, and he wanted to take her out. He smiled at the memory of how uncool he'd been. She'd rung her best friend for advice as to whether or not she should accept Lucas's invitation, and her friend had been all for it, confident he was 'the one'.

They'd had a terrible first date. Lucas had taken her to what he thought was a cool bar, but it was crowded and noisy, which made him anxious and awkward. Heather had been relaxed and, on their many subsequent dates, they fell in love. She was defiantly independent. She wanted his love, their intimacy and sex, but she also wanted the freedom her career brought. He adored her brilliance, her earthiness, their shared humour, their lovemaking and her laugh, and wanted their lives to be more entwined. They had fought this battle through their courtship. Money was also a flashpoint: she believed in his work as an artist but wanted him to earn more money.

They married two years later. He wanted me to know how bad the fights had been, for I had responded to his happy ending and not the turmoil. I thought perhaps fighting and still loving each other at the beginning of a relationship was an interesting foundation from which to marry, rather than fairy-tale blissful love. They had seen each other's worst sides, found ways to repair after a fight, and many of the key questions – sex, money, power and communication – had been examined, cross-examined, and they'd come to terms, or not, with them, but knew the difficulties.

It had taken them five years to conceive Lee, with four rounds of IVF, which Heather, as the major breadwinner, had paid for. I acknowledged how stressful and difficult for the relationship the years of trying for a baby must have been, and Lucas agreed it had been awful – the endless terrible waiting, for treatment, for results, to get past risky dates. They'd both had massive meltdowns through the turmoil of the treatment, the psychological rollercoaster of needing to have hope, and those hopes being shattered when it failed, picking themselves up for each new attempt, plotting dates on their calendar for sex (just in case they could bypass IVF) and possible due dates, wrangling to gain control over nature.

We laughed at the having to have sex. He agreed it was a little mechanical at times but 'For men it's less mechanical when you're with someone you love, and is there such a thing as bad sex?' I countered that there certainly was, but I was glad he hadn't known it. I realized I only saw couples who were in despair while infertile, and perhaps Heather had found it more extreme, but in Lucas I sensed a quiet pragmatism. Or perhaps his coping mechanism was denial. I suggested to him that the awfulness of the procedures hadn't stayed with him, influencing his view of the future. Now they had Lee, Lucas's distress had fallen away, and he was left with both the happiness of being a dad and the added strength of having survived and succeeded. His sharp response, reiterating how the painful memory of it remained with him, startled me.

On reflection, I should have known, better than most, that a positive experience rarely wipes out painful ones. Even if, over time, there is a sense of growth. Old psychological injuries can lie hidden in the back of one's mind and spring to the front, with surprising force, when triggered by a new painful experience or an echo of the old. This led me to discuss with my supervisor the disconcerting truth that I had consistently missed Lucas's suffering, and had leaped to the hopeful. We explored together that perhaps Lucas's clean-cut look and his positive energy had blinded me to the reality that his appearance did not necessarily match his internal battles. His shiny green eyes did not express a shiny happy heart. How could they? He had done the therapeutic work in adjusting to his 'gaslit' childhood, but nothing would erase it. I wondered if there was also a surface Canadian sensibility of optimism, which further obfuscated my seeing his truth.

As thrilled as Heather was at becoming a mother, she had been thrown by it emotionally. The initial physical discomfort of stitches and sore nipples, combined with panic that she didn't know what to do, or how to do it, meant she felt permanently anxious. Heather needed her sleep to function, and its sporadic unpredictability had led to her obsessive preoccupation with it – to the extent that she couldn't sleep even when Lee was asleep for fear that he was about to wake up. The negative spiral ratcheted up, evidenced by a written log tracking the dismally few hours she'd slept. More sensitized by my supervision, I stopped myself telling Lucas that everything Heather felt was normal. It can be diminishing to have one's unique experience cast as 'everyday'.

Lucas had been on a high initially, holding Lee in his arms, crying with joy and relief. It had felt surreal, hard to believe that what he'd dreamed of and longed for, had feared would never happen, was a reality. But a few weeks later, he had felt overwhelmed. He was someone who resolved difficulty with actions, and although he could help by soothing Lee, changing his nappy and looking after Heather, he felt a restless vigilance, as if he was looking for danger. We agreed that we know we are actually in the process of adapting to change when we feel that edginess. Learning new ways of living is always uncomfortable to begin with. The necessity for Lucas and Heather to sublimate their own needs to meet Lee's wasn't something any antenatal class could have prepared them for. It was shocking on every level, and he realized as he spoke that he had by no means adjusted to this. He vehemently wanted me to know how much he loved Lee, how being with him was an absolute joy. He shook his head, trying to hold the love he felt for his child and the fear that his responsibility for that little being engendered in him. How hopeless he felt at times. He felt like the child.

I wondered who had been able to support them, in those first months, with that cocktail of intense emotions. Both sets of parents had come for a week each. Their presence had eased the isolation, and Heather's mum had helped with the nights, but that had come with its own demands: Lucas had had to see his parents separately, and his mum had needed looking after more than she was able to care for them. There was rivalry between both sets of parents: they had totted up who had spent most time with Lee. It seemed to come more from their insecurity than love of the baby. Lucas wanted to take back his words, worried he'd been mean: he knew the grandparents had suffered during his and Heather's period of infertility, too, and were thrilled at Lee's birth.

Lucas and Heather had been aware for the first time of the price they paid by living far from home, missing the old bonds of college friends and other family. Heather's National Childbirth Trust class was her closest network, but its WhatsApp group was a mixed blessing, sometimes giving helpful information and tips, but other messages were competitive – 'Who has the most perfect baby/is the most perfect parent?' – which triggered toxic feelings of inadequacy. Heather had told Lucas that finding the mother in her was a similar process to an actor using a prop, like a pair of red shoes, to step into a new role. She had to consciously work on and develop herself as a mother, try out ways of being, practise until it became second nature.

I saw Lucas looking out of the window. When he turned back, he said quite forcefully that he didn't want to use up the session looking back. It had been helpful to describe the beginning but he wanted to look at their present. Heather was about to start work again. It raised complex issues.

Over the next few sessions, Lucas discussed Heather going back to work and how it brought up the matter of money and the division of duties. He described it as the conversation they'd been having throughout their relationship, which they'd never resolved. He felt it was like a tennis ball: they batted it back and forth but it would hit the ground and, eventually, they would have a fight. Heather wanted him to make more money: she no longer wanted the responsibility of being the main breadwinner, and she wanted to be able to change her role at work, to put in shorter hours with less travel. She reiterated what she'd always said: she believed in him as an artist, she wanted him to pursue it, but also wanted him to earn more.

Lucas's dilemma was that he had tried to give up on the dream, doing other jobs that paid more, but he'd hated them and gone back to being an artist. Everybody said to him, 'Don't give up on your dream. It's who you are.' He felt it was indeed who he was but could see the difficulty. On down days he wondered if he was being delusional, a Peter Pan, and whether he needed to grow up. But then he shook his head: he wasn't ready yet. He had an inherent need to be an artist and felt an unwillingness to let it go. He looked down as he said, 'The poker pot is heavy – I'm deep into the hand, I can't turn back.' Lucas asserted, really speaking to himself, that for now he'd continue. He'd hold on to the fact that when it worked it was very lucrative, and he'd had some successes, good feedback, some sales that had kept his hope alive. The art business was fickle and mainly out of his control. He could control his work, though, and its quality, the one day each week he put aside for his own creative output and studio visits to let people see what he was doing. He'd put his energy and hope into that. Decision made. Until it came around again.

We went deeper into the relationship between him and Heather to unpick how it had changed since Lee was born. Lucas was energized: looking inwards, he realized how much the years of infertility had depleted their resources as a couple, and the extent to which the birth of Lee had enriched them. As he spoke, he was excited at being able to articulate that as parents they had found a way of aligning and working together which was new and felt like growth. We celebrated that, for a couple who had fought their way into marriage, they resolved parenting issues relatively simply. If they disagreed they fought better, quicker, to find a resolution. Lucas said, 'I want to hang a lantern on that point. This is really what I've uncovered here that I needed to work on, and we've done it.'

It cannot have been a coincidence that in the next weeks their sex life sprang back: they felt desire and connection at a depth that empowered them both. He said quietly, 'I didn't know how lonely I'd felt until we got that back. It had been such a huge part of us.' Lucas spread his hands in front of him, looking at this new landscape. As if he was making a promise, he said, 'This thing is for ever.' I could see that their commitment to the family unit had built a more stable bond between them. It is what couples hope for when they have children, but often the reverse happens: the chaos of a new baby can create bigger rifts in the pre-existing fault lines.

Lucas wanted to explore further how their parental roles influenced the power dynamic between them. As he laid out his role, he sat more upright in his chair, rubbing his hands along his thighs: 'I'm a very involved dad. We just about play the reverse gender roles. It is a modern marriage.' I learned that most of the duties had a natural division, although there was always the odd battle over whose turn it was to do what. On the whole Heather would have the idea, and he would implement it. When Lee was being weaned, Heather had been insistent that he had healthy food to an extreme degree, homemade bone broth, only organic, nothing processed. I sighed inwardly at the thought. Lucas had fought it originally, how much work it would be for him, since he was the one doing the shopping and cooking, but his chest expanded with pride as he described how much he loved doing it, the satisfaction he felt in giving Lee wholesome food. It was his equivalent of breastfeeding, enabling Lee to thrive. He was determined to do this for the rest of his life and grinned at his commitment.

I acknowledged that their shared enterprise in loving and caring for Lee had brought Heather home, and their relationship closer. But their arguments about money were continuing, and although we had already discussed it, it remained a risk factor.

Lucas sat silently. He pushed the palm of his hand against his jaw, his discomfort signal. 'Money is the boulder in the river.' He knew the conflict would intensify in the future 'because you can never fully figure it out'. He was right.

My experience has taught me that there is often one fight that runs through an entire marriage, usually about being loved enough, sex or money. Leaving them unresolved, with no movement from either side, means that over the years the arguments pile up. Each partner holds their position tighter, until it becomes a stand-off, each side going silent or attacking. Over time it builds an impenetrable wall that brooks no resolution. I asked Lucas if he could imagine changing.

He didn't speak. Then, as if continuing the fight with Heather behind her back, he told me even she would admit that since the birth of Lee his flexibility had been a boon, for he took up a lot of the slack. Lucas looked proud as he described their routine. He looked after Lee one day a week, when he'd take him out to do something creative in the morning; they'd joined a playgroup at the local library in the afternoons. He got Lee up, did the drop-off and collection at his crèche, and gave him tea, did the bath-and-bed routine. Heather tried to get home before Lee was asleep, and always did the nights: her time alone with him was very precious. Lucas had clearly argued his case: now wasn't the time for them to resolve the money problem; his job fitted their life extremely well.

I wondered what the internal adjustment of becoming a dad looked like. 'It is believing I have . . .' His leg was kicking, which told me more than his words. He looked up, tears in his eyes, and finally the word 'Lee' broke out of him, as the reality of having a live, healthy son began to sink in. He sobbed tears of relief, mixed with the tears of pain he hadn't cried during the years of white-knuckle ride on the baby-making rollercoaster of hope and heartbreak. We let the image of Lee hang between us as we smiled into each other's eyes. Daring to trust that he had a healthy son was a long, complex process. What else was there?

Lucas wanted to be a relaxed, fun dad, but a dark force presaged doom in the background of his mind. As he talked, he realized he feared that the moment he really believed all was well, the bad gods would come down and smite them. It shaped his behaviour: he hated friends picking Lee up for fear of infection, was hyper-vigilant when they took him out, and the idea of an aeroplane practically gave him a panic attack. We explored how he might hold both feelings, his fear and his trust, side by side, one not knocking out the other. It would help him make choices for Lee in the future.

Lucas had booked only a few sessions and soon we were on our final appointment. I wondered if it had been useful. He told me that, in talking and being heard, he had let himself know what he already instinctively knew but he could hold on to it now with more confidence. We talked and he reiterated that life was all about change. People tried to make sense for themselves as to why certain things happened at certain times, as if there was some overall design to life, which he didn't think was useful. What he did know was that having a family marked him as having fully stepped into adulthood. His own family was a significant new base from which to grow and change. Growing and changing he was certainly doing.

Wande

Being a Working Mother

Wande, short for Yewande, was thirty-eight years old and contacted me via a former client. She wondered if I'd heard of her, as she was a well-known stand-up comedian and scriptwriter with her own show. She grimaced, a kind of twisted half-smile, when I told her I didn't know her, biting her bottom lip, as if I had proved a point to her about her worth. Wande told me she was married, with an eight-year-old son. She wanted therapy because she felt she was struggling with authenticity issues: she was a performer with a public persona, then went home where she was a mother and wife. She couldn't quite make them fit together. Her head dropped and her voice faded when she said 'how to be a mother' was the part of her that carried most disquiet. She played nervously with her thick black hair, cornrow-braided and held in a loose ponytail, her legs crossed, while her green Dr Martens boots quietly kicked the air. She tipped her head back, and drank her tube of Smarties in gulps. I could see that her great beauty and success did not anchor her confidently. I had a sense of her scattering internally, fragments of herself blowing just beyond her reach.

I wanted to check how she felt about seeing a white therapist, given she was black. When we met our life stories met, too, our different histories informing and influencing us. I am a privileged white woman born into a white culture with its history of dominance over people of colour, and she a black woman, middle class and educated, yes, yet with a very different story. I asked her to tell me if I made assumptions that were wrong or if I inadvertently upset her. She agreed it was an important part of her identity and she was glad I had named it openly. She felt it might be useful if there were misunderstandings between us because this was a rare place we could actually unpick them – rather than hold the injury silently.

Wande felt she shouldn't be coming to see me: so many others were suffering more than her. She was 'lucky' but that luck was swiftly followed by her fear: 'I worry more about money than I ever have. I have this foreboding of scarcity and being unlucky – that it will all go wrong.' As her words tumbled out of her, a wiser, more understanding thought emerged, spoken in a quieter, reflective voice: 'Fundamentally I believe whether we are a cell-mate or fortunate, we are the same, and we can all feel insecure.'

I acknowledged that she seemed to hold at least two opposing views of herself, one rather more forgiving than the other, and I wondered if there were more. Her eyes widened, and there was a note of excitement in her voice as she told me about herself as a 'frozen daughter'. Her father had had a devastating car crash, which had taken many years of slow rehabilitation for him to recover from and had thrown the whole family into a state of suspended shock. In contrast to that, she felt alive and confident when performing on stage, although once she came off she would be lambasted by loneliness and fear – there were days when she couldn't get out of bed and was overwhelmed by crushing sadness and weariness.

The two versions of herself flew across her face as she spoke. I noted to her that they didn't seem to listen or speak to each other, and we needed to get to know each important facet better. I didn't say much: she seemed to take a lot from hearing her own swirling thoughts spoken out loud. It can take months to uncover so much information from a new client, but as a writer and performer, she'd interrogated herself for her material, making it readily available in therapy: a bonus.

It wasn't until the session was over that I realized with a thud of anxiety that Wande had asked, 'What's the point?' but hadn't answered the question. This was where we had to start the next session. Was she suicidal? Or was it simply a question about the meaning of life? She told me that she had discussed her suicidal thoughts with friends and, as a group, they'd agreed there were times when they believed the world would be a better place without them. I gently questioned whether she was talking in the third person, almost outside herself.

She held her breath – sat stock still, boot pointing sharply upwards. There was a long silence as she looked past me. She murmured, 'I'm haunted I won't win the battle.' I left space for her words to land, for us both to take in their full meaning, and asked her to tell me about the battle.

It took some time to unravel. Her words caught in her throat. I had an image that they were in freefall, endlessly whirring in her mind, but dragging them into the light, speaking them, was painful, and it took grit to expose them. In the end I understood she had layers of fear in her, some of it traumatic fear from her father's accident. She'd built a carapace over it, which meant she didn't feel authentic: she felt she put on 'me' for people, and could not absorb the positives or her success. Most of her energy was used in blocking her self-harming thoughts. She beat off her despair with alcohol and social media – 'I run around in circles like a beaten dog.' She knew her son, Kemi, would suffer if she died, and that helped to tether her, but it connected her to another cavern of disquiet: herself as a mother. I suggested we put that on hold for now and focus on the thoughts she was suppressing. We needed to hold them up to the light.

There was an endless 'ladder of musts', some of which were about telling herself she was lazy but needed to work, about trusting and feeling afraid, about being found out as a fake. The battle she fought with alcohol: she knew she should stop but couldn't make the decision. The geography of herself had changed, and she didn't have the map. But in the voicing of her worries the map was emerging. We did a relaxation exercise at the end of the session, for me as much as for her: I'd felt tight too. I could see she was calmer. She gave me a twinkly smile as she left. The session had been intense.

That high kick did not last. Wande had left my session feeling calmer but jumped straight into a relentless schedule of shows all over the country. Away from home, adrenalized when performing and then anaesthetized by drink to wind down, she had not wanted to wake up in the mornings. I gently reflected back the toxic pattern she'd described, careful not to shame her but to show her I could feel how much distress she was in. She sobbed deep noisy tears. For a long time. Snorting with laughter, while apologizing for using my tissues as she rhythmically pulled them from the box. We both felt the relief in Wande owning the truth of her pain.

Her tears subsided. She pressed the tissues hard on her eyes, breathed deeply, then looked up at me, bang in the eye: 'I've got to stop drinking.' I nodded. Letting herself know this conclusively – no more exhausting shall-I-shan't-I – brought the sun into her face. She gave me a 3D colour film of what a sober life would be like: waking up fresh, energetic, free . . . The list went on. I asked how she planned to stay sober, which was maybe a bit tough but it was important to bring her back to basics. 'Take each day at a time,' she said, with confidence. She reached her decision quickly between us, but it had taken Wande months of thought, research, ambivalence and turmoil. Our conversation was part of a long process: we aren't always open to a new beginning. We can't switch ourselves on and off as we choose. We need time. Time to withdraw and retreat, to freeze even, before we try again. In this instance, something chimed. There was an alignment, a hum of energy, between the permission she gave herself to be sad and being heard, her problem, her choice, her decision, and she clicked. Boom.

We spent a number of sessions bedding in her developing sober trust in life. She'd start each session with 'Week two, I'm sober', 'Week three, I'm sober', badges of honour that I cheered and celebrated with her. Wande was more reflective and smiled into my eyes, quite often laughing at herself. I didn't question this as a defence, more an expression of relief that she wanted to live. I felt the leaching of her poison.

Wande's speed in bouncing back was, in my experience, unusual. It showed a robust underlying resilience: her secure and predictable childhood, with loving parents, lots of friends, enough structure. Her core sense of identity and beliefs gave her foundations that held firm when threatened. Her father's accident was a fault line that had shaken those foundations and skewed her trust in herself as a woman, a mother, and as a successful scriptwriter and comedian. Alcohol, the false god she had called on to make her feel better, had exacerbated the fault line. There was work for us to do, many layers of her experience to be explored and understood, so that she could make the shift from her past self to integrate it with who she was now. I was confident that she would configure her new self over time.

When Wande focused on herself, she looked up at the sky, towards the light, where she'd access joyous memories. When she felt a wave of sadness or pain, she looked to the left as if a bad guy was sitting on her shoulder. Part of Wande's struggle to find who she really was, as opposed to who she thought she should be, was whether to allow herself to know how much she disliked the sheer grind of mothering. It felt taboo to complain, as if complaining would make bad things happen. As the child of parents who'd been imbued with the importance of hard work as the route out of poverty (the reason her grandparents had left Nigeria), she felt it was wrong, even transgressive to complain. She cried hot tears of frustration with herself that she was having a 'crap time in my privileged life', when her grandparents had had no expectations and would never have complained. Then she breathed, and I helped her imagine talking to her grandmother and seeing the warmth in her eyes. A moment later Wande's excitement burst through, remembering her grandmother's rich laugh. When she talked about these hurdles I could see the stand-up comedian performing, and knew this was giving her material, but I didn't want to lose her feelings beneath. She had moments when she really craved a drink, but did a breathing exercise we'd agreed on, and moved her attention to something else, to disrupt the obsessive thoughts.

Inevitably Wande had fought with her husband, Ty, circular fights in which both were hurt and upset, blaming yet knowing there was no one to blame, and all they really needed was to hold each other. A clearer picture of Ty emerged. He'd been bullied and had a lonely childhood. He was analytic and mathematical, the opposite skills from Wande's. But he was patient and fundamentally kind. He wanted to do the right thing for the right reasons, and when Wande could explain things to him, and he could understand her, he would practise them. Since Wande's therapy had started, he had developed a skill he was proud of: letting Wande download her worries and listening without giving her answers. Wande was immensely touched to watch his serious face and see the effort it took him not to give her a solution. She felt she had the equivalent of a PhD in emotional intelligence, to his GCSE. She laughed as she noted this, and then a light went on: her knowledge of how different they were helped her to be patient and clear in translating how she felt to him.

When Wande spoke about her parents she whispered, as if they could hear her. She held them in huge affection and respect but, as with many aspects of her life, some confusion. She felt guilty even talking about them. Her father, prior to his accident, was a traditional dad who spoke to her as if he was a teacher, expecting her to obey, which she rarely did. Since the accident, he had become more like her mother, warmer and softer, but she missed his power.

The car crash had happened on a wet night, very near home. He'd swerved to avoid an oncoming car going too fast in the middle of the road. He should have died. He'd been unconscious in intensive care for days, and when he came round his doctors were unsure as to what brain function he'd have left. Over weeks he found his voice, and slowly learned to converse, but he'd also broken his neck. He was in hospital for five months, had been told he would never walk again. He'd overcome that through years of physiotherapy and sheer determination, although he couldn't use his left side, and walked with a stick. Sometimes in pain he had to resort to a wheelchair.

The accident was a minefield that Wande didn't want to go over again. She held her breath and swallowed whenever she mentioned it. She'd had Eye Movement Desensitization Reprocessing (EMDR), which reduces trauma symptoms, and therapy, but the wound was just below the surface, and could be reopened faster than she could stop it. While they were close, she felt a gap between the person she now was, how she lived, and her roots. At university and then through her career she mixed with 'posh people . . . this thing they call social mobility is a mindfuck if you're the one doing the mobilizing . . . At uni I felt like I lived in two worlds. There was the world when I was with my friends – very English, mainly white – and then I went home to another country with exotic foods and colours, different attitudes and rules. A sick father. But I didn't know the rules of the posh white people either.' She felt her parents' pride in her but – this remained unspoken – she being a black woman comedian working in a predominantly white space felt scary to them. They had accepted a system that didn't treat them as equals, borne the harshness, yet had succeeded in making a good life for themselves, while staying within their own community. Wande had stepped into an unknown world, which felt risky, as well as exciting.

Our recurring preoccupation with transitions centres around identity: who we are, autonomy; our sense of freedom, and making meaning; the underlying purpose we ascribe to our lives. All of this is disrupted when we have a child. It seemed to me that Wande's process of adjusting to parenthood had been blocked by the traumatic birth of Kemi, which had been intensified by the trauma of her father's car crash decades earlier. Becoming successful and publicly recognized added further pressure to her identity issues because she felt people liked her too much for no reason, and others probably disliked her, also for no reason. While she enjoyed her sense of competency when she performed, she felt shame as an incompetent mother, which hit her when she tried to write at home: 'I always feel a bit like a slug that someone is about to dump salt on. Every time I sit down to write, I confront all of that.' And she felt conflicted about self-exposure, embarrassed by having put out stuff about herself into the world which was against her family values. As she recognized her hunger for attention, self-disgust flowered in her, like hemlock, and blocked her openness to take in the good things. Once she'd spewed her disgust, she was free to be pragmatic. She realized she was doing a job that was 'Amazing. I can do this thing which means I get to pick my son up every day.'

Her parents were committed grandparents and regularly helped with Kemi, who adored them, while Wande and Ty were busy working. She started crying as she talked about her parents, not painful tears, tears of tenderness and awareness. I could see her clenching her fists and asked what that was about. She was worried they did too much, which led her to realize that 'The thing that distresses me, I compare myself negatively to my parents. I think I'm doing something bad to Kemi, but I don't know what it is.' She felt they instinctively knew how to be parents better than she did. They'd been steady and present. Also, there'd been a shift in her relationship with them all those years ago, after the accident, when she'd felt she had to make them happy, while suppressing her own fear. Part of her felt sad that she hid her true self from them. And she'd paid a price too. She was no longer blissfully ignorant that loving someone was risky, and that devastating accidents could happen to those she loved most.

I asked Wande if she was ready to talk about Kemi. She looked down, pressing her beautifully bejewelled fingers into her forehead. She felt their foundations were 'wobbly', that he'd turned from a happy toddler into a complex boy. More shamefully, she was happy to escape him and go back on the road for her show. While she was away she'd imagine this happy family, and yearn to get home, but once she was there, she'd be greeted by this furious child. 'Kemi could dismember us both and put us on a bonfire.' She struggled to admit to the cocktail of rage he set off in her, finishing by saying heavily, 'I'm not sure it was a good idea to have children. I don't feel safe enough.' She added that intellectually and as a feminist she thought it was absolutely fine to go away for work, but the reality was entirely different from the theory, which offered no solution for the guilt she felt when she was away, or the fury Kemi felt towards her when she came home.

Instinct told me to ask her to take a step back and tell me about the early years with Kemi. When had she felt it go wrong? Wande told me she'd had a gruesome birth that ended in an emergency Caesarean. She'd been in agony, screaming and powerless. Men in green coats had come and cut her open, and she'd nearly died. Kemi had got out, but he'd nearly killed her. The consultant had said to her afterwards, in a chirpy voice, 'We nearly lost you.' But Wande hadn't felt chirpy, she'd felt 'screwed over'. I understood that Kemi's birth had set in train a complex process that was only being revealed as we spoke about it eight years later. The agony and fear of her father's accident had been reignited by Kemi's terrifying birth, the image of men with knives, and her sense that loving him was like loving a time bomb. Her determination to be a good mother meant she could override it when she was breastfeeding Kemi, but when she started working again, becoming successful very quickly, it destabilized her and, in particular, her connection with herself. She loathed herself for enjoying the praise so much, turning to Twitter and alcohol to numb her predominant feelings of being a 'useless worthless person'.

Our work wasn't to eradicate the negative, and celebrate the positive, but for her to find permission within herself to allow both voices, and adjust her perspective to a more manageable image, which allowed her to get on with her job.

In the weeks that followed, Wande thought a lot about Kemi, talked to Ty and consequently changed how she spoke to her son, realizing he wasn't in the least bit interested in her work life. He saw it as competition. Now she was letting him be in charge of their time together and showing him more attention. She'd tell him how much she'd missed him and, as boring as it was, played the games he liked: Pokémon and Match Attax. He loved it. There had been a moment one morning before school, always the stormy time, when he'd kicked off, and she'd managed it better. She felt they'd got to a place where he could express his feelings and she'd been the parent she'd wanted to be. Over the next weeks she was surprised to find how much she had grown to enjoy being with Kemi. She'd read a book that said, 'All types of love need work and fierce commitment.' Having that in her mind as a focus helped her get away from the shame.

We'd had a break for the holidays, and when we next spoke I could see Wande had a buzz about her. 'I really like sobriety,' she said, with a proud grin, looking like a teenager who had won a prize. She enjoyed the clarity of it, but at other times she could hear this gremlin on her shoulder, questioning whether she really was an addict: 'Do I really have to do this? Why can't I be a normal person?' This was the key to her sanity. Before, there had been a clamour of voices. Now, in hearing clearly the cross-messaging that was pinging into her mind, she could choose which message was the right one for her. It put her in the driving seat of her own life, in a way she had never experienced before.

I could feel Wande's growing confidence in herself, her authentic self, with all its complexity. She was giving it her sober time and attention, which meant a great deal happened inside her between sessions. She said, 'It's our secrets that make us sick.' The strange magic of voicing her thoughts and being heard was working. We agreed our work for this phase of her life was complete: Wande now knew herself well enough to give herself the attention she needed to keep herself on track. 'I realized that if I spend time being aware and noticing the good stuff, but also noticing, and not pushing away, the bad stuff, it works for me. Living intentionally in the moment and being grateful.'

Reflections on Family

The etymology of 'family' is interesting: it comes from the Latin *famulus*, meaning 'servant in a household'. That sense of being in the service of our family, and vice versa, is a fresh perspective and rings true. Family relationships can be our most rewarding and crucial connections, yet they are by no means simple. Even the word 'family' will conjure different images and sensations for each of us.

The traditional Western picture is of a family unit consisting of parents and children living together as a stable and supportive base from which the children develop into adults. For the 19 million families in the UK, there is no norm: every child, parent and couple is unique and creates their own way of being. Family is no longer defined by biology, marriage or even a home. In the last few decades new ways of creating a family have developed: there are single-parent families, same-sex families, extended families, polyamorous families, families made up of friends with no blood relationships, and blended families consisting of the couple, the children they have had together, and the children from their previous relationships.

For all its complexity, the role of a family could not be more essential to our wellbeing, and the wellbeing of society. Family is, for most of us, the closest network of people we consistently love, who know us inside out, and are a reliable base to turn to in need. Family is the single most important influence on a child's life and their outcome, and it is essential for children to feel loved, connected and protected to grow and thrive. Children learn from their families how to form relationships, function in society and at work. Happy, secure children are more likely to be happy, secure adults.

When families work, they are the source of a deep-seated and profound confidence that we are loved, that we have our team who wants to support us, believes in us and cares what is happening in our lives and in our inner world. Family forms an invisible glue of togetherness and we know we are not alone. It gives us the strength to face the brickbats of life. A strong family will even support the fight for turf between each other, and the fight for its members to be who they are. There isn't a greater gift. Yet family is often the source of our most searing pain, for where we love most, we can also hate and hurt most. Hence the saying that a parent is only as happy as their least happy child. Each family member has a profound influence on every other member, for good or ill.

Families are complex systems in which much more goes on below the surface than we can see on top. Beneath each grandparent and parent are the hidden legacies from their own childhoods, 'the ghosts from the nursery', which create patterns of relating. These patterns trigger all those primitive feelings when we love and fear losing love: jealousy, rage, obsession, hope and despair. The territory of love in families is the hidden ground we consciously and unconsciously fight over. It is to my mind the root of most of the function and dysfunction in all of our lives.

Life is difficult and brings tough challenges for families, like losing jobs, bereavement or illness, which have to be accommodated. Even without negative events the juggling demands of work and home often feel relentless. It takes enormous psychological resource, time, money, patience, self-awareness, endurance and commitment to develop a functioning family. By this I do not mean idealized perfect relationships: I mean Winnicott's idea of 'good enough', which allows for our flaws and vulnerabilities, but overall creates a sense of reliable loving between family members, where the intention is for the good of the other, and they are loved as themselves, without conditions.

A healthy family is one in which there are more positive interactions than negative, in which each person feels respected, valued
and heard, in which conflict is acknowledged and repaired – there
is always conflict: where you have people, you have disagreements. The strength of a functioning family is in its members'
ability to communicate openly with each other, their sense of
belonging, in which they choose to spend time together, have fun
together, laugh together, and in which they are boosted by the
love and warmth of seeing each other. A healthy family has a basic
level of trust: they know there is someone, a group of people, who
is on their side. It also allows for each person to be celebrated for
their successes, without the fear of condemning envy – a familiar
problem in families. All of this requires a dedicated commitment
to family: it has to be prioritized over other life demands. Going
back to the Latin meaning, families require our service.

My case studies focused on the parenting aspect of families:
Leena's difficulty in recognizing Anita as an adult who needed some
autonomy; the transition into fatherhood for Lucas; the adaptation
Wande needed to make as a working mother to her eight-year-old
son. Every story in this book has a significant part focused on family
because family, whether it is functional or dysfunctional, forms the
bedrock of our lives. What was important about Leena, Lucas and
Wande was their self-awareness in recognizing that they held the
responsibility to change. They were willing, despite it being painful, to explore for themselves their difficulty, to protect themselves
against the inevitable 'stuckness' and damage that would have
ensued if they did not confront it. The problem with dysfunctional
families is the inability of family members to take responsibility for
the consequences of their actions, and continuously to repeat those
damaging actions, rather than working to change them.

Family Systems

Each member of a family contributes to creating a pattern of
beliefs, ways of behaving, and the permission or injunction of what

may be talked about within their particular family. Roles may be played by each person – such as the fixer, the difficult one, the clever one – and there is a dynamic between each family member which affects everyone. All of this makes up a family system and, as in all systems, it likes balance: each element has a part to play to keep the whole balanced. When one member behaves out of character, it becomes unbalanced. Parents are the primary agents of change in holding the responsibility for addressing their family's difficulties. Families that have open communication, consistent boundaries, self-awareness, goodwill and trust are more robust in managing the transitions and thereby disruptions that inevitably occur. It is not necessarily the solving of problems that matters, but the trust that is developed by having open discussion.

A dysfunctional family does not know how to deal with difficulty: no one knows what to expect, either verbally or behaviourally, or trusts that their difficulties will be acknowledged and resolved. At its worst, conflict, bad behaviour and often child neglect occur continuously. This causes high levels of distress for everyone, which can lead the family to break down.

Tolstoy wrote, 'Happy families are all alike; every unhappy family is unhappy in its own way.' I disagree. I believe every family is unique. No family remains the same, and it is unhelpful to think of them as either good or bad. Most families operate in a spectrum that will, at different times, be pulled towards functional or dysfunctional.

An image commonly used to represent the family system is a baby's mobile above a cot. When the family is working well there is a dynamic movement between each element of the mobile, which recalibrates to find a balance depending on the environment. If one part of the mobile goes missing or is tilted, it tips the mobile on its axis, and it takes a great deal of work to recalibrate it. One member of the family may act out the poison in the system, often through mental or physical illness, destructive behaviour or addiction, and unless the whole family system takes responsibility and addresses it collectively, the dysfunction continues for everyone.

Those patterns become embedded and the rupture is increasingly fixed. Sibling rivalry is a painful example, a poison that often runs in families: one sibling has to put the other down in order to raise themselves up. As a result approximately one-third of siblings describe their relationship as rivalrous or distant.

We all know how family feuds take a terrible toll on the people who hold the grudges, and impact everyone close to them. This is as true for divorced parents and their children as it is for siblings. Monica McGoldrick, an American family therapist, reflects that we can't run logic through an emotional system, meaning we have to seek ways to process emotion, however painful and disruptive it is. For example, logic will tell the divorced parents they have to get on for the benefit of their children, when every fibre of their being wants to annihilate the other. McGoldrick also points out that even if, for our mental health, we make the difficult but ne-cessary decision to cut all connection with our family, its members never entirely leave us. There is always a part of us that suffers the cold chill of disconnection from them.

Family systems can be influenced and informed by the gener-ations before, either consciously or unconsciously. Theorists believe that unexpressed losses, secrets or negative events travel alive and untouched across generations until someone is willing to deal with them. Typical examples would be the tragic death of a family mem-ber, or cousins who don't speak because their grandparents fought about money. Family therapists often use genograms to uncover these stories and messages from the past that hold such power in the present. McGoldrick advises, 'We make the best decisions if we pay attention to where we've come from and the future – what do we owe our grandparents, parents and our grandchildren?'

The Importance of Fathers

In what is thought of as the traditional nuclear family structure, the mother looks after domestic matters while the father is the 'breadwinner', working away from the household; the pair have at least one child. In this model, fathers tend to be condemned for not being involved enough and the importance of their role is ignored. In the past fathers held the position of all-powerful patriarchs, and later their value was measured by their income, even being sidelined by psychology research, where the focus was on the mother. It is different now, not least as the range of fatherhoods (for instance, in gay relationships) has broadened the general perception of the role of fathers.

Research shows the increasing importance of fathers in modern-day parenthood. Fathers are changing, and how that change evolves is not always clear. The expectation of modern men transitioning into fatherhood is multi-faceted: they can be expected to act as breadwinner, lover, guide, friend, playmate and carer. The phrase that is often repeated in the studies of new fathers is the importance of 'being there', which is certainly different from previous generations, whose experience as children was of often 'absent' fathers. There is certainly a generational shift: fathers, like Lucas, want to be more involved, feel sad and upset when they miss out on key moments in their child's life, and don't want to carry the pressure of being the sole breadwinner.

As children grow up, the father's role is as complex as the mother's and unquestionably as important. From their child's infancy the father's involvement has a direct influence on that child's development of self-esteem, more so than the mother's. This links to their educational and, ideally, career success. Children with a father who is invested in them and spends time with them are more likely to be emotionally secure: it gives them the confidence to explore and step outside the safety of their familiar surroundings. Children who have a secure relationship with their fathers are more likely to form stronger social connections with others as they mature. Fathers set a positive role model for their child, which helps build gender-role qualities in adolescent boys and girls. For adolescent girls, it models for them positive opinions and experiences of men, which has a profound influence on the quality of their future relationships.

New Fathers

After Lee was born alive and healthy, Lucas and Heather assumed that, since they had spent many distressing years trying for a baby, their relief and joy would outweigh their exhaustion and the turmoil of learning to care for him. That was not the case. Their joy in and love for him knew no bounds but it did not protect them from the turbulence his birth unleashed.

New parenthood is difficult on many levels. There is the neurobiological level of change: oxytocin levels rise, and sleep/wake patterns are radically disrupted. At the interpersonal level the couple's relationship has to be renegotiated as they form a new relationship with their baby and have almost no time for each other. At a practical level they are learning many new skills in how to soothe and care for their dependent baby while needing to reorganize their work and handle financial challenges.

This massive shift in themselves happens at a time when the demands of their new baby are intense, and their own needs for love, sleep and care are unlikely to be met. It is the phase when the relationship is under severe strain. Paradoxically, as they become a happy family of three, the mother and father can feel more alone than ever. They may see versions of themselves they haven't seen before, and really don't like; there may be a build-up of resentment and criticism. It requires lots of deep breaths, commitment and very good communication skills to protect against fractures in the relationship. Support for each other is key: it creates the trust to dare to be open to new ideas and, through reflection, to change. Hopefully, through the bumpy ride, they learn that the reality is different from their dream, and if they had a picture of their ideal family, they learn to accept, even embrace, that 'ideal' does not exist.

Being a parent inevitably forces the adult, like Lucas, to examine their own childhood, and brings out both the agitated child and fear of repeating the pattern. It comes as no surprise to learn that a National Childbirth Trust survey in 2015 found 38 per cent of new fathers are concerned about their mental health. In a 2015 study, what surprised men most was the amount of tension that having a new baby caused in their relationship with their partner. In some ways you can never be prepared for the full impact of having a new baby, but it seems men are not talking enough to each other or don't fully expect this to be a time of turbulence, tension and chaos.

The Office for National Statistics (ONS) statistics from 2017 show that there are 232,000 stay-at-home fathers, which is, interestingly, the lowest number since 2014. The number had been rising since 1993. Commentators believe stay-at-home fathers are re-entering the workplace because, like women, they feel society does not value or reward them for the work they do at home. They feel they are only given high status through paid work. Lucas and Heather may represent the future in that they will need to negotiate with each other who works and who stays home. It is unlikely to be a fixed role, but one that changes over time and circumstances – for a couple to see themselves as sharing breadwinning rather than there being a single breadwinner. All the research points to the necessity to reinvent oneself through life, and to have the adaptability to move in and out of different occupations.

When the mother is breastfeeding it can leave the father not knowing how to 'be there' but, with some thought, it is possible to find other ways to be physically close to and caring for their child. Having skin-to-skin contact, bathing them, or soothing their baby after a feed are ways to create connection with their infant – and have the added benefit of giving the mother a rest. Research from 2006 shows fathers who spend more time caring for their babies on their own are less likely to separate from their partners than those who are less involved.

Parenting: My Way or the Highway

The noun 'parenting' came commonly into use in 1959, but it certainly wasn't a concept familiar to most parents of that generation.

Since the late 1970s there has been an increased understanding of the importance of parenting, and consequently parenting style has changed. In our culture today, parents, more frequently mothers, take seriously all areas of a child's wellbeing, daily life and success. For some people, being a parent can become all-consuming, with their time and resources spent solely on looking after every aspect of their children's lives. With the advent of social media, parenting has, for some, become a competitive sport, one parent outdoing another through perfected images of family life – although there is a movement against this, with new and honest blogs, like Susan Kirby's 'Unmumsy Mum' and Gill Sims's 'Why Mummy Drinks' to name but two, which try to redress the balance.

It was in this environment that Wande felt she was failing as a mother. One of the arguments she battled with was her absolute right as a feminist to work, and the painful reality of her son's fury over her absence. For any parent to be the parent they want to be, the parent they can be proud of, it is necessary to unravel the many complex emotions that live within us. Journalling is a good way of doing this – jot down thoughts and feelings over a number of weeks and clarity will emerge.

One of a parent's key transitions is to love and respond to the child they have in front of them, rather than the child they might wish to have. We might bond with our child because they are like us, or withdraw from them because they are like us, or even hate them for having the qualities of the father we've divorced, but that is unacceptable. We have a responsibility to see them and love them for who they are.

Among the reams of advice on parenting, I find the idea of building resilience in our children most helpful. I turn to the work of Dr Michael Ungar, the Canadian family therapist who is among the best-known writers and researchers on resilience in the world. The message of his book *I Still Love You* – whose title alone says it all – is that if we are to build resilient children who flourish in a complex, ever-changing world, they need nine things: structure, consequences, parent–child connections, lots and lots of strong relationships, a powerful identity, a sense of control, a sense of belonging/culture/spirituality/life purpose, rights and responsibilities, safety and support. I like his simple clarity – I like at least knowing what I need to be giving my children – even if it seems a tough ask.

Parenting Adult Children

Leena faced the challenge of her daughter's wedding, her own loss of control over Anita. As their lives progress, there will continue to be thousands of smaller and larger versions of this dynamic. Our Western perspectives value self-reliance and separation as our children become adults. One of the definitions of success has been that parents have done a good job when their children no longer need them and are not beholden to them.

However, the separation is now far less clear for contemporary parents than in previous generations. Most 'Baby Boomers' (see page 295) have a more involved and connected relationship with their children than they had with their own parents, who expected their children to leave home and get on with their lives as soon as they were eighteen. As a parent today, how do we negotiate the line between being available and supportive, and neither abandoning nor intruding on our children? It is a difficult balance to achieve, which changes over time from when children are young adults to becoming parents themselves to eventually, ideally, supporting their parents as they age.

It is helpful to be thoughtful and discuss with adult children what the areas of tension are likely to be and how to manage them. As with all difficult conversations, how you communicate, as much as what you say, will predict whether or not it will be well received. The tone of your voice, your body language, being open and discursive, rather than directive, all aid collaborative discussions.

Some parents believe they deserve more acknowledgement, even payback, than they receive. They may extract it by still controlling their adult children. Perhaps parents can never get back all they have given, or the reverse: they may be richly rewarded. Maybe their children only realize in retrospect all their parents have done for them, often when they have their own children. Be that as it may, new boundaries between adult children and their parents have to be defined, where the power no longer resides solely with the parent.

Parents need to respect the decisions and choices of their children and, in the main, give an opinion only if they are asked. Questioning our children is difficult, because we want them to know we're interested in them and their lives but difficult topics, such as finding a partner or having a baby, are best responded to when the child brings them up.

Money is always complicated, on many levels. It is imbued with potent feelings, which have to be acknowledged: power, love and favouritism between siblings. The problems of children borrowing money from parents, the terms of the borrowing, or what they can expect when you die, to name but a few, are some of the common challenges. It helps to be clear, transparent and discuss openly the issues that will protect against later resentment and battles. Every family is unique, which means there can't be catch-all, age-specific rules around when we jump in to help our children with money or rescue plans, but our attitude matters: that we come from a position of trusting their view, respecting their plan, not making them beholden to us, and not taking control. The difficulty for the adult parent is that we are wired to protect our children, to keep them alive and well, and that instinct to protect them doesn't fade when they are adults. To us, at some level, they are always our baby. But we do have to love and accept what is happening to them, and back off while finding other ways to soothe our own anxiety.

A new person in the family, through marriage or cohabitation, changes the make-up of the family, and when that couple have children together, even more so. For the person marrying or cohabiting, it is worth noting that, unless there is a rift, you marry your beloved and their family. It brings together two worlds and ways of being, which can cause real conflict at one end of the spectrum, disquiet or, at the other end, absolute joy. Families of multiple generations who get on well together are more resilient in dealing with life's difficulties, simply because there are more people to turn to for help. It is the responsibility of everyone to adapt: be open, flexible, sensitive, and co-operate together. Timing matters: offensive remarks or behaviours made at the beginning of the relationship, before the trust and love have developed, can haunt the relationship long term.

Being a successful parent means giving your child roots *and* wings. The adult child needs to step off the 'mother-ship' (or 'parent-ship') and create their own ship. Their life is not our life: we have to acknowledge that they are different from us. We need not only to accept them but embrace them as they are and accept who they love. Wanting to exert control or influence over your child only causes fracture. It is clear from the research of Dr Deanna Brann, psychotherapist and author of *Reluctantly Related*, that the adult child has to be loyal to the spouse/partner, not their family of origin. If children remain loyal to their family of origin, the love relationship is at high risk of breaking down. In my experience it is never wise to criticize how our children parent theirs, particularly with non-verbal sighs and 'hms', or passive-aggressive remarks such as 'It's interesting you're doing X . . . I did . . .' It is guaranteed to cause offence, and what you once believed may be outdated so no longer considered good for your grandchild.

The power parents have to influence the wellbeing of their adult children has, to my mind, been underestimated. It is important we recognize that, and do our best to reconfigure the relationship and recalibrate the power balance. Do you remember going home as an adult and reverting to your childlike self or, worse, a grumpy teenager? This is because our relationship with our parents is embodied in us, and is triggered at the speed of light, far faster than our thoughts. We needed our parents' love and care to survive when we were babies, and the power of that connection never entirely dissolves.

This is true, too, for the parent of their adult child. The emotion parents and children have for each other can be overwhelming when the parents are concerned for the child or they disagree intensely. I'm not referring here to minor squabbles that are forgiven and forgotten. Leena, whose rage meant she wanted to punish and crush the child she had loved and protected with all her being, was frightening in her fury. It is catastrophic for the relationship to act on those feelings: it develops into a reciprocal punishing of each other, hurting each other, which escalates to become a stand-off. You can never take back the words you said in anger, and they can haunt the relationship for ever, re-emerging in the next altercation.

When angry with your child, or very worried about them, it helps if you avoid sounding off in the heat of the fury. Stamp around with a friend or partner: get the rage out – but not on your child. We have to exercise self-control, however difficult that is. Furious hurtful words tear holes in your bond. They usually come from a place of hurt, maybe based on rejection, but your child is an adult who needs to reject you and get on with their life. Let the fury or worry settle, then practise what you are going to say – write it down. Really think about it, so that when you do speak, it will be received as thoughtful and not an attack.

There are many stories of the agony caused to parents when there is estrangement between them, their adult children and consequently their grandchildren. The causes of the rupture are as varied as people. There are some circumstances over which the parents of adult children have no control, however hard they have fought to reconcile the relationship. They are left with the painful task of having to find a way of living with this new and devastating loss. There are also stories of the reverse, when parents choose to have no relationship with their children, or a scant relationship, which is an equally painful living loss for their children. In my experience, it is likely that the person who has cut themselves off has done so because their feelings are so overwhelming that the only way they can cope is to shut them down. Indifference is the opposite of love, not hate.

Estrangement is toxic, with many innocent parties damaged along the way, and often this can be transmitted to the next generation. I would urge each person involved to fight as hard as they can to repair the relationship, which is no easy ask. It requires the courage to overcome the profound hurt from the rejection, and to dare to withstand further hurt. But, however hard that is, it is important to know in your heart of hearts that you personally have done everything within your power to build the bridge of reconciliation. You can fight for the relationship by offering small tokens of connection, like sending cards or photographs, even something funny: it doesn't need to be a big and demanding gesture. Often it is small steps that slowly rebuild the connection. In some cases, getting professional input, a therapist or mediator, to help unpick what happened in a safe and contained place, can be transformative. The residue of hurt that remains from a permanent estrangement never dies, even after death, and is often ignited further after death.

'Boomerang Kids'

Increasingly adult children like Caz (who appears in Work, pages 136–45) are unable to – or choose not to – leave home, or come back after some years away. The number of 'boomerang kids' is increasing: in 2015 the ONS reported that 3.3 million young adults (aged 20–34) are sharing a home with their parents in the UK. That is the highest number since records began in 1996. The main reason may well be economic, or delays in formalizing love relationships or getting careers off the ground. Yet it is worth parents examining their part in it: are they providing so much for free that their child doesn't want to leave? Are they infantilizing their child? Are they frightened of children leaving and being alone with their partner? Children staying at home is not necessarily a good thing for either party: new research from the London School of Economics shows that the quality of their life together decreased for the parents when a child moved back home. There can also be an increasing financial worry too, that parents' savings are being spent, which leaves them exposed in old age.

My view is that, in this scenario, parents need to create a new set of rules for their adult children. Consider the following:

- Agree from the outset a fixed term for the length of time the adult child is to live with you – it is harder to do this later on.
- The adult child makes an agreed financial contribution to the household.
- You all agree to share household tasks.
- Discuss disagreement flashpoints that happened regularly before the adult child moved out, and explore ways of circumnavigating them in the present.
- Agree house rules about friends, music, etc.

Culture and Parenting

I am focusing on Asian culture because it was relevant to Leena, but the complex weave of heritage, culture and integration in present society would be true for any immigrant and the subsequent generations.

Research shows first-generation immigrants from collectivist cultures – which emphasize the needs and goals of the group over the needs and desires of each individual – practise what we in the West see as controlling authoritarian parenting styles. Parents may insist on an arranged marriage, or that their child goes into a particular profession, in order to hold on to their sense of identity in a foreign land; they may even be somewhat stuck in a particular historical-cultural time from their past. This creates tension, even big clashes, with second, third and fourth generations, who have acclimatized to the more individualistic Western culture.

Other Asian parents wish to transmit to their children the rules and obligations that reflected their race, ethnicity and culture, to uphold their heritage culture and remain part of their Asian society in the UK. Yet they also want their children to be immersed in British culture, to learn English, navigate institutions, such as school and university, and celebrate mainstream British traditions and holidays. It requires a complex oscillation between the two cultures to find a way to encourage the children to hold on to the norms of their heritage but also to integrate and become part of their existing culture. When this is successful, it gives their children the bonus of greater depth of experience and the flexible creativity to move between two worlds.

When second-generation British Asians become parents, surveys show they actively consider the diversity of where they send their children to school. They feel extremely upset (more so than their parents before them) if they are subject to racial abuse, although they tend to face it less overtly than their parents (mostly in the form of microaggressions). They often wish their children to have a diverse mix of friends, since for many this was frowned upon by their own parents. Their heritage remains important to them – as it does to all of us – and they may turn to their parents (the grandparents) to teach their children the important aspects of their cultural heritage, including religious practices and cooking, which they may have rebelled against and didn't fully learn.

These second, third and fourth generations create their own rules, which may, for example, disapprove of intermarriage or the reverse. We all know families, or are in families, who have particular traditions, perhaps over religious holidays or birthdays, that may come from many generations back. What is true of all families is they develop their own rituals and accepted behaviours. It is part of human nature to create rules and habits to enable us to live more easily together and in society. It fulfils that key family requirement: to keep the family system stable.

Grandparents

Wande's parents were very involved in their grandson's care. Lucas and Heather's parents stepped in to help when their grandson was born and overall they found it rewarding. Research on functioning families reveals that grandparents find this fulfilling and spend an average of just over eight hours a week looking after their grandchildren; in the UK, 2.7 million grandparents are regular care-givers.

Grandmothers, like mothers, are likely to do more of the care and are more likely to change their own working life to take on care duties. Those who work part time do as much as those who are retired. The research found two-thirds (65 per cent) of grandparents across the UK provide some form of care for their grandchildren, making it easier for parents to go out to work. It saves families around £1,786 in childminder bills per year – a £16.1 billion saving across the UK. The financial saving is highly valued, even vital for some families.

In the case of separation and divorce, grandparents often resolve the financial problem that ensues by providing childcare for free. The highest levels of grandparental help take place in families that break down, but that is not matched by satisfaction levels. These are lower, presumably because it is much harder work helping distressed children and parents. A recent survey showed 90 per cent of grandparents believed it had a positive impact on their life. But many saw they had to 'put themselves out' and almost half felt their children did not appreciate them. Others felt pressured into taking on more of the care duties than they wanted.

The most common difficulty was that grandparents felt powerless in terms of exercising control over their grandchildren when they didn't agree with their children's discipline style.

There are important benefits: the grandparents enjoy better health, with all that running around after little ones, and the grandchildren are enriched by the input of two generations of people who love them deeply. For parents, the comfort of knowing that their children are looked after by someone they trust and who loves them is immeasurable.

Love

'It is easy to hate and it is difficult to love . . . All good things are difficult to achieve; and bad things are very easy to get.'

Confucius

Maria

Marriage and Affairs

Before we met, I spoke to Maria on the telephone, and heard a warm American accent, and a rush of words, as if she had more to say than there was space for. Maria wanted to see me because she was at a crossroads in her life: she was in her mid-fifties, had been married for twenty-six years, had three daughters, and there were fundamental questions about love and marriage that she needed to answer.

When we met for the first time, she hurried into my room, and sat down, taking a deep breath. She smiled a lot. Her lively brown eyes were set in a face that had spent a great deal of time outside, which made sense when she told me she was a gardener, waving her mud-caked nails at me for evidence. When she spoke, she tugged at her fringe, as if it would help her to pull the thoughts out of her mind, while the rest of her shiny brown hair fell in waves around her face.

Maria was questioning her marriage to Ken, whether to accept the status quo, try to change it, or leave him. The present situation was complex: Ken was no longer interested in her sexually, and even mocked her attempts to seduce him. He shut down conversations about their relationship, saying versions of 'Why would you spoil a lovely day by discussing our marriage?' He was only interested in talking about their children or work. Maria, a Catholic, found this hurtful and felt that he was reneging on the deal they had signed up for. More than anything she craved the intimacy that opening emotionally, being vulnerable together, having sex gave her. When Maria accepted Ken's viewpoint they got on well: he was funny, she respected him as father to their children and knew he was a good man, who worked hard.

To add to the mix Maria had had a lover, Andrew, for the last five years. She'd felt unrequited love for him for decades, and now had a close and sexually satisfying relationship with him. She had squared this with her faith, knowing that she believed in God but didn't have to follow Catholic doctrine to be a good Christian. Andrew showed her for the first time how life-enhancing 'mind-blowing sex' could be, breathing new energy into her whole being.

However, what had 'smashed into' this already complex story was Ted, a gardening colleague, with whom she'd had an additional year-long affair. Ted was twenty years younger than Maria, and wanted to end their relationship, to reinvest in his marriage and family, particularly as he was father to a two-year-old son. This lover leaving her was causing Maria much distress, destabilizing her life and her marriage. She cried all the time for him: although she could logically respect his position, she felt the love they'd had was unique. She'd never connected with anyone in that way before, not even Andrew, and believed it made them better people. Their intimacy was not only shared in the bedroom but alongside one another at work. The closeness, the sweat, the hard work and physical contact they experienced creating beautiful gardens together made going to work without him almost unbearable. Her time with Ted had produced some of her most fruitful work. Maria agreed they would have to end their physical relationship – as much as she'd found it thrilling, part of her didn't feel at ease with having two lovers – but she couldn't accept an end to the friendship.

Interestingly, there were no secrets. Ken knew about Andrew and Ted in a distant, minimal-information way. And she had told Andrew about the younger man; they'd both respected her relationships.

I was relieved to find that I didn't feel judgemental, only

sympathetic to Maria's distress, and committed to help her find a way of living her life that worked for her. Maria was happily surprised to discover that talking honestly helped her to understand herself. When her thoughts had been hidden, they circulated in her mind, building to the extent that she felt she was drowning. We wanted to explore the root of her love for Ted: how come she had the capacity for another lover? What was the unmet need in her?

Over a number of sessions some insights emerged: it cannot have been a coincidence that her affair with her first lover had started after she'd had cancer, which at one point had seemed seriously life-threatening. Sex is the ultimate life force, an instinctive counter to the possibility of death. Not having quite enough money was a recurring theme throughout her life: she'd never wanted more than enough, but constantly worrying about it wore her down. We wondered if there was a connection between being enriched through multiple relationships that helped to dampen her financial deficit. Through both of her lovers Maria had discovered aspects of herself that felt entirely new: each man had opened up a different version of her that had been hidden through the faithful years of her marriage to Ken.

Two of her daughters were in work and her youngest was at college. They lived at home, so she didn't feel her nest was empty, but we agreed there was unquestionably space available now from active parenting. Pride emanated from her face as she recognized her sexual self, which had to some extent been sated by being a very physical mother: she'd breastfed her three daughters until they were eighteen months old, 'they ate me up', and they had been attached to her at all times.

Her parenting style was different from her father's: he had believed love was shown by what he did, not what he said. He had been distant, which left a longing in her to be desired, and a vulnerability to rejection. All three of the men she now loved had wounded her by rejecting her at different times: Ken by withdrawing sexually, Andrew by rejecting her when she was young and had believed he was the love of her life. She now realized she had married Ken on the rebound from Andrew. And now Ted had rejected her by ending their affair. It was complicated.

From the outside it would appear clear: let Ted go. Although there would be a painful process of adjusting to his loss (and work would be a troublesome place for a time), how could she hold any hope for a younger man who had made clear that he saw her as a threat to his stability rather than a desired lover? The hope she held that they would be together was contaminating her life daily, sucking the joy she felt from her love for her children, and the satisfaction she got from her work. We all know our lives would be infinitely happier and easier if we could match our desires with what is best for us, but most decision-making is not rational: it is influenced by our feelings and previous experience. It takes a great deal of psychological work to align those thoughts and feelings.

In Maria's case, talking had given her the insight as to what had led to her affairs but it did not prevent her hoping that Ted would come back to her. She kept reiterating his words: 'If we are meant to be together, we will be together.' The fact that she'd finally got her lover, Andrew, to fall for her, all those decades later, led her to believe hope is ultimately satisfied. She thought if she waited long enough it would happen.

I acknowledged her love for Ted, and how painful she found it, and I offered some perspectives of mine. However much she wanted it to be true, her past experience of her lover coming back didn't predict the future with Ted. I questioned whether she could envisage a future in which all of her needs were met by one man. Or was she shaped by her father's coldness, which was expressed mainly through lack of interest, almost as if she didn't exist? It had ignited in her a longing for attention, and I wondered whether she believed she could never have all she wanted.

Maria's response was robust. She had thought a lot about this, telling me she was surrounded by girlfriends whose marriages were imperfect, and she believed that perfect relationships were an illusion, or extremely rare. It felt far too risky to end her current relationships in the hope that someone better would emerge.

We had a gap for a few weeks when Maria had gone back to South Carolina to visit her family: her mother, who was sprightly and energetic, and her father, who was housebound now. She felt guilty at not being able to do more, and sad when she left, with the thought that her father might die and she wouldn't see him again. It brought up the familiar split she lived with, never fully belonging in the UK, her birth family being across the Atlantic. We wondered together whether this had facilitated her ability to have an affair, to hold these different relationships separately inside her. We didn't come to a clear conclusion, but what we did understand was that Maria was drawn to new territory, to pushing boundaries. She had met Ken in the UK when she'd needed to get away from home, taste new life, have adventures, and that drive was still alive in her more than twenty years later.

Maria needed to spend time going over in detail 'this great love you don't normally have in life', to find the words for what in her mind had been indescribable. Ted and she had met working on a gardening project, she the more senior gardener. Initially Ted had looked up to her expertise; over time they found themselves talking and talking about everything. The project ended, Ted texted that he missed her, which soon led to endless messaging and long discursive emails, opening up about themselves and their lives, building up a momentum of excitement in them both. I felt touched by Maria, as she pulled on her fringe, saying, 'When does an affair start? He says I seduced him when I came to him to make love to him. For me it was that first kiss. It felt like a promise. When he caressed my hand in the café, it felt like making love.' For that year they had made love when they could; it was happy and creative, joyful sex. She was able to show him ways of connecting that were new to him. Sex had been a bit of a fumble for him up to then. They listed what they loved about each other, sent each other poems, laughed together, cried together, all the time knowing they would never leave their respective spouses.

Maria trusted Ted in a way she had never trusted anyone, and believed that trust was inviolate. She cried out as she acknowledged it was her absolute trust in him that cut deepest in her. She'd believed the love at the heart of them was untouchable, and now he didn't even want to speak to her. She thrashed and raged against it and, in doing so, realized he held the power, a reversal of their original position. When she recognized how much power Ted had, Maria woke up and, for the first time, she felt the beginnings of anger.

Maria's anger shifted her away from being a victim, and she managed to persuade Ted to see her, which he'd refused to do for eight months. It was an important meeting: he was cold towards her, and physically recoiled from her. When she left she was shocked and hurt that he could be so cruel. But in processing that, it allowed her to see that this was a different Ted: no part of her wanted this Ted. She didn't even like him. I wondered if he had said anything that let her know for certain there was no hope of them coming back together. I was surprised by her response: 'There is nothing he can say that will change my mind. I will always love him, and believe he loves me.' I'd thought we were seeing the same picture, but she explained that, while she adamantly believed at some point they would be together, she knew *she* had to reject *him* now. I saw that she could hold both aspects, find a place inside herself where their passionate love could reside, and recognize the man she loved was no longer present. I voiced my concern that her hope that 'When I give up on him, he will come back' was a kind of magical thinking, that she was bargaining with a higher power. It used up a huge amount of energy, which, if invested in her present, could be richly rewarding. But that wondering fell on stony ground.

Although Maria felt stronger, we went back and forth with this process. She looked for Ted on WhatsApp, hit a wall of sadness that he'd gone. Then she felt positive about her life, enjoyed her lover, her children. I was adamant that if she was to find a way of moving on properly she had to stop all contact with Ted: every text evoked their whole history, and the promise of the dream. She agreed in principle but found it impossible in practice. I knew how hard that was, the dopamine hit that even searching hopefully for a message gave, and the crashing disappointment that generated a further need to search.

A pivotal understanding emerged when Maria talked about her daughters, how proud she was of them. As an aside I asked if she'd ever wished she'd had a son. Her initial response was no, and she gave me quite a strong validation of how wonderful it was to have three daughters. But it had planted a seed in her that grew over the next week, and when she returned she tentatively said, 'Ted's used up a part of me that is there for a son. You'd never give up on a son, would you?' Another time she wondered if one of the three miscarriages she'd had had been of a boy. This new awareness developed in her mind over the next weeks. She remembered Ted had said how maternal she was. She felt that in some unconscious part of her psyche he had filled a place in her heart that was meant for a son: he was the son she'd never had. It helped release her from her stuckness, and her dream that one day he'd beg to come back, when she could triumphantly reject him, hurting him in the way he'd hurt her.

Maria came in with a new haircut, and rather jauntily wiggled her new boots at me. Jolly nice they were too. I waited to see if it represented an internal shift. The boots were a birthday present from Ken, who'd sought their daughters' guidance; the memory made Maria grin from top to jaunty boot. They had had a lovely birthday dinner, roast chicken, and she felt gratified at the family she and Ken had built together, the home that the children and so many of their friends came to – she saw this was the central purpose of her life. She realized as she looked at Ken that if she left him her problems wouldn't be solved: there would be new ones. She wanted to protect her daughters. While she was married to Ken, his difficulties were hers to resolve, and vice versa. If they divorced they'd fall to their children. She didn't see herself as a martyr to her daughters, but as a role model of how to live an adventurous life. She realized much of the work with them had been done: now was the time to celebrate the joy her daughters gave her and reap the rewards of those tough parenting years.

Ideally Maria would have preferred not to have a lover, but she knew life wasn't perfect. Andrew filled the gaps in a loving and meaningful way yet didn't encroach on her life. She could put him in a box. Ted, however, had derailed her life. She'd had a dream about him: they were walking down a street in her home town in the US; he had his arm around her. She looked up at me, smiling with those twinkly eyes, 'He's deep inside me, there's no option,' and then she said rather triumphantly that she no longer felt rejected, and wasn't living in hope. 'I don't fully understand it, but I don't feel sad. I feel I have so much to be grateful for, and I really love Ted. I'm very pleased it's happened. I have no regrets.'

I felt warmth towards her, and proud she'd found a way of coming through such a painful process. A moment later she set my alarm bells ringing by mentioning, 'I might be seeing Ted at Hampton Court Flower Show.' I felt cross that all her work could be potentially unravelled by seeing him again and said clearly that I thought it would trigger all her body memories and set her off on a new bout of longing. She felt she had to go for work. I wondered whether she was using it as an excuse to test her heart, being pulled back to him just at the point she was saying she felt she'd made the transition into this new settled phase of her life. As she left, she told me she'd think about it.

Maria had seen Ted, and it had shaken her up. He'd set off her desire to touch him, which he then coldly rejected. He begged her not to contact him, telling her how threatening, to his happiness and marriage, contact with her was. It took her quite a few weeks to centre herself again, telling me, 'I'm unhappy. I don't feel not being in touch with him works. It makes me really sad.' I could see in her face a little hot spot that was throbbing with pain, and her breath was short, holding in the pain. I wanted to understand what she was holding on to, what meaning it was giving her, and what part of her couldn't let go, when Ted was adamant it was over, and even blamed her for seducing him, as if he was a victim of her love. She cried, telling me, 'I almost believe the man he was is dead, but I believe he can come back.'

Ah. I felt a thud of energy. Maybe we were getting to the nub of it. What was the coming back about? I wondered if it was linked to her Catholicism, the Resurrection. She thought for a long time, pressing her fingers into her chin, like Rodin's sculpture *The Thinker*, talking slowly, as if exploring a new alien territory, telling me she had to find a way of dealing with it that was authentic, and she knew she was a romantic, loved mystery and the idea of redemption. A little breath of excitement as she continued: perhaps she had been holding on because she thought she'd lose the love they'd had if she gave up hope of getting him back. But she finally saw the reality, calling it a 'turning point for me. I can finally understand. I was in denial before. He doesn't want me now, although he did in the past. I don't want to colour my whole life with missing him. It's positive to know what we had. I can hold on to that, and visit it now and again, but it's not there any more.'

I felt relief for her that she could now find a way of living the life she had and not the life in her dreams. It would be painful facing the reality of the end, but better than the suspended hope of reconciliation.

In the next weeks, Maria felt she was in a better place, despite the ups and downs, and great pangs of missing Ted. She crackled with energy, telling me her life was rich, she was enjoying her work, taking on new, interesting projects, and she was able to enjoy the time with her children with renewed pleasure. She went to a work dinner with Ken, quite a rare event, where people came up to her saying how much they admired him, which she enjoyed, laughing, 'If you're married to a workaholic, better he's a successful workaholic than a failure.' And then she looked up, as if she'd discovered new words to describe him that surprised her, and told me, 'I believe in Ken. He's true to himself.' Having thought endlessly about Ted, she thought now that he wasn't living his true life, which diminished her infatuation with him.

I let her know I could see how rich her life was: I could see it in her face and how she sat in the chair. She relished that, getting more excited as she told me, 'My relationship with Andrew is in such a good place. I am so happy with him. I do understand him. I'm grateful for all we do have. I'm hungry for experience and our affair, since we're both married, works. We love our sex life, we are each other's closest ally – we love each other very much.' She gave me a warm hug as she left. 'I think I can get on with my life. I feel I've folded a lot of my past pain into my heart. It will never disappear – I understand that – but I am more at peace with it now.'

Jackson

Love, Health and Family

I have never been patient in my personal life, but until Jackson walked through my door, I could rely on my patience when I worked. Jackson tested me on many levels. He was twenty-five years old, slight of build, dark-eyed, with black hair tied neatly in a ponytail, fragile-looking, and he didn't speak. He was as tidy as a new pin, punctual to the minute. I imagined his drawers would have had Marie Kondo cheering.

Jackson would sit, his leg jiggling, hunching his back as he pressed his elbow on his knee, looking between his foot and his bitten nails, somehow giving me the message that his part was to show up while mine was to read his mind and give him the answers that would fix his problems. Words imbued with feeling or empty of it are my familiar territory. Silence between words is the cadence and rhythm of a session I easily navigate, which meant that with Jackson I felt useless.

For weeks I would try to connect with him, the weeks leading to months as I did the equivalent of therapeutic cartwheels trying to access what was going on in him. I received the occasional sentence or a nod, but mainly silence. Through intense supervision to soothe my frustrated anger, eventually I adapted: I slowed down and calmed my drive to dig into him. When I accepted this was where he needed to be I learned there were different hues of silence emanating from Jackson, some tense or angry, some profoundly despairing, others brooding, and yet others quite peaceful. But mainly I sensed his deep well of loneliness, his lack of capacity to climb out of that dark hole. I would name what I experienced in the room with him and saw his body incrementally unfurl as I made my simple observations.

When we discussed our beginning, much later on, we both understood Jackson's behaviour had not been a conscious choice, but a reflex: he automatically shut down as he stepped into my room, and whatever messages were swirling in his head, he couldn't voice them. It gave me an image of a tortoise retreating under its shell; tapping on it would ensure the animal didn't pop its head out. Jackson could only build trust with me when I didn't push him, when I gave him my non-judgemental attitude, the warmth of my gaze, and when I paid attention to his whole being, which allowed him to respond in his own time, without having to dance to my tune.

There wasn't a breakthrough moment but slowly, after six months, Jackson began to tell me his story. His mother was a successful black woman, a senior adviser in City Hall, whose relationship with his father had been brief, her pregnancy unplanned, and his white dad, a journalist, now had a wife and two children to whom he was much more committed. The themes that recurred over the years we worked together were mainly concerned with Jackson's love life, his health and his relationship with his family – it was unusual to have a session without him talking about each one for they were profoundly interconnected, but for the sake of clarity I will separate them.

Jackson had been a 'good child', who worked hard, succeeded in getting into a top university and now had a well-paid job in the tech industry. I could see from the force with which he spoke how he'd worked his whole life, in that gritted-teeth, head-down, be-a-machine, only-perfection-is-good-enough way of working. But while ticking all the required boxes, from early childhood Jackson had had multiple health issues, eczema, allergies, and whenever a virus was going around, he would get it. He suffered badly with regular respiratory infections, which required endless rounds of antibiotics, and glandular fever in his first year of university. As he was telling me this, I noticed him scratch his eyes, a familiar sore red spot set against his pallid complexion, and I realized again how exhausted he was. I reflected that his foot had been hard on the accelerator to succeed in order to please his parents, while his ailing health had kept the handbrake on, and he was revving that poor tired body of his to breaking point.

This time he heard me differently, and whispered, 'I'm an empty husk.' I felt a flutter of relief as I heard Jackson acknowledge this, for we now had a small foothold of mutual understanding, and we could build on it together.

As he became more confident with me Jackson talked easily about the minutiae of his daily life – his expensive tuna sandwich that he treated himself to on Mondays and Thursdays. I understood it was important for him to do this to keep a hold on his outside world, because he knew that, for our therapy to make progress, he needed to delve into the unknown scary world of his feelings and be curious about what was going on inside him. Our focus was to discover the messages Jackson was telling himself, and their source. They were difficult disjointed sessions as he began to feel his real pain beneath his illnesses and exhaustion. He did feel loved by his mum, with heart-warming memories of her reading him stories in bed, and funny games they'd play, but I could see the hurt in his eyes as he remembered her exasperation with his constant stream of illnesses, how difficult it was for her as a single mother. The messages he received were 'It's your genes', 'This is your lot', 'You are weaker than others' and 'You must keep going . . .'

Jackson's mum had had to overcome many impediments to succeed, so worked long hours, often over weekends, and modelled how to work to the extreme. She congratulated Jackson when he did well but he had minimal experience of being cared for, and didn't know he needed to care for himself. He knew only how to override his illnesses and learned it was not okay to ask for attention. This meant he was imbued with a sense of shame for making a demand or wanting something. As I took in what he was telling me I felt a chill in my stomach, and wondered out loud that I was perhaps feeling what he hadn't been able to feel. I could see the startled look in his eyes, when he realized that he had impacted me. This was an entirely unknown concept to him, let alone experience, and he nodded with a sweet, shy smile.

His and his mother's best times together were holidays, precious happy memories in Jamaica, spending time with cousins and family friends in a tiny wooden hut on a sunlit beach. On one of the few occasions when Jackson looked me in the eye, he was describing playing catch on that beach, the sun shining through his smile, and I felt the bittersweetness of how precious that memory was, and how scant. It pulled tenderness from me: I wanted to let him know he was worthy of far more than he had received.

Jackson caught a debilitating cough that lasted for weeks, and we wondered together whether his memories had triggered it. We were developing a language that helped us understand that his mental and physical wellbeing were inextricably linked, that when he didn't feel his body, he didn't feel himself. As he said in a powerful moment, 'I am not.' In three words he'd told us how unwanted he felt and what a terrible price he had paid for that. A few sessions later he sobbed, his whole body shaking, trying to calm himself by wiping his clammy hands down the sides of his legs, as he found the words to say that, at his core, he didn't believe he had a right to exist, that he feared being humiliated at any moment, and had to stay hyper-vigilant, work harder than anyone else to ensure that he wasn't wiped out, keeping small so he wouldn't attract negative attention, and absolutely never fail.

We knew his relationship with his father had a part to play, but I was worried that if we didn't build up his immune system before we did that work he'd collapse. He had been close to the edge of collapsing many times, and I felt protective of him, not wanting him to push himself, but for once to learn that he could be gentle with himself and change his attitude, begin to take his health seriously, to learn he couldn't do it alone, that he needed the help of others. We looked at what he might do now, and I saw a gleam in those brown eyes of his, his energy sparked by the image of a research project he could get his teeth into and, in a moment of realization, he said, 'I can't keep doing this to myself . . . I have to find a way out.'

From all the books and papers he'd read, he decided to see a nutritionist, an acupuncturist (appointments a good distance apart to allow him to afford them), and experimented with various exercise regimes, settling for kick-boxing classes and a high-intensity interval training app. He tried meditation and relaxation, and told me rather triumphantly they were a step too far. We both enjoyed his sense of power, in finding his 'no'. There was no overnight transformation, but through the months, his disciplined approach to life was working for him. He created a tough but manageable regime and it reaped rewards. As his physical strength grew, his mental strength felt more robust; he proudly flashed me his Popeye arm muscles, not exactly bulging but certainly stronger. Jackson began to get a handle on how to monitor his energy: he recognized when he was tired and rested, rather than overrode it. The surprising bonus was that he felt clearer in his thinking, which he concluded was due to the change in his diet: it rejuvenated his gut, rather than depleted it.

For the first time in his life Jackson understood that boundaries weren't just the preserve of others, but were important for him too. Inch by inch he learned to check his authentic response and find his truthful yes and no. He told me, 'My body isn't screaming at me any more. It's like those Exocet missiles that attacked me have turned back . . .' A big breath, his leg slowly jiggling. '. . . I know when I'm super-stressed they'll come screaming at me again, but most of the time I'm out of the war zone.'

I wanted to high-five him, but radiated a version of it instead, and told him how proud of him I was that he'd committed to such a difficult project, persevered despite his frustrations and now was reaping the rewards.

Meantime when Jackson talked about his father the anguish and fury on his face were heartbreaking. The sharpness stung my chest. His feelings were entangled and intense but the story, the many different versions of it I heard, was painfully simple: as a child his father had seen him once a month out of duty, not love or pleasure. When his dad looked at him Jackson felt his irritation or, worse, his indifference. Jackson, who had no way of protecting himself, believed he was worthless and turned it into a self-attack. During his adolescence, Jackson had been sulkily silent with occasional outbursts of fury and its predictable outcome of further rejection. Once when Jackson's hurt broke out, he remembered his dad spewing, 'Just looking at you makes me feel sick. You look like your mother.' As Jackson spoke the poisonous words that had cut into him for years, it was as if the floor fell out beneath him. He raked the air, trying to hold on to something solid, not to disappear. With his permission, I came beside him, put my hand gently on his back, and encouraged him to breathe slowly, to ground him. As he found his centre, he whispered, 'How I look isn't down to me . . . It's Dad's issue . . .' An important and healing clarification.

Jackson's stepmother's resentment towards him played out in numerous ways. Hating his need for money, and his illnesses, she refused to let him come to stay to protect her children from 'infection'. There wasn't a place in the house that was allocated for him: he slept on a Z-bed in the sitting room while his two half-siblings had their own rooms. Watching them live the loving childhood he dreamed of was a bitter twist. The cruel truth of our bad design as human beings was that the more Jackson longed for his dad, contorting himself to please him, the more it turned his dad off and the more anxious and needy Jackson became. Even when he was congratulated, Jackson didn't trust it and wanted more. It reminded me of a research paper I'd read that said lack of attention was more painful than being hit or shouted at, which at least left one feeling as if one existed.

At university Jackson had formed close and important friendships with three other students, his homemade family (thank goodness for them). They persuaded him to stop putting himself through the cycle of agony so he reduced his contact with his dad to a meal every few months, enough to be connected but defend against the evisceration he experienced when he saw him more often. We couldn't mend his wound, but we could give the young Jackson a voice that was heard, and ways to self-soothe. We used visualizations to access little Jackson more easily – describing visualizations sounds like therapy woo-woo, which I hate. In practice, they are a powerful tool to enable my clients to access parts of themselves that thinking and talking cannot reach. The Heineken of therapy!

The place that most commonly emerged was a dark forest of tall pine trees where little Jackson sat on the ground, not doing anything or looking at anything, just alone and still. I would ask him whether he wanted someone. What did he need? I heard, 'Nothing, I am nothing.' He held on to that victim position with brute force, freezing his hurt and desperation because this place was familiar. Daring to shift, to expose the years of vulnerability, was unknown and terrifying.

Returning from holiday one day, months later, Jackson came grinning into my room, and sat in a different chair. I smiled and wondered what was up, hoped he'd found a girl, but, no: he'd had a series of powerful dreams where he'd been a flame-throwing ball-busting superhero. He'd blown up his dad's house, crushed his car with his foot, thrown his stepmother across the universe and, best of all, picked up his father by his shirt collar, roared his rage into his face and seen fear in his father's eyes. Finally his father was the victim. Who knows what had triggered his unconscious into such power, but the creative force of his imagination enabled Jackson to grow. It shifted the noose of victimhood, and Jackson was freed to explore himself from a different position.

Jackson showed me again that people need to want to get better – we all suffer, but maintaining victimhood is optional. Over time, a long time, Jackson was sustained by the results of his courage, small daily actions, and after lots of mini-breakthroughs he sat bolt upright in the chair, his eyes closed, breathing deeply, tears streaming down his face, but his voice calm and strong, as he gave himself the affirmation 'The universe wanted me to be born. I am worthy of love . . . I deserve to exist.'

If he'd opened his eyes he'd have seen tears running down my face too. I wondered if the change in him would result in a different response from his father. I hoped it would.

When Jackson started opening up to me the only thing he was clear about was that he wanted a girlfriend. Some of his mates were still happy playing the field but he wanted someone to love. He described the 'tribunal of girls' who'd dismissed his overtures at university and how nervous and hopeless he'd felt around them. They had left him with a sense of shame that meant he had rejected even the possibility of love for many years, resorting to porn to meet his needs. Despite his fantastic friends, who certainly made a difference, I could see the vicious circle of sadness and loneliness that had built up in him, but now he didn't want to be that 'stone-hearted person who fears love'.

Wanting a relationship gave him the motivation to face his health issues, and his father. I learned about the dating landscape Jackson found himself in. It was thought of as slightly creepy to go up to someone at a bar, and apps where there was mutual agreement to date were the norm, though some still met through friends. Apps suited Jackson because they gave him time to think what to write, offered plenty of choices and he was good-looking enough to be right-swiped; he knew his less good-looking friends often lied about their height and found ways of glamorizing their photographs.

After a number of successful dates, there were gateways to be got through, usually led by the young woman: first, 'We're dating', which meant they were meeting up and having sex; then 'We're exclusive', which meant being faithful to each other but not boyfriend and girlfriend; and finally, usually three or four months in, 'We're boyfriend and girlfriend.' Phew. He knew it was common to go on many dates each week, but Jackson could only muster the courage to do it once a week, and I could see his anxiety as he rubbed his hands together, dreading it and desperate for it at the same time.

I heard in detail about an afternoon date Jackson had one Saturday. There were many personal hurdles for him to overcome as he headed out: first, how he looked – he took ages to get dressed, wanting to be perfect, trying on different trainers, clothes, brushing his hair into various styles, but never felt satisfied. His self-image versus his dream image was another hurdle: he had a romantic Hollywood picture of falling in love at first sight but he didn't see how he could be that leading man, being naturally shy and introverted – he didn't know how to be flirty, but to add a final twist he also feared he would be seen as sexist if he was.

That date hadn't gone well: the girl had decided he wasn't right and started looking at her phone in a desultory fashion as poor Jackson tried to make conversation. He left utterly flattened. There was a revolving door of similar dates, some a little better when they met twice, some they had sex, but nothing lasted. I felt for him: he was getting affirmation of the negative message he had always shouted at himself, 'You're unlovable.' If it hadn't been for his best friends he'd have given up. They took him out, cooked him supper, and when he told them he was broken, they hugged and loved him, kept in touch every day by text. We agreed Jackson's improved health and fitness meant he was more resilient.

Then he met Suki. She was lovely. He couldn't believe his luck because she took the lead and seduced him. They overcame those first awkward sexual encounters – she even taught him that good sex came from pleasure, the dance of desire through communication rather than a mad dash to orgasm. Over time he learned to overcome his performance anxiety and trust in their mutual touch and connection. I told him I was impressed by her assertiveness, and we agreed, laughing, she'd done a good job as coach and confidence builder. They'd happily got through the dating and exclusive hoops.

Jackson was excited, he felt alive and proud as he introduced her to his gang. He grinned at me, describing her interest in his looks, even cutting off his ponytail at her suggestion. He felt a new version of himself was growing and it was touching to witness. But six months later there were alarm bells he wanted to ignore. She started putting off their meetings, withdrew sexually, and stopped replying to texts; her withdrawal sent him into a crazed panic when he couldn't sleep or concentrate, his whole life seemingly dependent on the ping of her message, but then she'd tell him not to be ridiculous, acted as if she was the injured party, and soothed him with sex. When he tried to do special things with her, she seemed uninterested, even cold, but at other times she'd be warm again, say the things he wanted to hear, how much she cared about him, even giving pictures of a future together.

When I questioned him, he looked sad, and told me he didn't have the luxury to be choosy and dump her; he needed her more than he cared about the rollercoaster she put him through. He didn't believe that if he lost her he'd find someone else. He couldn't bear the idea of being on the dating circuit again. I acknowledged there were many reasons not to break up with her. We talked about how her hot and cold behaviour ignited a madness of overvaluing what you cannot have and not cherishing what you do have.

In the end it was Jackson's friend Haz who gave him the cruel wake-up call. Suki had two Facebook accounts: one where they were friends and she was displayed as 'in a relationship' with Jackson, and another, which he didn't know about, which showed her partying and getting with other people. This was too much humiliation for Jackson, who confronted Suki. She instantly broke up with him. That led to desperate weeks of misery. His body took the hit: his asthma and eczema kicked in, he couldn't sleep and he'd slump on the chair in my room, as sad as he had been in the first months of our work together. He sought comfort from his mother, who was loving, and they went for reviving walks together. However, she had never had a successful relationship of her own, which fomented a doomed vision of love that found an easy target in Jackson's broken heart. It brought up the needy child in him, the ghosts of his father's disgusted glances. I wanted my warmth to reach across to him, to let him know that he wasn't alone this time, that I heard the depth of his sadness, and was there to support him through it.

As I spoke he'd give me a gimlet eye of disbelief, but I also felt something landed in him. The mechanism he'd learned as a child to keep going despite his loss came to his aid; the distraction of work and exercise broke up the wells of sadness that lay in wait for him as he walked home. We both wished we could get his head and heart to work in tune with each other, as he knew deep down Suki was a bad 'un. Yet the mark she left in him echoed his early wound, and he couldn't imagine trusting again or believe that anyone would truly love him. While he knew she'd toyed with him, it didn't stop him missing her, or going over scenarios when he wished he'd said the right thing, been the person he imagined she wanted him to be. Then she'd love him. The madness of obsessive love.

Jackson did the work of grief: he cried and yowled, retreated to the past, curled up in a ball, and then he would kick-box and scream. He had the sense to see his acupuncturist, who centred him, and to let his friends love him. They took him away for weekends in the country and organized regular outings together, which soothed him. This was different from the emptiness of that boy in the well, who screamed silently, who never asked for help because he knew none was available. This was a man who had coping mechanisms and, crucially, people who loved him and whom he loved.

At this point I had been seeing him for two years. That Jackson was now twenty-seven, not decades older, meant that therapy could take hold more easily. The natural bounce of youth was on his side, a primitive drive to procreate, to get on, with less-entrenched patterns of behaviour, as he wallowed in victimhood. Six months after Jackson broke up with Suki, he started going out again, inevitably with some dread but a glimmer of hope. The good sex with Suki meant he was more confident on that front, giving me a rather twinkly smile as he told me so. I was confident, too, for I knew he now had skills of emotional intelligence and relational self-awareness that would serve him even better than fancy moves. Again he had a number of dates, some more fun than others, but this time he made a friend, Katie: they laughed a lot together, enjoyed going to exhibitions and movies, and they expanded their friendship group through each other. He told me pointedly he wasn't attracted to her, but it had perked him up no end. New friendship is exciting.

Now when I look at Jackson there are times I can still see that fragile, wounded young man, yet I can also see a young man who has dared to face his own demons: he has literally faced them down. I see a young man who bravely allows himself to be vulnerable, to express the messiness of his feelings, while keeping his drawers tidy, of course, and who has shifted his position fundamentally from one of not being allowed to exist to that of a young man who is truly alive to all that is emerging in him and one who is creating his own story. I cannot wait to hear the next chapter.

The work continues.

Robbie

To Have Loved and Lost

Robbie wrote to me requesting an appointment. It was a short, almost rude email, with an air of entitlement that got my back up. My instinct was to tell him my caseload was full, but I gave myself time to reflect. I suggested an assessment session to give us both the opportunity to see whether we could work together, and the option to withdraw. Despite folklore about first impressions being reliable, I think they say more about me than the other person. It is important to hold back from my reflex response.

A few weeks later, Robbie, sixty-three years old, rang my doorbell. I could feel my defences edging upwards, assuming his abruptness would be transferred from his keyboard to me. He walked slowly up my stairs, needing to stop many times on the way, his red face shiny with perspiration by the time he collapsed into the chair in my room. His jacket was as tired as his face, worn and shiny beyond dry-cleaning. Robbie spoke achingly slowly, planting one word in front of another, not helped by a streaming cold. I found myself twisting in my seat with impatience.

His wife, Susan, had died of a brain haemorrhage two years earlier – he had returned home from work, where he was head of an academy school, to find her dead on the kitchen floor. She'd been dead a few hours. The tone of his voice let me know that this was a story he had told many times: it was empty of feeling. Robbie, with his three adult children, had pulled through those first bleak months together. On strict instruction from his eldest daughter, they had accessed family therapy, which he'd been surprised to find helpful. All of their reactions to Susan's death had been different, reflecting their personalities and relationship with her. Talking them through together, practically and emotionally, had protected them from big disagreements. He found it extremely difficult when his children overrode his wishes, but learned that, on the matter of their mother, he had to listen to them.

Robbie smiled when he told me his children were getting on with their lives. His daughter Jess, a digital content producer, was married, his son Phil worked in finance in New York, and his youngest son, Rich, was an apprentice carpenter in Cumbria. If there was a child to worry about, as there always was, it would be Rich. He worked long hours, lived alone and had never had a girlfriend.

A close friend had told Robbie he needed to 'move on', which infuriated him, but part of him knew he was lonely. He looked at me with uncertainty. Could I help? I was wary of Robbie's headmaster tone, which brought the 'stupid pupil' to the fore in me. But that was my issue to deal with. My stance had softened. Beneath his brusque exterior, I could see Robbie's vulnerability and his battered heart. I told him I hoped I could help him. Obviously I didn't have answers, but I would like us to work together on how he might go forward in this next phase of his life. It wouldn't be about forgetting Susan and moving on, but remembering her and finding a way of living again – hopefully loving again. I saw him ease a little in response.

I asked him to tell me about Susan, which triggered a coughing fit. Out came his blue spotted handkerchief, which became an old friend and signal of his distress. Eventually he told me Susan had been his 'soul-mate', warm and loving, the person he turned to for advice. She kept him grounded when work overtook him and, most importantly, she took most responsibility for their children. He sobbed at the loss of their parenting together. She had been a part-time GP and it felt particularly cruel that she'd been thinking of retiring just before she died, wanting to do something more spiritual with her life. He described his grief: the first year he had felt numb, while getting sledgehammer hits of pain out of the blue. There had been the crazy juggle of work and organizing her funeral, her will, waiting for the post-mortem results. Friends, neighbours and her family had regularly been around, or dropped food in, but that had stopped after six months. He had no siblings. Robbie's default response of keeping going had worked for him to a great extent – although he missed her in every corner of the house. Memories would assault him, and he would find himself crying, longing for her, realizing anew that the whole world they had created together had gone.

Rich had then still lived at home, and they had grown closer, which had been the surprising boon. Robbie had found cooking for him a way of loving his son and therapeutic. He looked up at me, with the edge of a cheeky grin, glad to surprise me with his domestic skill. He went on to tell me his grief was less raw now, the physical pain had eased, but there was a vast emptiness. I wondered whether the slowness of his words reflected that emptiness, or was it exhaustion? Or both? I asked him if he slept. Since the day of Susan's death, he had slept badly. In the first months he'd resorted to sleeping pills but had stopped for fear of becoming addicted. I felt in my stomach the chill of his loneliness and the disruption of his being. I found myself wanting to pump warmth into him, sitting on my hands to stop myself rubbing his arms, as one would a child coming out of cold water.

For weeks I heard different versions of the same experience.

Robbie felt the future was difficult, he could see time stretching out in front of him with no point to it. He found it bleak to be on his own, especially since Rich had left home a few months ago. For Robbie, turning the key in the lock to an empty house, the endless chores, a cold bed and not having his companion, who was his sounding board and 'soul-warrior', was utterly debilitating. The weight of his pain sat in me. I realized, with a sense of shame, this wasn't the therapist I wanted to be, that I rather dreaded our sessions. I didn't want to yank him out of his pain, since pain was the agent of change, and told myself this was a necessary part of his process. I needed to be patient and accompany him.

Until one session. As I sank deeper in my chair, I had an image that I was being buried alive, suffocated by his ponderous repetition. Tentatively I found a way of telling him what I felt, and I wondered if my image of being buried alive had any resonance in him. He took his time, of course, breathing heavily, and told me, 'I feel dark. I want to be with Susan, on the other side.' I told him gently I could hear how much pain he was in. Robbie began to cry quietly, which led to big shaking sobs and primitive howls of pain. I went to sit beside him, instinctively felt he needed the warmth of my hand on his shoulder, as his pain built up through his body and flooded out into the room.

When Robbie's pain subsided, I went back to my chair, and felt lighter. He lifted his head. He had no words. I suggested he should take care of himself that evening, doing the things that soothed him: go for a walk, cook supper, listen to music (he had a playlist he used to calm himself), and definitely not resort to his habitual pattern of working until midnight.

Over the next sessions our focus became less oriented in the past and more towards the future, which was a shift, although by no means straightforward. I was relieved when I heard Robbie say he wanted to find a partner – 'Life without love is no life' – but he wasn't sure how to do so. While I agreed that finding someone to love and be loved by would give him much-needed hope in his life, I worried whether his level of exhaustion would be a barrier to successful dating, which could undermine him further. We talked about how he might re-energize himself before he joined a dating agency. Robbie told me his spirituality was important to him, that even in his bleakest moments he'd felt connected to a higher power, God. Both Buddha and Jesus had meaning for him, and he wanted to find a spiritual practice that recognized their importance.

We worked out a regime together that he had to stick to, no 'Shall I today?' ambivalence, but commitment. His homework. I could see him liking being given concrete rules: three mornings a week a fast walk or a run, three evenings spent in spiritual contemplation, and visits to his local church when the spirit took him; on Saturday or Sunday a longer stint of exercise, ideally with a friend. To improve his sleep, we agreed he should have a cold bedroom, an eye mask for darkness, no digital activity two hours before bed – and no working after 7 p.m. No wonder he wasn't sleeping: his brain was racing with work stresses.

In the months that followed, Robbie's energy levels gradually improved. He'd stuck to the new discipline. He still puffed his way up the stairs, but he was less ponderous and spoke with more vitality. We were both more awake. He was sleeping better, having added a set of mental exercises a friend had told him about as a prelude to sleep. With his best friend, whom I mentally thanked for being a proper friend, and his daughter, for the feminine perspective, he had worked out his online profile for the dating agency he planned to sign up with. Unusually for Robbie, he came to a session with a topic in mind: he wanted to discuss what he was looking for in a possible date. I wanted to check where Susan was with regard to his dating. We both knew logically that he was single, but what about in his heart?

Robbie was way ahead of me. He'd thought about this a great deal, and believed she would want him to love again, but he needed to do something tangible to release her hold on him. He believed the past was in the present, and the present influenced his future. Susan would always be part of him, but he needed physically to represent a shift of perspective. After much discussion,

Robbie decided he wanted to go to the coast, a place the family had often been to, and go out to sea to release her.

As the dawn was rising on the morning of his plan, he'd sat on the beach, breathing in the energy from the sea, and breathing out his pain. He could feel layers of sadness fall away. Then, on his little boat, he visualized Susan. While holding the last part of her ashes, and her favourite flowers in his hands, he was telling his head to let them go, but struggled to open his hands. He battled with himself as he held the ashes tighter and gasped telling me it was the hardest thing he'd ever done, eventually scattering them into the sea. He'd slowly rowed back to the shore, knowing he had done the right thing. He had spent some time in the medieval church nearby, praying for Susan's spirit, and for peace on his path to enlightenment. A week later he signed up with the dating agency.

Robbie began to picture his future. He called it a new book, more than a chapter. The new woman in his life couldn't simply be a companion; he wouldn't settle for that. He wanted another soulmate. He sounded excited at the possibility of no longer being alone. After a few weeks it became the 'parade' of dating, looking at people's profiles, rejecting those with teenage children. Or those with no children, although they often looked attractive, because he knew he couldn't deal with having another baby. He would go for drinks with hope and come home disappointed when there had been no spark or, worse, the woman had been dogmatic, with opinions he didn't share. He spoke of his sadness in seeing their loneliness and desperation, which matched his own, wanting to make it work, but knowing this person wasn't right. Robbie longed for the innocence of dating in his youth. He had had no idea that dating in his sixties would be so complex: everyone came with their baggage and fault lines – and sex was complicated. The sex he'd had felt empty. He'd remembered it as being fun and exciting, but that innocent joy seemed long gone. Everyone had a story of loss, bitterness or betrayal, which lay beneath the smile and promises of hope.

Robbie had experienced a kick of cold disappointment, which

had set him back, when he'd met a woman he liked and she hadn't wanted to meet him again. Sometimes he forced himself to date a second time. He even kissed a woman he hadn't really liked, but then had to deal with the additional complication of saying no to her, having offered a sliver of hope, which made him feel bad. All the not-knowing and longing, hoping there was someone for him and at other times thinking he might have to learn to live alone, was crazy-making. It intensified his missing Susan, and he decided he had to stop.

I felt a little crushed too. I'd thought it might be straightforward, assuming that, being a man, he would be spoilt for choice. But, as with all assumptions, I was wrong.

Robbie reverted to his old way of coping: working hard. It didn't block out the pain, but it gave him a break from it, and connected him to his strengths. He'd had considerable success with his academy, turning it around from 'inadequate' to 'outstanding' in the previous five years. He had sorted out bad behaviour and improved the quality of the staff so the board of governors and the parents were, on the whole, pleased with him. His difficulty was the relentless toil of having more things to do, and be responsible for, than he had time to deal with: his overflowing in-tray, all the risks of radicalization, safeguarding, and being at the whim of political policies over which he had no control.

But beneath all of that Robbie found meaning in his work. Walking around the school, knowing a lot of the children, enjoying their spirit, doing what he could to sort out those with problems, sustained him. He was passionate about his new garden project and improving the school canteen. Robbie continually had new goals to reach, which kept him energized. He was good at his job: he liked leading and making his vision a reality. It built his self-esteem, when he felt personally fragile. As long as he kept it in perspective, did one thing at a time, turned off work when he got home, it was good for him. He had to retire in five years, and his dream was that he would find a new partner with whom he could 'reinvent myself'.

Over the summer Robbie spent time with his children, which he enjoyed. He found the smell of them and the familiarity of their hugs and closeness consoling. But sometimes when he was with them, he would find himself silent as they talked and bantered together. He felt more keenly the space where Susan should have been; it tilted him to feel like half a person. Also, they had started bossing him around, telling him what he should be doing, being a version of Susan, but most indubitably not Susan. Quite patronizing. I could see his fierceness in repeating his version of 'Back off' to them.

Fortunately, the long summer holidays allowed Robbie to take a spiritual retreat on a Hebridean island, with an inspiring leader. It profoundly enriched him. Being with like-minded people, their openness in talking together in a way he didn't in his usual life, fed his soul. I could see light in Robbie's eyes as he told me, 'The desire of my heart is stillness . . . and I've clarified my purpose to live with love, show up and be of service.' As he spoke, he cried. Tears of release. I could feel there was more space in him for joy and felt how much we both wanted him to have it.

A photograph of Lou popped up on his screen from his dating agency and he asked her for a drink. There was a spark the moment they met, and within days they were in a whirlwind of excitement and passion. Robbie was too happy to meet me and cancelled appointments. When I did see him, he had lost weight and was skippy with joy. He even wore a different jacket, no dreary 'old friend' any more. The grump disappeared. It made me smile. Lou was alluring, an artist, from Lebanon, divorced, with grown-up children. To his astonishment, he had the best sex of his life with her. Sex had been a minute part of his relationship with Susan. With Lou he had discovered an aspect of himself he hadn't known existed. They met as much as they possibly could, although both had commitments that often got in the way. He felt alive and renewed. Love is not dependent on age: it makes us feel new, how-ever old we are, when we fall in love. The only dampener to his joy was Rich, who refused to meet Lou – not because he was against his father having a new relationship: he had told him he didn't 'want to go there'. Robbie was angry with him. He felt Rich was being unfair, given all they had been through.

Then, after those intense two months, Lou suddenly cut all contact with Robbie. She stopped replying to his texts, didn't return his telephone calls, disappeared from his life. He was utterly devastated. He wrote her a long letter telling her what he felt for her, how special their time together had been. He knew there were problems about making time for each other, but he felt that their budding relationship was precious, and needed to be treated tenderly. No response. He raged against her silence.

Eventually she texted him, but it was opaque, citing busyness, which left him angrier. It was a different kind of death, leaving his imagination to fill in all the gaps. Robbie left furious messages on her mobile, telling her people said goodbye after a coffee, after a phone call. They had been lovers – she had jumped into her hello quick enough, how dare she not have the decency to say goodbye? He stopped himself driving to her house, or checking her social media, but only just. His job forced him to keep going: putting on his headmaster cloak every day kept him sane when he thought he might fragment. He hated being in his house on his own, unlocking that door to emptiness again. The loss of the thrill of his newly found sexual excitement hit him anew every night and triggered his insomnia. But the bigger loss was connection. He was skin hungry, contact hungry. He longed for the closeness of their bodies fitting together, holding her as she slept.

I felt angry with Lou, this woman I'd never met, and found her silent withdrawal unfathomable. We bolstered our outrage by agreeing that if she couldn't end their relationship cleanly she clearly wasn't the right person for him. We tried to find an explanation for her behaviour, looking at her relationship history: was it an indication of her way of being? Robbie wondered if he had been 'too keen'. The line between being needy and loving can be hard to gauge, neediness being experienced as wanting the other person to fill a gap in you. Loving is more open, although loving can be experienced as a demand. Perhaps it was a factor to keep in mind with a new date in the future. We were clutching at straws, trying to make sense of something for which only Lou knew the answer.

When Robbie's fury died down, he came to see me, heart sore and uncomfortable inside. Nothing fitted or sat right. I suggested we do a visualization to stop the whirring of his mind. He saw a space in the small of his back: it was red and raw, like a squidgy ball. When I asked him if it could speak what would it say, it yowled. For a long time. Then he breathed in light and love, and exhaled the darkness, the pain. He could see the red ball bathed in a silky light, and could feel his heart as a balance, telling him they could do this together. He couldn't kick out the ball, but he sensed that although it hurt now the pain would pass. This was not for ever. There was no route map, but he had a sense that a lighter time lay ahead: he needed to listen to the wisdom of his body, trust his body and nature. The images from the visualization succeeded in shifting his focus from what he couldn't control or influence to himself, the person he could influence, support and have compassion for. Robbie knew, again, the path for him was to be less frantic in looking and sit with his discomfort. Then paradoxically peace would emerge.

Robbie hadn't talked about or, in fact, mentioned his parents. Perhaps I'd picked up an unvoiced message not to go there for I hadn't asked about them. His father had died in his mid-eighties. But his mother, who was in her nineties, had become ill. He had to rush from school to join her for hospital appointments or visit her at home. Going home was grim: she hadn't been able to keep the place clean and refused any additional help. He hated the smell of decay, the sticky surfaces, and looking after her was a thankless task for she constantly moaned. Robbie knew she was no longer safe to live alone – she might easily leave the gas on or have a fall. He dreaded the fight it was going to be to get her into a nursing home. He was overstretched, and the reality that everything always came back to him hit him anew. Nothing happened in his life unless he did it. This weighed heavily on him as a burden of endless responsibility, which he'd carried from childhood.

As he spoke I could feel the weight of it in my body, and he'd reverted to speaking slowly with much sighing. It keyed into a part of him he felt guilty about: he resented having to look after his mother. There wasn't a bank of goodwill and love from his childhood he could draw on. Both his parents had been 'emotionally arrested'. His mother preferred her dogs to children and his father had been absent – 'He never made me a bowl of Heinz tomato soup or even a piece of toast in fifty-five years.' The care his mother required felt like a life sentence of time and money he didn't want to spend. He was angry that the situation brought the worst side of him to the fore.

In a moment of touching insight, he apologized to his eight-year-old self, for what was ahead. When he was thinking, he twiddled his rather hefty eyebrows. I could see his younger self doing that in school lessons, concentrating at times or dreaming, that sweet young boy's wide-eyed innocence being knocked out by Robbie's drive to succeed, to be good, to please his parents, which overrode his authentic self. When he was crunched down with pain, Robbie was again that eight-year-old boy, peeking out of the rather older redder face. It was in those moments that it was hardest for him to unfurl enough to do the things that helped him, like breathe and take in some of the life and love that restored him. But with the space to reflect in our session, Robbie reminded himself that nature calmed him, as did being close to his children. He needed to prioritize what fed his soul. He sighed deeply, looked down at his hands and smiled, then heaved himself out of the chair looking sad, yet with renewed intent.

After the summer Robbie knew that he wanted to start looking for a girlfriend. Lou had given him a taste for joy, and he wanted it again. But he was in a dilemma. He'd been hurt and was scared of being hurt again. The quest for love said, 'Take me, eat me, love me, find me,' but fear said, 'Stop, no, hold still.' Part of him dreamed love would find him, if he stopped looking for it. How was he to go forward? I didn't have the answer. I trusted Robbie would work it out for himself.

Robbie was right in not pushing himself to go faster than his poor bruised self could take. He was listening fully to his heart. He spent the time working hard but also seeing friends, allowing his confidence to build, and restoring himself with his spiritual practice and walks. It took him eight more months before he was ready, longer than I had thought. He decided not to sign up with a dating agency or any apps: he wanted the meeting to be natural, as it had been in his youth. He knew it would limit his field of choice but he couldn't face the emotional toll that went with it.

He met Jane quite by chance through an old university friend. I could feel the optimism in his voice as he spoke. He liked her. They laughed together and saw the world through a similar lens. He wasn't madly in love, as he had been with Lou. He held himself back as he wanted to take it slowly and for them to get to know each other properly. He lit up as he said, 'I have someone to think about, who is thinking about me . . .' It sounded as if they were growing in intimacy. It was dawning on them both that they were no longer alone, as they revealed their true selves to each other, and felt seen, known and accepted as they found themselves to be. Long may it last.

Our work continues.

Esther

Starting Over, Love at Seventy-three

Esther had read my book *Grief Works* and wrote asking to see me. There was a directness in the way she described her need for therapy that I found compelling. Six months previously her divorce from her second husband, Richard, had been finalized, and she seemed to be doing well enough. 'My friends say that I am getting better: I see my son Michael a lot with his two children, and I have visited my daughter Rebecca in the States a few times, even looked after her two-year-old daughter. I'm an active member of the synagogue in Pinner, I have joined a gym, taken up art again, go to concerts, read a lot. I've made new friends and caught up with old.'

She told me she was seventy-three years old and had divorced her children's father in her early fifties. The relief she felt that her second marriage was over was overshadowed by an enormous sense of failure. She argued that a divorce was as much a loss as death, with its own complexity, sadness and grief. She wanted to see me to make the most of the life she had to live, not sit in her feelings of fear and disappointment, which she'd hidden from those around her. That she was intentionally doing all she could to process this loss suggested to me our work was likely to have a positive outcome – she was already on her own side. I responded positively, and we agreed to Skype sessions.

Esther was large, tanned, with thick grey hair cut to her shoulders, and dressed in a brightly coloured shirt. She gave me a slightly mischievous smile, as if to say, 'I got you.' I was touched as I became aware she trusted me immediately, as if she already knew me, through my book, and we could skip the three or four sessions that initially build the relationship between client and therapist. When I spoke, and I didn't need to say much, my words landed right inside her. She would examine them for truth, let her emotional response emerge, then find the words to describe what she was feeling. She would often lean forward to write a few notes that she would think about later. This pattern unfolded throughout our work and reminded me that trust is key: she knew I didn't judge her, that I would be honest with her, and that I, too, was invested in her living her last years to the full. I could tell she intuitively saw in my eyes that I found her inspirational. I didn't have many good role models of older women other than famous people. The only image I had of ageing was one of slow withdrawal and deterioration, which meant I feared old age.

Esther told me, 'I think that the fact I cried at your chapter on a parent dying, rather than the one on a partner dying, is probably telling,' and gave us both the insight that she felt young inside. Our initial work was to support her vulnerability while we unravelled what else was 'telling'. I asked her about her relationship with Richard.

Over a number of sessions Esther clarified for us both the story of their relationship: she'd been fifty-seven when she had met him at a conference; she had been an events organizer and he an engineer who'd come to present his work. From the moment he met her, he'd made his attraction to her obvious, and it was his desire for her that had bowled her over: he was radically different from her rather reserved first husband. Richard promised to take care of her emotionally and financially, offering Esther the stability she had always longed for. She had moved into his home within a year of meeting him, relocating from hers in Oxford, away from her previous life and, most importantly, her two children. Her son, Michael, aged twenty-three at the time, had felt abandoned by her, and was extremely angry. Richard's lack of willingness to include her children in their life exacerbated this. The initial intense spark between them remained for many years: they stimulated each other and found a way of living together that was both interesting and happy.

The fault line was Richard's controlling nature, in particular the wall he erected between Esther and her children. It caused endless arguments that were never resolved and left Esther in the uneasy position of feeling both a bad mother and a bad wife. Over time this corroded their relationship, and Esther told me, 'Being made to choose Richard over my children was impossible. In the end it was too high a price to pay. It tore us apart.'

Esther had been the one to call an end to their marriage, which brought back difficult echoes of her first divorce. Richard had been shocked, having failed to heed the warning signals of their rows and Esther's pleas for him to change. He was enraged and did all he could to wrench back control: he refused to move out of their house, and used the financial settlement as a way to punish her. He wouldn't speak to her and she had a hellish year of legal battling. For Esther, living alone, fearing dying alone and financial insecurity, threw waves of anxiety through her system, leaving her physically weak from the anxiety and sleeplessness. She cried with me noisily, as she voiced her guilt, relief and the profound sadness she had felt when the wrangling was done. She would rock on her chair as she cried, holding her fists tight, clenching against the pain, then breathe and feel the relief of allowing herself to cry. We both knew that recognizing her complex feelings in words wouldn't magically make them go away, but it was the crucial first step in enabling them to change.

I suggested she write Richard a letter, not necessarily to send. As soon as I said it her face crumpled, and she cried with great heaving sobs, trying to speak. I told her gently to breathe, to let herself cry, until she could find the words to say, 'Yes, yes, that is what I can do.' Esther wrote and rewrote a letter to Richard over the next few weeks. It was a long letter that I never saw. Words that had built up in her mind for years came out, without any guidance from me. She told me she spoke to him of their initial love, the strength and happy memories of their marriage, and their difficulties. She wrote of the things she wished she'd been able to resolve with him, and how sad she felt that their conflict had destroyed their love. Through it she began to see a more forgiving picture of them both, and it reduced her circular thinking, the endless attempt to try to get him to understand her. She would have liked to continue a relationship with him in some form, but he had adamantly cut her out of his life, and blocked all contact. It was a living loss. Esther felt Richard behaved as if she had died, but for her the relationship remained alive and unresolved when she wanted to be at peace with it.

Our relationship grew in depth and trust. My simple but accurate reflections meant Esther felt heard and, crucially, seen as she really was. I thought she also picked up my unvoiced warmth and admiration for her. Esther began to talk about being a grandmother, how she wasn't the relaxed, happy grandmother that she wanted to be. Her friends kept telling her how much fun they had with their grandchildren, and she'd nod and smile, but it wasn't what she felt. Her anxiety rose because her son, Michael, wanted to go for a week's holiday with his wife and had asked her to look after the children. She'd agreed but rather dreaded it – doing it alone would be difficult. Even having the unhelpful presence of Richard would have felt better than being 100 per cent responsible, and she became panicky. She knew there would be moments she'd enjoy, but she felt stressed. She remembered the last time she'd had them: she'd had to stop herself shouting at them when they made a mess or didn't do as they were told.

We recognized it was about control: control from her own childhood. As a child she'd never had a tantrum or complained. She was good – she'd had to be, for fear of not being loved, living under her mother's intolerant regime. An early memory of being slapped when she spat out broccoli drew pink-cheeked fury at the shame of her four-year-old self. Those encounters had unconsciously lived on in her as a mother, which she hadn't really enjoyed either for the same reasons of needing control and feeling anxious. Looking after two children was her absolute limit. More than that and her brain got 'fuzzy'.

We explored the source of her fuzziness, and found she had a critical parental voice in her, constantly putting her down. We saw clearly, for the first time, how she'd had no experience of joy, of playing, no body memory of how to have fun. She'd never had it as a child or with her own children. There was real sadness in her voice as she began to make sense of it, haltingly recognizing her inner child, who was never allowed to have tantrums and now had to tolerate her grandchildren, who could have tantrums. It triggered an internal tantrum in her, hence her 'fuzziness'.

I wondered with her about how she could soothe her inner child, and how we might take the perfect version of mother/grandmother out of her head and allow herself the more realistic messy version. Maybe one in which she could have a tantrum – spit out broccoli without recrimination. The possibility sparked energy in her, and we had a lovely moment when she laughed and the playful side of her came alive. I talked with her about how this vibrancy I saw in her outweighed the constantly worried version others commented on, and she smiled into my eyes, and went away to think about it.

Esther's week with her grandchildren was a success. She'd managed her anxiety by making her flat childproof and organizing a whole raft of things to do. Occasionally her critical voice emerged, particularly when she was with other grandmothers, who, she felt, had magical child skills she lacked. She recognized that she may always have some anxiety, wondering whether that had intensified as she aged. But pride shone in her, with an expanded perception of what she was capable of, at the real pleasure she and the grand-children had shared. As she described their glee when she pushed them down a slide, I could see in her eyes how those moments of spontaneous hugs, their bursts of laughter, had kindled love in her in a new way, breaking through some of her own hurts as a child and as a mother. It had been tiring and took a toll physically – her knee hurt and back ached – which put her in touch with her mortality. She told me as an aside, as she said goodbye, as if commenting on the weather, that she was frightened of the act of dying, but not death itself. I was left pondering on the paradox of this: how awareness of vitality when we are older inevitably raises awareness of deterioration and death.

When Esther went to spend a day with Michael, she was interested that our therapy gave her greater insight into those around her. Her first husband was present, and she observed that he wasn't an involved grandparent either. He spent most of the time reading his newspaper and muttering to himself. It gave her quiet satisfaction to see that what had annoyed her when she lived with him was now annoying her son. She noticed that Michael didn't get down on the floor and play with his children either: he was distracted and his children fought to get his attention, sometimes brutally. They didn't heed his injunctions to behave, and she reflected that they wanted the very thing she'd wanted as a child: his gaze, his emotional openness and his time. They had his presence, and didn't have the fear she'd been imbued with – they even tele-phoned him when he was at work – but his busyness, the armour he used against true connection, was as present in him as it had been in the generations before him.

Esther's dilemma, which we wrangled over for a number of

sessions, was whether to say anything. Was it her role? Would it be felt as criticism? Did she have a responsibility to say something or was it interfering? Her bond with Michael was still fragile, slowly being rebuilt following the years when he'd felt that Richard had robbed him of her, and there was a lot of anger in him, which spewed out now and again, particularly when he'd had a few drinks. She tried writing to him, tore up many versions of the letter. She didn't think he'd take the time to read it properly. The mother in her wanted to help him, protect him from repeating her mistakes, find a way of saying what she now understood. But, in the end, she said nothing. She hoped that in the future an opportunity would arise when they could have a collaborative discussion, where she could acknowledge her part and her understanding. Therapy had enabled her to travel across time, to step out of being a seventy-three-year-old grandmother and learn from her past. She vehemently wanted that learning to go forward and change the transgenerational pattern of her family's future.

Esther's sadness for the end of her marriage was a thread that ran through most sessions. She didn't miss Richard *per se*, but aspects of their life together were a recurring loss. Not having such a nice flat really bothered her, though she wished it didn't. Although she was proud that she lived happily within her means, Richard's money hadn't brought her happiness. She felt relieved not to have to deal with their constant arguments, but she missed the simple companionship of sharing life's small moments: a great TV programme, offloading the daily battles with traffic or the internet.

There was also loss that shocked me: the social response to no longer being in a couple. She sat upright, fisting her hands, as she told me how certain people now treated her with disdain, as if she had fallen down the pecking order of importance, dismissing her when she spoke. She would be placed at dinner next to the person she knew was also seen as unimportant. If staying with friends, she would no longer be put in their guest room, which was reserved for couples, but instead in the child's room in the attic, with its accompanying 'Batman wallpaper'. Esther felt for the first time the invisibility of being a single older woman, people glancing past her.

We unravelled how the presence of Richard socially had given her confidence: a couple was a strong unit when going out, and now she felt more exposed. She didn't dare argue or be the strident version of herself without the armour of being in a couple to defend her – which was tricky, since she felt more annoyed when she did go out. The idea of couples being twice as strong as a single person felt wrong in the twenty-first century. Perhaps it is primitive, our hard-wired unconscious response that a single old person is no longer a threat, or of value, and can be cast aside.

The other losses and gains of divorce were her friendships. A whole recalibration had to be endured. Esther felt other women saw her as a potential threat rather than as a friend. There were friends who, she felt, were disloyal to her (she was furious with them), one in particular who'd seen Richard for dinner but lied about it to her. Other friends were fantastic, and she felt her open sadness had brought them closer. Her two closest friends, whom she loved deeply, were married; as much as she drew strength from their time together, she recognized the shift in balance now she was single. They returned home to their partners, and she went home alone. When one brought her partner to her meeting with Esther, they were a threesome, which felt off kilter. There was also an unvoiced tension from the women's husbands, who didn't like her 'stealing' their wives and felt intimidated by the openness of their conversations: she knew more about them than they'd have liked. But her eyes twinkled as she remembered how her friends fought to see her, sometimes sending texts insisting that she meet them when they sensed she held herself back, fearing she'd be seen as intrusive.

Yet despite these challenges Esther had more energy, enjoying her new-found freedom. She was working as a volunteer in the synagogue, supporting refugees, which she found meaningful. She was taking seriously behaviours that protected her from dementia: exercise, art classes, Tai Chi. I was impressed by her energy and told her so. She wasn't limiting herself with clichés that she was too old to try something new. At one point, she looked down and whispered, with a sense of shame, that she kept thinking about men. She bit her lip, looked sideways. There had been a man at the synagogue whom she found attractive and she was embarrassed that she felt sexual around him. I wondered if her shame was sexual conditioning about her age or religion. We went down a few blind alleys until we found it came from an early experience of shame for her mother, who was such a flirt. Her hobby was men, except, of course, her husband, whom she had treated with disdain. It had left a silent injunction in Esther not to flirt.

I acknowledged the power of that, and held the other side of it, that she was a vibrant and attractive woman, who might live for at least another twenty years, and reminded her that she'd first contacted me because she was lonely. She laughed, and we agreed on the delight of being desired. Then it was as if a door snapped shut. She sat up in her chair, crossed her arms and gave a brilliant argument as to why she wouldn't and couldn't be in another relationship. How her children needed her full attention, and she wanted to be free to travel to the US to see her daughter, Rebecca.

I smiled inside: the greater the defence, the greater the feeling. I was happy a seed for a future relationship had been sown.

Over the next months Esther's resilience continued to grow. Although she found travelling and strange places more discombobulating since she'd grown older, she'd had a good visit with her daughter in America and took great pleasure in the uncomplicated nature of their relationship. Her work and connection in the synagogue were rewarding: her sense of Jewishness, the belonging to a tribe, had increased in older age, and it sustained her on many levels, although she didn't go to services very often.

Her preoccupation with Michael was a recurring worry, and I reflected that they seemed to have a mutual ambivalence towards each other. Whatever feeling there was, there was also the other feeling at the same time – his anger with her showed how important she was to him. I questioned the silent bind they seemed to have got into: it was as if he believed he had limitless rights to punish her for the years of her absence with Richard, and her duty was to comply, or she would somehow be a bad mother again. I saw a quizzical spark in her eyes, as if instinctively she wanted to agree with me, but she took her time: her old critical voice was battling with her new awareness. She smiled, 'You may have a point,' then wondered how she might talk with him openly, without a big row. Finally she said vehemently, 'Parenting is literally never over, is it?' We laughed at the truth, and I agreed, but added that it changes – it can change, and it needs to change as the children grow older.

The next time I saw Esther she started the session giggling, as she pressed her newly manicured hands against her cheeks. 'A week's a very long time, and completely transformed my life. I've met a very, very, very important person . . . It's gone off like a rocket. Day nine feels more like nine months.' She had met Peter at a lecture. He had invited her for a coffee the next day, and from that moment, they had spent every possible minute together, talking and laughing, being open and loving. When they weren't with each other physically they were on the telephone for hours or texting constantly. Laughing and talking, wanting to share everything they knew about themselves with each other. Peter was a few years younger than Esther, twice divorced with a daughter, and worked as a scientific journalist. He was self-conscious that he was a leg amputee following a bad car crash fifteen years previously. It meant they hadn't had sex yet, but he'd said, 'Our brains have had sex. We haven't had sex,' and Esther felt the same, giggling as she told me how her body sexually lit up at the mere thought of him.

Esther wanted to use the wisdom of her two previous relationships to inform this one, have the difficult conversations and maintain her independence. She didn't want to repeat the suffocation she'd felt with Richard. I told Esther it was heart-bursting to witness the joy on her face. I could feel the contagion of being in love, how it gave her boundless energy and optimism. How being desired, and thought about by a man, being the focus of that

longing and attention, met a deep need in her. The acknowledgement made her cry, telling me, 'It throws into sharp perspective
the pain.' She knew she wanted one more love in her life but hadn't
thought she'd get it. Now, through talking with me, she wanted
to grab the opportunity, recognizing this was rare in any life and
very rare at her age.

Over the next weeks their relationship blossomed. Most significantly for Esther, Peter wanted to meet her grandchildren, and
had fun playing with them. That alone broke down any barriers
she might have put up. Peter was entirely different from Richard.
He had met her son, and they'd got on well. They spent time with
important friends and family; everybody was happy for them,
which Esther found immensely touching. She laughed at the sigh
of envy a friend in her forty-seventh year of marriage gave. Happiness was pouring out of her: she couldn't stop smiling, she felt
optimistic about life and confident in herself.

The blissful next chapter contained a few reality checks, which
shook Esther. I was interested that I felt I could have been listening
to a twenty-year-old talking about a new relationship, as she
talked about days on which they texted less, in response to Peter's
recent abruptness, then a night they'd both got 'smashed' and
ended up in bed together, had a 'lovely time, he knows what he's
doing', and her disquiet that maybe he wasn't as kind and open as
she'd first thought.

Esther could feel gossamer but steely threads of hurt, rejection
and helplessness, an echo from her past history, and this held them
both back. She could also feel shoots of optimism, wanting to be
more open with Peter and show him that she longed to hold him,
and be held. All this was going on while they were drinking coffee
and reading the newspapers. Her feelings, her worries, her preoccu-
pations, her wanting and not wanting were universal responses to
love. Feelings do not age. I could see Esther calmed down as she
began to make sense of what was happening between them. They
both had painful relationship histories, which, naturally, were now
coming into play. The golden haze had faded and the reality of their

strengths and vulnerabilities was more present. In talking about Peter, she had greater understanding of him, and felt less angry.

She was about to ask me a question, 'Do you think . . .', when she started crying. Sobs shook her strong frame, for she knew the answer immediately. She was wondering if her fear of his withdrawal had anything to do with her father's inattention. She knew, deep down, it did. That four-year-old longing for her father's love was alive in her, hurting her, damn it. Then she laughed.

They had a cooling-off period, a number of weeks when they spoke intermittently, and she thought it was over. The pain of it was written clearly in her face. She couldn't concentrate, settle, or enjoy anything. She went over and over their different conversations, wondering what she'd said wrong or wished she'd said, how she could get him back. She fixated on the relationship by writing messages she didn't send on her phone, seeing he was online and wondering if he was thinking of her.

They had booked weeks before to go to a local concert together, which they agreed to do. Over the next few months they slowly built up their connection again, and with it their understanding and trust in each other. They talked through the hot spots that had triggered their rupture.

Esther told me, 'I know myself now. I can go into my heart and choose how I am going to relate to him. I will be more truthful about the core of what I feel, good and bad.' Esther's sunburst smile told me all I needed to know. She was happy and more realistic about their relationship.

It meant she didn't need me now: she had made the transition from being married to being single. She had done the work to adjust to this new life. Despite the cliché that you can't teach an old dog new tricks, Esther had made a remarkable turn-around in her outlook and feelings. She had examined and clarified many of the sinkholes of pain from her past: some she had reframed and the pain had softened; others were lessons in what to do differently. She had come to terms with her divorce to the extent that she dared trust to be in a relationship again. Most importantly, she had come to trust and value herself. Her gift to me was the memory of the boundless joy on the face of a woman in her mid-seventies, who was curious, vibrant and sexual, with plenty of living to do.

Isabel

Divorce and New Love at Forty-three

Isabel, forty-three years old, swept into my room, wafting elegance, and a confidence that brooked no vulnerability. I looked down at my scuffed shoes with irritation, then smiled at myself: she'd triggered a competitive response in me, and probably did in others. I'd need to check that, if I was going to meet her fully. As she pulled her designer skirt neatly beneath her, she examined her nails, with a short intake of breath, and a responding bob of her thick black ponytail. She looked at me from her fringe and told me she didn't know how to start. There was a crack below her perfected gleam.

To give Isabel time to settle, and check me out, I told her how I worked: my contract details, that we regularly had reviews to ensure she was getting what she wanted. I emphasized the importance for me of honest feedback. To ease her difficulty in finding words, I told her she didn't have to dive in and bare her soul the minute she met me, a total stranger. How could she? I felt it was important to let her find her own way into herself: we had time. I saw my role as facilitating her relationship with herself. To discover together what gave her life joy and meaning, what caused her pain, and what was going on beneath her actions. Where did she feel thwarted? What parts of herself was she suppressing? What had brought her to therapy, and why now?

Isabel took the cushion from behind her and hugged it to her tummy, letting us both know that what she was going to say was painful. I saw she was going to jump in, no gentle getting-to-know-each-other, which led me to wonder if, perhaps, she was someone who didn't have internal gears: she was either in neutral or fourth.

Isabel was divorcing her husband, Guy, with whom she had a four-year-old son, after a twelve-year marriage. She had started and ran a successful designer-handbag business, which at times took over her life completely. She gulped air, tears in her eyes, and spoke fast, wanting to get the facts out, racing to the end before the tears won. To add to the mix, she had been having an affair for two years with, in her words, 'an irredeemably unsuitable man', Gunner. Isabel crossed her arms, as a defence and a challenge, her lip trembling.

I didn't speak. I wanted to give her space to gather herself, after the ordeal of voicing what had been a deeply held secret, which felt scary when exposed to me. I could feel the tremble of her lower lip, such a contrast to her elegant façade, and recognized how helpful defences are: we need them to get on with our life. But it meant the neatly packaged story she'd held inside had grown messy as she spoke. I could see her startled eyes taking in the ramifications of what she'd said. The whole structure of her life was being ruptured, and it was her doing.

I spoke gently, letting her know I was aware of how raw this was for her. I wondered what her hopes for our therapy were. She rubbed her arm, her eyes darting between the floor and me, then gripped her chair as if to stop herself flying out of the door. Eventually she replied that she didn't know. She was used to solving her own problems. I could almost hear, under her breath, a voice shouting at her, 'For God's sake, woman, get a grip.' I acknowledged that her natural coping mechanism was not to touch what hurt her, step away from it by being busy and getting on. Seeking help seemed weak. But I was glad she was with me, and I wanted to help her.

Isabel sank further into the chair, then forced herself to speak more, her voice tight with reluctance. Her father was 'old-school' English, married to her Spanish mother. They lived in Cornwall and disapproved of her divorce, seeing it as her failure. She had been the one to make the decision to separate. Their sympathy was with Guy, who had seen her kissing Gunner in the street — sheer bad luck for it wasn't his usual route.

Isabel growled with rage at her parents' judgement: 'How dare they judge me?' I suggested that often hurt lies beneath anger: was she perhaps hurt by their lack of loyalty? She was hurt, but as she breathed deeper and spoke more slowly, she realized, as if for the first time, that confusion was wrapped around everything and she now sought clarity. She felt frightened, chaotic and lost, and wanted to understand what had got her into this position. I let her know that our work would be to find out together what the underlying causes were, explore the more hidden aspects of herself, grieve for the marriage she'd had, and enable her to rebuild her life going forward. I told her it was likely to be a painful process, letting herself know what the end of her marriage would mean to her.

Before I finished speaking, she had picked up her bag, and was reapplying her red lipstick to go out into the world. I had been dismissed as she switched to her public face and next meeting. Her capacity to tolerate that confusion had been used up.

I heard more of her back story, which came out in short bursts over a number of weeks, hidden under the paraphernalia of everyday life. At first I thought it was an avoidance mechanism, but grasped that it worked as a balancing technique for her highly sensitive feelings. If she could talk about work, her leather supplier, for example, something she had knowledge and agency over, it gave her the ballast to be vulnerable. And her mother was an area of vulnerability. She was glamorous, and had been a successful set designer, whom Isabel's school friends had looked at with envy. She had been the fun parent, creating brilliant games that would be utterly exhilarating. Isabel remembered being taken shopping, for no reason other than pleasure, and on one occasion coming home with her favourite outfit, a white miniskirt and T-shirt. Her joy quickly alchemized to shame, the moment she caught the familiar glance of disapproval from her father. Her dad had wanted to share their joy, but he was stressed all the time, particularly about spending money. He tried to exert control – and be the grown-up. Without obvious success. There was no stopping her mother.

I could picture her mother vividly, and my bias against what I term 'child mothers' reared its head. They infuriate me: mothers who love play and high jinks, who seek attention, but do not double down and take responsibility, or do the job of being the adult parent. They don't hold boundaries. Their charm seduces but the damage done to their children is unrecognized. As Isabel's story unfolded, my anger with her mother whirled inside me, unvoiced for now, as it wasn't useful for Isabel to be taken from the focus of understanding herself. And my compassion for her grew.

Life had begun to unravel at a faster pace when Isabel was in her late teens. Isabel described with haunting clarity the day she realized her mother was an alcoholic. She had come home from university for the holidays, knowing something was not right but uncertain as to what it was. One evening she had walked into the sitting room and seen her mother drinking whisky out of the bottle. Isabel had challenged her, questioned what she was doing. Her mother had tried hiding the bottle, defiantly telling her, in a drunken voice, she wasn't doing anything. It was a shattering moment, when the truth of her mother's alcoholism could no longer be denied. Twenty-five years later, the situation had only got worse: her mother had never succeeded in staying sober, and her parents' marriage was one of co-dependency and dysfunction. There could be weeks of sobriety, then the chaotic rollercoaster of her mother's binges. I heard the toll her mother's lies took on Isabel. 'My mother totally believes her own lies. She'll substitute her version for the truth in every story she tells. Blaming everyone but herself. I'm exhausted by it.'

As Isabel was speaking I noticed her go numb. She had too many feelings: fury for all the hurt, but also many layers of love, resentment and disappointment. I could see the anguish of the child, who couldn't trust her own mother, and the adult, who didn't want it to hurt as much as it did.

A few weeks later Isabel came in, wearing no make-up and a tracksuit. She couldn't speak for a while. She put her hands to her mouth, not wanting to voice what had happened. She'd had a terrible time with her boyfriend. He had accused her of being unfaithful:

a position of outrage steeped in hypocrisy, since he'd never for a moment pretended to be faithful to Isabel. They'd had hours of circular fighting, he yelling about her infidelity and she denying it, escalating at each round. Isabel spoke as if she was outside herself, wondering how on earth she'd found herself in this place. She was forty-three, with a good business, a child and a husband, and now she was being verbally abused by this man. She couldn't blame anyone but herself, yet couldn't understand herself either.

I felt afraid for her, seeing the fear in her eyes, and wondered about her safety, the safety of her child, who, fortunately, had been with Guy. Part of her was relieved, because this meant she had to end her relationship with Gunner. At least it was over.

It wasn't the end of their relationship. After a couple of weeks of his relentless messaging she had succumbed and started seeing him again. She couldn't resist him sexually. Even after their terrible arguments, thinking of him turned her on. He had incredible sexual power over her: she would become his plaything; he was confident and domineering sexually, and she loved the feeling of her femininity surrendering to his commands. At the beginning the relationship had been her pleasure zone, a light party place where she could get away from being the boss, wife and mother. He wasn't interested in her business success, which added to his attraction; he just wanted to have fun. Isabel discovered a sexual version of herself she had never known before. She'd always liked sex, and I could hear that in the intensity of her voice, but this wild, uninhibited sex blew her away. She would do a deal with the gods, promising this would be the last time, telling herself Gunner was bad for her, she had to end it, and then she went back for more. When her husband Guy had found out, as horrendous and painful as that had been, she explained it as helping her extricate herself from her marriage, which was dead. She had tried for many years to bring it back to life, to be happy with him, but there was no more she could do. She was beginning to hate him. It was over. Polite alienation had replaced the warmth of their love. Gunner had brought her alive. But now their relationship was dark, difficult and complicated and she couldn't seem to get out of it. She loved him.

I challenged that this was love. It didn't look like love to me. Love, to my mind, would let her be a version of herself she liked and brought her happiness. As the words came out of my mouth she crashed right in front of me, looking startled, tears building in her eyes. She didn't move a muscle. I said quietly that I could see something had happened, but she couldn't speak. We sat there for a long time. I asked her to breathe. I had come across as harsh. She turned away in shame, and told me she felt worse. I tried to reach her through the tone of my voice, and I told her that I understood she felt criticized, telling her my intention was to be truthful, but I acknowledged it had hurt her to hear that. She pressed her palms to her temples, to stop the whirring in her head. I suggested she closed her eyes, take some deep breaths until she felt centred. She looked young, opening her eyes, as she told me she knew so much and then so little. I reassured her: our job was to find out what she didn't know. She smiled, calmer.

Over the next weeks Isabel came in as *soignée* as ever, but much more turbulent and distressed inside, and cried constantly through the sessions. Our focus was between her son, Alex, her marriage, Gunner and her business. Alex was confused and found the good-byes between his parents distressing. It was upsetting to witness his sadness, but Isabel had found joy in being in their original family unit of three, eating together, hanging out at home. When she'd described their marriage as dead, that did not include her and Guy as parents. She loved parenting with Guy: he was exactly the father she wanted him to be – loving, predictable and kind.

Recently Alex had been inconsolable on seeing her leave and had cried 'Mummy' all night. He also took time to settle in Isabel's rented flat, wanting his old bedroom. As much as it tore at her heart, she agreed with Guy that they couldn't play with Alex together until he had adjusted to their separation. They had been advised on how to tell him they were divorcing: to be truthful and clear, support him to express his feelings, answer all his questions and discuss with him what it would mean practically for him. It was important to reiterate that it was not his fault. The more consistent and loving an environment, in their separate bases, they could create for him, the better. Isabel sobbed as she talked about him. This was the centre of her feeling of failure, and she grieved for the loss of the family unit Alex had thrived in.

They'd agreed on shared parenting, Alex splitting his time between them each week. Guy was a good father, but he was furious with Isabel, which made regular contact with him painful. She cried, remembering the times they had been happy together. She wanted to tell Guy she was sorry for the hurt she'd caused him. She felt guilty. Part of her still cared for him; as the father to her child and the man she had once loved.

I questioned if she was sure divorce was the right course for her. Isabel sat bolt upright. Yes, the marriage was over. Her love was for how they'd been in the distant past. She explained that their relationship had been good for a long time; their sex life had been ordinary, boring in fact, but she had put it to one side believing it was not the important part of her life. For the last three or four years, though, whatever she did to try to connect with Guy hadn't worked. He was incapable of listening to her. He would forget whole conversations they'd had. He was often late home from work, looking tired and hassled. She felt as if she didn't exist. He was a car salesman, and it was as if he was having an affair with his phone. Guy stroked and held it far more than he did her. He was obsessed with getting new sales. They would fight about it: he'd argue that he was bringing in the greater slice of the income and wanted her to value and respect that. It would end in days of mutual stonewalling. Whatever she did to rekindle their love seemed to fall on stony ground, and it made her feel ill, her anxiety soaring, which affected her ability to sleep and function. In the end she had felt so frozen out that her hate had morphed into contempt, which was the death knell to her love for him. Yet they had stayed together because she saw how much Alex worshipped him.

When we were talking about boyfriends before Guy, Isabel

unearthed an unconscious belief about her relationship with men. She believed, deep down, she would never meet the person she really wanted, who would feel the same about her. She remembered at school being attracted to a boy in her class, but he had gone for the pretty girl – she hadn't been a pretty teenager but she had been sexy. She could attract men but they wanted her for sex, not for a serious relationship. As a consequence, she'd consciously dated the less cool, more eccentric boys, such as Guy. Isabel sounded sad as she realized that when she was with Guy she had felt alone and had never fully given herself to him: she had held something back, for as much as he was reliable she didn't look up to him. The brutal truth was that he bored her and she'd married him fearing she wouldn't find anyone better. She wanted to change that belief and find someone who matched her in energy, sexuality and ambition.

Tears fell gently down her face as she said she was floating above the ground, that she had left one place but not landed safely anywhere. Isabel cried some more as she went deeper into herself, understanding that she didn't know herself well enough to know where to land. There was a long silence while she took in what she'd said. Then she continued, reflecting that she'd been running a race, as she'd said before, to escape her parents. Some of it was to earn enough money to have control, but also, she said, after another long silence, it was about escaping *herself*. I felt a sense of relief, that she had found the track inside herself to access this knowledge. It had been suppressed up to now but would guide her into her future.

The more Isabel talked about Gunner, the more I felt their relationship mirrored the addictive cycle of her mother's drinking, a different drug but the same cycle. She did not want to think about it in that way. She would change the subject. This continued until one day Isabel came in, the elegance of her beautiful jacket contrasting with her pallid skin and the don't-look-at-me message her eyes were transmitting. Her voice was shaky, and she took short breaths, talking to me about everything except what she needed to say. I told her I could see something was distressing her. She pressed her handkerchief hard into her eyes, covering her whole face and howled, rocking back and forth. I couldn't decide whether to move towards her, for her to feel my hand on her shoulder as a comfort, but decided she might interpret it as me wanting to shut her down. It took some time for her tears to subside, and with the hanky still pressed into her eyes, she spoke haltingly.

Isabel had had another terrible set of experiences with her boy-friend. She didn't want to go into them in detail, but she felt full of shame and self-loathing. She used the word 'degradation' a number of times, which set off alarm bells in me. After one terri-ble evening, she woke feeling ill, and promised herself she would stop contact with him. But once she was home from work, all her feelings of loneliness and desire overtook her, which set up a poi-sonous cycle. We had looked at what was going on for a while when I found myself asking her, 'Do you hate yourself?'

She put her hands and her hanky on her lap, and looked at me directly. 'Yes.' There was no obfuscating or covering up. She hated herself. Every day was a cycle of destruction and she didn't know how to stop. There was a pang of pain in my chest: she felt so bad that she had been choosing self-destruction over life.

I let her know how much I felt for her, and was then clear: she had a choice. I acknowledged most of what had happened to her was out of her control, but this was within it. Only she had the power to make that choice. We discussed her options: continue seeing Gun-ner, see him less, or not see him at all. She said she really wanted to stop, and I could hear the renewed energy in her voice as she said it. She was powerless to say no to his control of her, which to me meant, as tough as it was to hear, she was in the addict category. She flinched. It threw up images of drunks on the street. I asked her what would help her, suggesting A A as an option, maybe Al-Anon, A A's support organization for families of addicts. Isabel went to and fro as to whether she'd go. I sympathized – who wants to acknowledge being an addict? The shame of it, the thought of exposing herself to a group of strangers went against everything she had trusted up to now. Her body quivered at the thought. I didn't push as I knew that would be counterproductive. Eventually she decided to go – just the once.

I wanted her to find ways to build up the muscle of delaying gratification. If she could learn to say no to Gunner, it would mean her tomorrow would be happier. The short-term high of the yes ensured that her tomorrow would be unhappy. We discussed habits she could develop to help her when she got home: do ten minutes of Pilates stretching, have a bath with a candle and music, eat her supper. She didn't want to watch TV, it bored her, but she'd find comfort in classic books – she was going to buy *Pride and Prejudice*.

When she left I couldn't shake off her distress and felt a pull the next morning to send her a text, checking she was okay, as I would a friend. I didn't. I knew I needed to hold the boundary, trust she would take responsibility for herself. It wasn't helpful to overstep it. I talked about her at length to my supervisor. I described my earlier urge, and discussed how to hold the dynamic between us, where I facilitated a relationship that empowered her to trust herself and fulfil her potential in work, love and as a parent. Only she could fully know that. Aren't we all addictive in some ways? On the other hand, with addicts denial is their weapon. It is entrenched and could cause her downfall. I was truly worried about her safety. But if I continued to confront her with her addiction, was I being overly controlling? Talking it out released some of my tension, clarifying it. At my best I would need to hold both parts in balance: her potential to know her own answers, and my responsibility to her.

Isabel arrived in an optimistic mood for a number of weeks, red lipstick in place, and visibly calmer. She had gone to some Al-Anon meetings where she knew she was not meant to judge anyone but judged everyone, checking if their problems were worse than hers. She appreciated their honesty and then resented them for taking space, even found them boring. But once she had left, she wanted to go back: there was something about their energy that made her feel safer there than in the outside world. Isabel had begun to take in their message that she was two different people: as I framed it, she had different versions of herself. There was the highly successful business woman, who was creative and strong, even a leader. That was the public version. But she had a secret life

where she went when she felt unhappy, triggered by the hurt child
in her. Being naughty and rebellious was her fight against the
hurt, an emotional V sign to her parents, and all figures of authority, although, of course, it mirrored her mother's behaviour – a
dangerous addiction. It kept the pain in place, untouched and
available to be hauled in so that she could act out at any point.

We discussed the concept of emotional sobriety, as well as
physical sobriety. As the child of an alcoholic, she experienced
emotional intoxication, the excitement of clinging to dysfunctional
relationships in which the upset and stress block the original hurt.
Functional relationships are uncomfortable because they don't disguise or suppress that early pain. Isabel spoke reluctantly, and
admitted that she was used to feeling bad. Our work would be to
unite the different versions of herself, for each part had a voice that
needed to be fully heard and attended to: a choir that needed to
sing together, rather than clash.

Isabel started going to Pilates classes. It was a wake-up call as to
how unfit she was: she had no self-care regime at all. She found that
Pilates suited her body. I felt calmer with her, then relieved to hear
she had finally broken up with Gunner. There was no contact. It hit
her that for the first time she was single, which felt like a shock. The
intoxication with Gunner had anaesthetized the grief of leaving
the life she'd had. It had given her the false exhilaration of freedom,
but now she was in a new landscape: she was alone and crying for her
dreams. But it gave her the space to look at what she wanted, and she
wasn't at all sure she wanted to fit in with society's pressure to have a
conventional family. She had seen almost no families that worked
well together. Isabel sounded feisty and angry as she said she had
always found her own way, her own answer. This time she was going
to be the answer to her problem. Her path to love may be different
from that of others, and she was going to find ways of thriving. With
her, I was energized and curious, and felt we were making progress.

For a number of weeks, the organization of her handbag-
collection show in Paris took over Isabel's life. She described with
some excitement and an edge of fear the work it took to get the

samples ready, priced and displayed on the stand, to organize the fashion show, the whirlwind of meetings, with the press, retailers, and shows she had to rush through for the five days. It was a great success, with many new orders. When all the hype was over and Isabel had caught up on the backlog of work, she hit the buffers. Work excitement had replaced Gunner excitement, which I hadn't foreseen. She told me she had relapsed and she was in contact with Gunner again, even looking at her diary for time to go away with him in secret, not telling Guy where she was.

I asked if she could talk me through what had happened. She described a void that had opened up in her that longed for connection with him, in which she was consumed with the memory of their intensity, which took her over. Her exhaustion and loneliness hadn't helped. The AA acronym of danger – HALT: Hungry Angry Lonely Tired – came to my mind. It means an addict should ask themselves if they are experiencing any of the four: if they are, it lowers their resistance to their addiction. She had ticked three if not four of those boxes and done the reverse of HALT. She hadn't asked for help. She'd messaged Gunner. They used WhatsApp, which felt close and constantly on call. At one level, she couldn't understand it, saying it was the loser in her; at another, she knew she was utterly addicted. She had fallen off the wagon to her mainline drug. Sexual arousal lights up the brain in exactly the same areas as cocaine and she'd hooked herself in. I was worried. I could feel a knot tighten in me of concern for her safety, how to get her back on track, and frustration. Some of my own issues fed into it.

We reflected together on what Isabel knew and ignored: that her relationship with Gunner was an expression of her hurt when her trust in her mother was shattered. Isabel knew the child in her was replaying a version of that negative cycle, with the hope that this time it would fix the pain, make her better, while she also knew it couldn't. I could feel her strength and her vulnerability, and the kind of madness she got into with Gunner. It was like a spell, a different dimension she couldn't master. She didn't want to be this damaged child, who was addicted to negative behaviours.

The idea revolted her. She knew she'd been influenced by seeing how her father had been co-dependent with her mother for decades: he had always believed it would get better. I found myself urging caution, telling her she was potentially putting herself in the way of physical harm. I could see that I had only succeeded in shaming her. Isabel was in thrall to him, and whatever I said right now was not getting through to her.

My anxiety remained after our session and, restlessly, I paced my room. I wanted to shout at her, 'Will you please stop breaking your own damn heart?' I took my concerns to my supervisor again: there was a safeguarding issue for her son, Alex, if she was seeing Gunner. We discussed how I could help Isabel to grieve properly for her mother. I wanted to connect with the voice in her that was telling her she wasn't worthy of love, which was why she was abandoning herself. I needed to support her to find the adult in herself, who could choose to pick up the child inside and soothe her. At the moment she was recklessly letting that stroppy, rebellious, hurt child turn her life upside down. That child who was shouting, 'I should', 'I can't', 'I should', 'I won't.' I felt a pull to parent her, but knew she had to do this for herself. She needed help to find the life she wanted. I asked her what she wanted. Isabel was unequivocal: she wanted to end the relationship with Gunner. She just didn't know how.

Isabel's life felt surreal. Her private life continued in its chaotic whirlwind but her business was thriving and expanding. A-listers were seen sporting her bags, and they sold out in a matter of hours. With new investment, she was moving office and found a nicer flat to rent. At her most creative Isabel was joyous and ebullient. She would fly into my room pulsating with passion and energy for her new collection. There were always staff and supply issues, but Isabel knew the business was booming and she had absolute confidence in herself and her brand. How could we get this natural leader and winner to help the broken internal child?

In the last weeks, I'd stopped worrying as much. I had a new clarity. I told Isabel, 'I support you in figuring out what is best for you. I have no agenda in you ending it with Gunner. If you want it, I support you.'

Isabel was tearful. She wanted me to believe in her. I did, particularly when she didn't believe in herself. I trusted that, with time, she would get to the place she wanted to get to, wherever that may be.

We had an interesting discussion about what to look for in life, how high to aim. Her business life had exceeded her expectations: should she have the same dreams for herself? Isabel said, 'Don't we all dream that there are different, more exciting, more thrilling versions of ourselves? Don't we want to live those unlived lives? If only we could access them and let them out.' She recognized that her handbags were a metaphor of that, each representing a new version of the self.

I had to quieten my first response, my joy-killing thought: we should have goals, and realistic aims for what we want in our life. Weren't dreams a kind of magical thinking that only the very few attained? I needed to go back to trusting her. Having dreams was a key part of her ability to create, and she needed to hold on to them. They gave her hope and a place to aim. I wondered if she could access that creativity for her personal life and bring with it some of the commitment to take herself seriously. Then we'd be making progress. I asked her who she pictured in her future.

Isabel surprised me: she had a clear picture of the man she wanted. Someone who was as ambitious as her, attractive, sexy, but then there was something about finding her equal – a man she could respect, look up to, as well as lean on and trust. As she finished picturing him she smiled so widely the sun came out. She'd got me believing in that dream. Isabel looked excited. Energized. She wanted to have a new relationship, a good one this time.

Our relationship was powerful, but she often dreaded seeing me. When she told me where she was in her life, it made it real, and stopped her fooling herself. As she skipped out, kitten-heeled, she talked about befriending her dark side. It would help not to hide herself from herself. 'I want to be all I am, my past, as well as live my present.'

A few weeks later Isabel told me she had broken up with Gunner. Something in her had shifted when I no longer had an agenda for her to get rid of him. That defiant voice in her didn't have to fight me: she could surrender for herself. Isabel felt differently this time. She was ready for a new chapter. She spoke a lot about authenticity. She was 'so over him' that I couldn't help but laugh at her nonchalant dismissal of the man who had driven her stark staring bonkers for months.

We looked at what might hook her back. She was at her riskiest when she felt empty and went to Gunner to fill her. Isabel needed to heighten her awareness of what was going on inside her; she needed to acknowledge the hurt that triggered her SOS signals, and then she needed to meet the internal cry for help. She needed to learn how to delay gratification and be open to the good things in herself, and in her life. At present, she didn't take them in.

We had many weeks of good workaday therapy. Without Gunner there were no crises, which freed her to be available to herself and to focus. At last Isabel was emotionally sober. There were times of great sadness, when she held up and examined the pain her parents' lies had caused her, the inaccurate stories she'd made up to fill the gaps, and the bad patterns that had created in her. Her work was to learn to tell herself the absolute truth, not get lost in substituted dreams, then learn to live with that reality. She grieved for the parents she'd wanted, sobbed deeply for them all, the waste and the cost. I felt tender for the wafts of sadness as they ran through her.

Her separation from Guy came back into the room. She had no doubt she'd made the right decision: she didn't want to be married to him. She didn't miss the identity of being a wife, as many spouses do. In fact she felt exhilarated to be free. But she allowed herself to feel the pain of this loss. Her sorrow felt physical – it was in her bones, her head and her heart. Expressing her sorrow released her to be grateful to Guy as a father. She was proud of herself, too, that she'd had the wisdom to choose a great dad for their child. Their financial settlement had been difficult, more stand-offs with each other through expensive lawyers, which was incredibly stressful, but in the end, despite their striving, there wasn't much money to fight over and they'd found a good enough arrangement. She was enormously grateful for their mutual recognition that Alex's wellbeing needed to be at the centre of all they did as she'd seen couples' bitterness destroy each other, their children caught up and wounded in the crossfire.

Isabel's mood was improving. She was having fun sexually too, no commitments but enjoying the force of her sexual drive and the pleasure it gave her. Although the rebel in her feared being imprisoned by rules, she developed some new behaviours, which helped counter her internal chaos. She began to organize her time better (she'd heard many children of alcoholics 'lost time'), she exercised regularly, learned to delegate and wrote more – journalling let her know those secrets she'd stuck in the cellar of her being. A pivotal understanding was her rebelliousness, that powerful force of hers. She realized it had been vital to protect her as a child, but now it was an armour against trusting. She needed to allow herself to be vulnerable to take in love. As each understanding was brought out into the daylight, her awareness of herself grew, and along with it her self-esteem. Isabel grinned at me, her dark eyes twinkling. I felt warmth spark in me as I witnessed these shoots of growth, heard her infectious giggle at the excitement of her possible future. 'I have a good work ethic. I believe that in myself, and respect it in others. I like that I'm a successful business owner. I can now channel that into me. I can see that things are looking good. If I'm patient enough, move into this next phase, now I'm settled, then my energy will draw something better in. Perhaps one day I will meet someone who's got his shit together, but for now I'm happy just dating. I don't need a man to complete me. Actually, I don't want a boyfriend right now. I'm beginning to believe more in me and in what I'm building, and where my life is taking me. I can accept it and believe it and have fun.'

As a therapist these are the gifts of my job. The joy of seeing Isabel with renewed hope, and the deep satisfaction of knowing her internal sense of herself now matched her physical beauty.

Isabel had been in the grip of emotional addiction. It had hurled her around, left her emotionally battered. But with time she had overcome the denial that had perpetuated her self-destructive behaviour, she'd instilled the discipline of delaying gratification and she had dared take the first of many steps into recovery. There were key moments, like hearing her say, 'I'm a winner,' while gleefully laughing at the new knowledge. These steps, over time, had changed her internal perception of herself, which enabled her to progress. They were small shifts of perception, but their impact was far-reaching: it allowed her to love herself, to be someone worthy of love ... As that cycle gathers momentum, her story will take off into new happier chapters.

Reflections on Love

Love gives us our greatest joy and our greatest despair. It is where madness and murder reside, as well as meaning and safety. Love is a risky business. Yet those who build a mutually loving relationship are happier, healthier, richer, live longer and have greater zest for life than others. And the big bonus is that their children are happier too. To be in a good relationship is the elixir of life. It is not bought in a bottle, but the potential for it is within each of us. Like all good things, it is neither easy nor a given; it requires luck, and a huge amount of work on ourselves and as a couple.

The research is unequivocal: all our relationships matter – having strong, reliable ones with our partner, family and friends is vital, but working at keeping our love relationship alive is worth the sweat and the boredom. Finding ways of sharing life together and seeking better ways to manage conflict, however difficult it may be, are, for most people, better than being alone. The key isn't just having a partner, but the quality of the relationship with that partner.

Couples in long-term unhappy marriages do not gain the benefits. Those who have successful subsequent relationships, following a separation, revert to the thriving category.

In 2017 there were 7.7 million single-person households in the UK. The reasons for this are varied. For some, living alone was not a choice. In relation to love, there will be people who feel lonely and long for a partner and do all they can to find one but fail. As difficult a fact as it is, loneliness has many negative health conditions associated with it, which means some single people suffer more. Others will embrace singledom and flourish. They thoroughly enjoy solo activities, may want a varied love life rather than monogamy, and feel liberated in not having to limit themselves to meet the demands of a partner while having a wide circle of close friends. At the moment we don't know very much about this group of people for the focus has been on couples. How we live now is changing faster than the research is collected. In the years ahead it will be interesting to see what the data tells us of the outcomes for the new ways in which we live and love.

You may ask why there are five stories in this section, more than any other. The answer is simple: love tends to preoccupy us more than anything else. Maria, Jackson, Robbie, Esther and Isabel show how unique each of our relationships is, and how pivotal they can be to our sense of self and our wellbeing. Because love is central to our happiness, my reflections have been more extensive than usual. I wanted to relay concrete theories and understandings to help unravel the complexity of the case studies, and also love in your own life.

Through reading these stories we see that we change over time. One of the many challenges we face when it comes to love relationships is how we change separately and together. If we don't work out how to do that, it is a key risk factor in long-term partnerships. In the turmoil and questioning Maria went through, painful though it was, she found a way to adapt within herself, and maintain her marriage. For Isabel, Robbie and Esther, we see their loss and distress charted as their relationships ended, either by death or divorce. For Jackson, having the insight to examine the roots of his ill-health and insecurity in his twenties meant he went into his first relationships with more self-knowledge and resilience. Hopefully, that will protect him from a cycle of damaging relationships in his future.

Each one of the five suffered in their own particular way. The speed with which each of them returned to their childlike self when they were most hurt in love was immensely touching, and illustrates how we retreat to our earlier selves at all stages of our life. For each of them, the path to healing lay in expressing their pain, which, over time, freed them to seek love again. Age is not a good measure of how we love. I learned from them all how our desire for love does not age, but shines as strongly in a woman in her mid-seventies and a man in his sixties, as it does in women in their fifties and forties, and a young man in his twenties.

What is Love?

How we've been loved in our childhood gives us a unique experience of what love is and will shape our attitude and behaviour, but it is not fixed: our love relationships throughout our life are as influential. What we expect love to look and feel like will be coloured by what we see and experience around us, in family and friends as well as our culture: books, pop music, films, TV and social media fill our imagination with images and stories of what 'true love' is. They, in turn, are imbued with the work of artists of all hues through the centuries, from medieval courtly love to paintings, opera, sculpture and novels, with their spectacularly beautiful depictions of love and tragedy. The most common described form of love across all art forms and cultures is that of romance, the spell-binding vision of falling passionately in love, not the wear and tear, the quieter, more subdued love of long-term relationships. I have turned to psychological research for insight. For decades psychologists have studied love in depth yet the outcomes of their work have been slow to filter into public consciousness. With increased access to information online and podcasts, though, they are gaining traction.

When we fall romantically in love our brain is bathed by the neurotransmitter dopamine and we want and desire, with an unquenchable hunger, the object of our love. Helen Fisher, the brilliant anthropologist and author of *Why We Love*, who specializes in exploring how we love, explains that these unconscious tendencies to seek a mate come from our evolutionary requirement to procreate; it is encoded in our DNA, and still motivates our actions today. The system was evolved by our forebears in the African savannah millions of years ago. The strategy was to reproduce their genes, and they did that most successfully with an essentially exclusive mating relationship between one male and one female. The word 'essentially' is there for a reason: fidelity was not central to the success of the enterprise.

Every person will have their own unique story of love, but we are likely to follow a set pattern. Robert Sternberg, an eminent psychologist, theorized, 'Love can be considered to have three main components: passion, intimacy, and commitment.' Passion really means sex, the drive to copulate, when we feel 'madly in love', madness often being the operative word. Fisher showed that when the brains of men and women in love were put under an MRI scanner, many of the same parts of the brain lit up. Love fires up the dopamine reward system, often short-circuiting our rational thinking. That alone tells us romantic love provides a poor basis on which to form a long-term partnership.

Love is one of the most powerful drugs on our planet. It is a drive from the early reptilian part of our brain where it is deeply embedded in us. Men and women are wired to fall in love, and our physiological responses are similar. It is not an emotion that can be processed. Our body is no longer under our control: it can feel like a car permanently in fourth gear, and however much we want to take our foot off the accelerator and change down, there is no way to do so. We are hot and we want to drive with our whole being towards the object of our love, this other person whom we can never get enough of. We are hungry for their body, their smell, their words and their being.

As Robbie poignantly showed, being in love brings that sense of aliveness, elation, and of being a new person. When the dream is cruelly shattered, the pain of a break-up often lasts eighteen months to two years.

In the ideal scenario, if the couple finds ways to communicate honestly and openly while they are madly in love, intimacy may follow. Intimacy means deeply knowing another person and feeling deeply known by them. If we gradually and gently show our true self to each other, warts and all, and are accepted, even valued, we have achieved intimacy. Emotional and sexual intimacy are the magical components of love. Trust and respect between the couple develop further when they see themselves as a team who support each other, recognizing that they are more robust in dealing with life's vicissitudes together than apart.

Commitment is the decision to maintain this relationship, this love, for the long term, often through the institution of marriage and, increasingly, cohabitation. It is at this point, if the couple plan to have children together, that each needs to assess carefully whether their partner has the capacity to be a loving, committed parent. Most cultures around the world include fidelity as part of that commitment, but in all cultures, even where there is the death penalty, infidelity occurs.

From Sternberg's research, the level of love each person experiences will depend on the depth of their passion, intimacy and commitment. The kind of love they feel is defined by how these components play out in each individual and the couple. One person might feel very passionate but dare not commit; another might be a good communicator but not highly sexual. The key to protect against hurt and disruption is to be as clear with each other as possible about their feelings and expectations. In order for the relationship to put down secure roots over time, it has to change and adapt as the individuals' needs and experiences alter.

According to various studies, in a successful relationship we can expect to be reliably kind to each other, create a friendship of mutual respect, learn to value each other, listen and express our love and affection regularly. In a good relationship, finding ways of holding each other loosely, while working hard to keep the connection alive, creates a positive dynamic. It grows when we learn to fight each other, as we will and as we have to, and how to repair after the fight. And we should be having fun as we shape our lives together, building a meaningful partnership. To do this successfully in the long term takes will and desire.

The Impact of Genetics and Environment on Love

Helen Fisher's research highlights that the human mating game is complex, that sexual strategies differ from one individual to the next, but our evolutionary drive is written in us: 'We are born to love.' Fisher argues that genetics plays the determining role in our personality type, which is in itself shaped by our environment.

It was striking how in the stories of Maria, Jackson, Robbie, Esther and Isabel the influence of their parents' relationship created patterns within them: they wanted to change yet found themselves repeating those scenarios. Perhaps they could be more forgiving of themselves if they recognized the part genes play: as Fisher writes, 'Our biological nature whispers constantly within us to influence who we love.' Research on attachment supports their experience, showing adults tend to recreate the same type of relationship they witnessed in their childhood. Our script lies within us and is played out consciously and unconsciously in our lives. Not surprisingly, the example of secure, trustworthy parents in partnership helps their offspring to make secure partnerships in their turn, and the reverse. Insecure partners, who lack an internal foundation of trust or are unable to recognize who is trustworthy, also lay down a script for their children. Furthermore, the relationship those children have with their parents shapes them, too, and is a powerful predictor of how they will behave in their own love life. But attachment styles, and patterns once learned, can be changed. I wouldn't be a therapist if I didn't believe that, with self-awareness, determination and some luck, we can re-program

ourselves and develop sound relationships, despite our biology
and history.

What happens to us outside the family also influences our belief
system and thereby our behaviour. As in Maria's story, our first
love, good or bad, will shape our trust in future partners. Those
first sexual, more complex relationships, which usually occur
between the ages of eighteen and twenty-three, are a key time for
experimentation and develop our attitude towards love and sex.
It is thought that they link to the divorce statistics: if we are more
self-oriented in relationships, enjoy the lack of commitment of
one-off or casual hook-ups at that age, we may feel less inclined to
commit to marriage, or fear divorce less than others.

We are undoubtedly hard-wired to procreate, but how we do it,
and what is acceptable behaviour, are social constructs. This in
turn is influenced by what is transmitted into our minds. People
can be, and are, influenced by the content of the media they con-
sume, and if we see continual representations of relationships in a
certain way, we will be influenced in our relationship behaviour.
Today, as opposed to thirty years ago, there are more programmes
on our screens that show sexually casual relationships, rather than
committed relationships. This will influence us to see casual hook-
up sex as common. Interestingly there is a bias against women
having casual sex: it shows negative consequences for women
more often than for their male counterparts. I wonder, despite the
sexual revolution, whether there are echoes of those biblical
injunctions that for women sex is only for procreation.

For genetic and environmental reasons, there is a bias in society
against those who are single. It is assumed if they have divorced
they will find another partner, and if they have never had a long-
term relationship they are regarded with either pity or confusion.
It is as primitive as wild animals in nature, where the loner is more
likely to fall prey to attack. Single people can be dismissed, undervalued and criticized. They may want a partner, and even feel
despair at living alone, but being at the mercy of insensitive remarks
or assumptions makes it worse.

Statistics, and the Impact of Social Change on Love

Statistics provide a lens that focuses on how contemporary society is changing with regard to long-term relationships and what is becoming the new norm.

Fewer people are getting married than at any time in more than 100 years. In 2014 nearly 34 per cent of the adult population was separated or single. It is the biggest indicator of how much change there is in society. In 2014 51 per cent of people aged sixteen and over in England and Wales were married or civil-partnered. Cohabiting families are the fastest-growing family type, between 1996 and 2016 more than doubling from 1.5 million families to 3.3 million families. According to the Marriage Foundation, 'Cohabiting parents make up 19 per cent of all couples with dependent children, but account for half of all family breakdown.'

Looking at these changes from a historical perspective helps us make sense of them. For centuries marriage was not about love, but an economic contract, originally to share resources. Royalty married for an alliance of nations. Aristocrats married for money or land. Others had an arranged marriage between two families with shared beliefs and class, or peasant farmers because they needed a partner to share the toil. Nowadays 89 per cent of people throughout the world say they will only marry for love.

In the last fifty years there has been ground-breaking social change, which has transformed our view of the institution of marriage, and we have by no means adjusted to its consequences. Three social forces have spearheaded this radical change. The *psychological revolution* has reduced the power of social institutions and increased the importance of expressive individualism. The emphasis is now more on personal happiness than the institution of marriage as a stable force for childbearing and -rearing. The *gender revolution*, mainly due to the Pill and the women's movement, has emancipated women from constant pregnancy to go into the workforce; now typically both spouses work. While women may still wish to be married, their reasons for doing so are different:

rarely now will they marry for status, role fulfilment or legacy, as these may be found in a career. The *secular revolution*, the decline of religious belief and religious moral authority, has meant that marriages are not held together by fear of breaking faith with God, and it is therefore easier to exit without fear of social stigma.

Divorce

For Esther and Isabel, divorcing was painful but the right decision. It was not made lightly or without a great deal of care and heartache. Their experience echoes a recent study, which shows it is one of the most difficult things people have ever dealt with, but for those who initiated the divorce it was for the best. Recovering from divorce takes time: the research reveals that it usually takes four years for people to feel that their life is back on an even keel. For Isabel, a crucial part of feeling positive about her divorce was that she and her husband agreed equal childcare, which is also shown to be of significant benefit to the child.

The majority of divorces happen after ten to fifteen years of marriage, which means younger children are inevitably affected. A high percentage of divorced adults remarry, and 40 per cent of the remarriages also end in divorce. This means that any children have to face multiple changes in how, where and who they live with, which can be disturbing, with long-term negative consequences. The issues that most commonly inflict ongoing damage for those who have divorced are financial difficulties and single-parent families where often the father has much less contact with the children.

Esther joins those termed the 'silver splitters'. This age group has seen the divorce rate double in recent years, but the increase in older divorcees is counter to the overall trend where there is a 9.1 per cent decrease in divorce from 2014, and a 34 per cent decline from the most recent peak in 2003. Research suggests this is due to women's attitude in relationships changing as they mature: they become more assertive. They are often reported as saying they are more confident, less concerned by others' criticism and have more self-belief.

Forty-two per cent of marriages in England and Wales end in divorce. In 2017 there were 101,699 divorces. Analysis suggests the reason for the drop in divorce rates is because couples are marrying later, and there is an overall drop in marriage generally.

Esther's son was twenty-three when she first divorced, and it might have been assumed that, being an adult, he would not suffer as much as a younger child. That was not the case for him. Nor is it for most adult children of divorcing parents: they are often devastated. A study showed their initial reaction is profound shock, even if they knew the marriage had been difficult for years. Their experience is like grief, with all its complexities of loss, anger and deep sadness. They may question the veracity of their past, which in turn can raise trust issues in all relationships. Through their process of grieving, they often confront their parents, or the one they blame for breaking up their family, and it takes consistent committed work to rebuild their trust.

Adult Children of Alcoholics

Isabel was the daughter of an alcoholic. In general, the emotional legacy of an alcoholic parent to their child is often unrecognized, and in particular, how it impacts the child's ability to form loving long-term relationships. Children of alcoholics are predisposed to all addictive behaviours, *emotional addiction* as well as alcohol and drug abuse. I was struck by the importance of emotional sobriety and I shall be more attuned to it in the future.

A paper from Al-Anon states that the typical traits of children brought up in the homes of alcoholics include 'fear of authority figures, isolation, fear of abandonment, uneasiness with other people, clinging to dysfunctional relationships and addiction to excitement in which they show a preference for continual upset rather than workable relationships'. Children of alcoholics also have a higher risk of damaging behaviours, including substance abuse, antisocial behaviours, low self-esteem, depression, anxiety and eating disorders.

This is by no means a prediction of their outcome, Isabel being a case in point. Yet it is a risk factor, and greater awareness can offer protection. The treatment to support the emotional sobriety of adult children of alcoholics and rebuild their trust in themselves and life is the 12-step recovery programme Al-Anon (part of A A for the families of Alcoholics).

Relationship Dynamics: Gender and Love

Research supports our instinctive understanding that most men are first drawn to someone by sexual attraction and tend to fall in love quickly, while women look for warmth and occupational status. As the relationship progresses there is ideally a balance in affection and sex, as men become more affectionate and women more sexual. Both men and women want intimacy but express it differently. Men will more commonly show love through doing something practical: they are doers. Women are talkers: they use many more words than men, saying how they feel, getting excited by the emotional connection between words and feelings. It is often a source of tension in relationships that men want women to talk less and vice versa. What is important is to come to an understanding together as to what the other person's 'language of love' is: do they feel loved through gestures, words or physical contact? What turns them off? When we learn how our partner best receives love, it enables us to be more confident when we give it and helps create a positive cycle. It reminds me of giving presents: often people give presents they would like to receive, rather than getting into the mind of the recipient. It is a process of adaptation, expanding our psychological lexicon to include that of our partner, allowing us to move into their mindset, and also to step out of it to protect against co-dependency. In long-term relationships, language and the expression of love will change a great deal. It requires flexibility to adjust side by side.

Interestingly men, like Jackson, hold on to a waning relationship longer than women, and after the break-up, they feel lonelier and more preoccupied with what went wrong. It isn't clear whether this is because women have better friendships, which help fill the absence of a partner, but research on love in later life shows that women are less in need of companionship as they can access it via friendships.

Finding the 'One' Soul-mate

The story of finding 'the one' has been told and retold in every medium dating back to Plato, from where our search for the person who makes us whole begins to finding the perfect fit who can complete us and heal all we have been missing until we met them. This fantasy of 'the one' may continue after we have committed to someone yet still harbour secret dreams of finding them. Often in our search for this idealized other half, we overlook the person who is lying in the bed beside us. The myth of finding the perfect soul-mate is responsible for untold damage.

More is expected from marriage than ever before. Esther Perel, the brilliant couples psychotherapist and author of *Mating in Captivity*, explains that the demands of committed relationships are increasing: 'We turn to one person to provide what an entire village once did: a sense of grounding, meaning, and continuity.' We expect personal growth and fulfilment, as well as excitement and safety, comfort, great sex, financial security and someone to take out the bins. Increasing numbers of relationships end when those expectations are not met, when the relationship feels stagnant. We often decide that it is 'all or nothing' rather than looking to get some of our needs met elsewhere. Eli Finkel, author of *The All or Nothing Marriage*, notes that it is possible to have a partnership that fulfils all our expectations, but they are rare and require the requisite time and attention to nurture them, usually at the cost of that time investment in other areas of our lives, such as our careers. We cannot have it all.

Even if the ideal partner is a myth, it is wise to use more than our 'in-love brain' to help us make decisions as to whether or not to commit to the long term with this person. A study by Professor Anne Barlow on couple relationships found thriving relationships shared some fundamental qualities, and from that research, ten 'critical questions' evolved. All couples could discuss them to gain insight into their relationship and help it flourish, or to highlight the areas in a relationship that need work. They may also be of use to couples prior to committing long term.

1. Are my partner and I a 'good fit'? This can be broken down into the following nine questions.
2. Do we have a strong basis of friendship?
3. Do we want the same things in our relationship and out of life?
4. Are our expectations realistic?
5. Do we generally see the best in each other?
6. Do we both work at keeping our relationship vibrant?
7. Do we both feel we can discuss things freely and raise issues with each other?
8. Are we both committed to working through hard times?
9. When we face stressful circumstances, would we pull together to get through it?
10. Do we each have supportive others around us?

How does it help if you ask these questions in a committed relationship? Dr Ted Hudson's research shows we *create* a good partner, we don't find them. I think this is an absolutely crucial understanding. Research from his longitudinal study elucidates: 'There is no difference in the objective compatibility between those couples who are unhappy and those who are happy.' Hudson found that couples who feel 'content and warmth in their relationship' don't believe having compatible personalities is the issue. On the contrary, they believe it was their attitude that made the relationship work. The strength of the relationship does not depend on how alike they are, more their willingness to adapt and build a bank of warmth and affection that helps buffer the annoyance of their differences. This supports the concept of the development of compatibility, having a growth mindset ('I believe I can change') rather than a fixed mindset ('This is how I am'). Having an attitude of growth means going through difficulties and seeing them as an opportunity to know each other better and bolster the relationship through the resolution of the conflict.

I am not forgetting cohabiting couples, which is an increasingly common way of living in a committed relationship. Whether they are self-selecting or the framework of cohabiting means it is less robust, the US National Institute of Child Health and Human Development reports: 'Cohabiting relationships are less stable than marriages and that instability is increasing.' Cohabiting couples are more likely to separate than those who marry – and, as I said, 42 per cent of marriages in England Wales end in divorce.

For all the work and frustration that keeping relationships together entails, research shows that those in marriage, cohabiting or dating report higher levels of wellbeing than those who don't date at all or date multiple people.

Research on Sex in Long-term Partnerships

As we saw, Maria's desire for sex increased as her children grew up. She was no longer exhausted; as her intense parenting decreased, it left a space for new love.

Professor Kirsten Mark's recent research on sexual behaviour found 'Women who managed to maintain sexual desire in long-term relationships identified as being more sexual beings with high desire' even before the relationship began. This may be indicative of the overlap between individual-level sexual desire and desire for a specific partner. It would make sense that both men and women who have a view of themselves as a sexual being are more successful in maintaining sexual desire through their long-term relationships. I have met many couples who have a mismatch in their sexual desire, and the roots of it were clear at the beginning of their relationship, as we saw with Isabel and her husband. I've wondered why they would think that this would improve over the long term. But there are no rules. I have seen couples for whom it has improved, but it takes work and a conscious effort.

Society's attitude to women's sexual desire is slowly shifting. New research shows women have equal sexual desire to men, and are now exploring openly what gives them pleasure, and making confident choices to get their needs met. This is particularly true of women born from the 1990s on, but is seeping through to all generations, particularly through websites such as OMGyes.com. Far more open, useful and much-needed information, which isn't porn, is available now on sites such as The Pleasure Mechanics. The idea that men think of sex every seven minutes while women think of it on Sundays is clearly a myth: women are getting out there and owning their sexual power.

Maria, Robbie and Isabel found that their sexual relationships with their spouses had waned over the duration of their marriage. Kirsten Mark, who specializes in research on sexual desire and satisfaction, found in a systematic review that there is a circular motion to sexual desire: the more sexual desire you have, the more you want sex; the better the sex life, the more you desire sex. The hurdle in long-term relationships is to keep the sexual desire alive. Addressing the importance of your own identity in remaining attractive to one another makes a big difference. As does non-sexual touch: we are more likely to get 'hot' if there is the warmth of frequent hugs and kisses on a daily basis. It is logical that jumping into a passionate embrace from a cold disconnection is a much higher leap. If you merge into 'one' it may be that you no longer really see the other. As Esther Perel articulately clarifies, the dance between safety and belonging, desire and mystery, keeps the erotic flame alive in the relationship.

What is indisputable in all aspects of relationships is that the sooner the difficulty, whatever it is, is faced and resolved or accommodated, the more the relationship will thrive. Difficulties become entrenched and hard to unravel if left to fester over a long period. I offer 'relationship maintenance' to couples who are married or cohabiting in a committed relationship. We meet once they have made the commitment to be long-term partners and look at the issues they already have difficulty with; we touch on their own history, and look at their strengths as a couple. We meet two or three times a year. It gives them the opportunity to deal with conflict early, to reaffirm what works, and look at the consequences of changes brought by having children, moving to a new house or jobs. We have MOTs for our cars, and many of us have regular health check-ups: it makes sense that we'd do it for one of the cornerstones of our life, our love relationship.

What Sustains Long-term Partnerships?

We can never truly know what it is like to be on the inside of someone else's committed relationship. We can look at some couples and wonder why on earth they are together, and be astonished by others, who appear blissfully happy but then separate. There are mystery and magic, which are unpredictable and unknowable, to love and relationships.

Dr John Gottman has spent decades conducting extensive research with thousands of couples. He maintains that he can predict within ten minutes of watching a couple argue the likelihood of that couple divorcing. His beliefs best match my experience of working with clients and discovering what fundamental ways of being sustain and enrich long-term love.

Gottman's research revealed that if a couple commit equally to build a meaningful long-term relationship, it will tend to last. That sounds simple: two people agree to build their life together and find a way of staying together, whatever is thrown at them. My understanding is that the commitment is almost like flicking a switch in our head. Accepting that we are going to be with this person for life means we turn off the questions in our head that voice doubts about the long-term nature of the relationship, and we switch those internal thoughts to how we can make it work. That internal self-chatter, which I call our 'shitty committee', those questions and accusations about our partner, are quietened, even turned off, and our self-talk shifts: what do we need to do now? We consciously shut down one perspective to step into another. Then what becomes important is how we interact with each other: it is important to note that dynamic is co-created, both partners having a role in the creation of how they relate with each other.

My focus here is how we change within our relationships. What I understand from Gottman's Four Horsemen of the Apocalypse, as detailed below, is that this way of relating, if it is done regularly over the long term, predicts a breakdown in the relationship. Holding fixed views, which pull between the two poles of right and wrong, spells trouble. What starts as criticism, can lead to contempt, defensiveness and stonewalling. This in turn shuts down connection, warmth and trust. It is our capacity to adapt and bend towards the other, even when we disagree, that builds a robust relationship: the willingness to be flexible, to be open to new circumstances or environments, and at times prioritize the needs of the other. That does not mean being a passive doormat. You can be assertive, but also make choices that respect and value the relationship you are in and your partner. It creates a positive cycle: that flexibility, being well received, helps build confidence, which is nurtured by being loved.

Gottman's Four Horsemen of the Apocalypse

These are the four attributes that John Gottman believes are the enemy of a happy long-term relationship:

Criticism. This comes from a position of pointing a finger, a rigid 'you are wrong, I am right' stance, which the recipient experiences as an attack. It is often verbalized as 'You always . . .' It is felt as a personal attack, not criticism of their behaviour. It puts them on the defensive. A more helpful position to take is to own your own feeling: 'When you don't take the bins out I feel . . .' This may seem mechanical and annoying at the beginning, but keep at it: over time it has surprisingly successful outcomes. As an aside, women do tend to criticize more than men.

Contempt is looking down on your partner, from a position of superiority, showing contempt for their character and moral or ethical position. It is an attack on their sense of self. It is ignited by that cycle of negative thoughts about them that stew away and are just waiting to be hurled, which makes reconciliation virtually impossible. It often follows on from relentless criticism. Contempt uses words to inflict harm intentionally, and is often expressed with eye-rolling or disgust. Contempt spells poison for the relationship, for it is the most corrosive behaviour in a marriage. Again, the antidote is to be aware of the impact of your contempt, and start changing with small steps, taking responsibility for your feelings and avoiding 'you' statements. But the root of negative thoughts needs to be addressed, so that warmth and respect underpin the conflict. Building a culture of appreciation in the relationship is not easy, but it is possible. A ratio of 5:1 kindnesses versus criticisms is a good measure on the barometer of the relationship to aim for. They can be small – this isn't asking for Oscar-winning performances in romantic love – gestures such as a smile, a touch on the shoulder, a thank-you, a warm glance, a thoughtful note or message all build up a bank of warmth, which then protects the relationship during conflict.

Defensiveness. This is the default response to criticism, defending against the accusation, behaving like a victim who has been unjustly attacked – 'It wasn't me' – then often turning on the attack: 'Why didn't you do it?' The victim

position is held with brute force and is often accompanied
by that whingeing tone, which is off-putting. When two
people hold the opposite poles of attack and defend, there is
no possibility of resolution and the conflict escalates, when
couples dig up previous accusations to counter-attack. The
cleanest way to deal with criticism is to take some
responsibility, acknowledge the part of the complaint to
which you can hold your hand up.

Stonewalling is exactly as it sounds: a blocking-out
and refusal to listen, often triggered by a contemptuous
attack from your partner. It can be characterized by
walking out of the room, distracting yourself with
another object and shutting down. The reason is often
because you are overwhelmed, and it is the only response
you have. It is common for men to stonewall; when women
stonewall, it is a sign that divorce is nigh. As with all
things relational, awareness is the first step, and once you
recognize that this dynamic is happening, it is important to
stop. Not in an aggressive way but agree that it isn't possible
to talk constructively now. Similar to children's 'time out',
both partners need to go into separate rooms, wind down
their systems with meditation or relaxation and agree to
return and try to talk with more empathy and respect.

Trying to stop ourselves using these four behaviours so that we
can grow together requires awareness of what we are saying and
some investigation internally as to why we criticize: why do we
have to make the other person wrong? What is the dynamic
between us? Conflict is inevitable, even necessary, in a relationship.
Disagreeing from a position of respect and equality can nurture
growth, when it comes with the willingness to listen, to take on
board our partner's view.

If we don't know what is going wrong in our relationship, and
if we can't find ways of voicing it, then resentment and distance
will grow. It is essential to know what is going on, good and bad,

and in the process build bridges of understanding, which include, perhaps, shifting our position. That would mean at times letting go of having to be right, or at least being more flexible. As an example, a typical hot spot for conflict is the dishwasher: use it, don't use it, stack this way or that, rinse, don't rinse – who cares? – everyone has an opinion: the fight is really about power and control. We misguidedly think that if we have control we can protect ourselves from being hurt. But, if we dare to trust enough, we can change, and find we are more protected from hurt.

The way I think about communication in conflict is to imagine that the words we are transmitting out of our mouths are entering into the mind and body of our partner, the person we love, with whom we've committed to build our life. Surely it is worth taking the time to learn how to have conflicts that do not cause serious injury to the other person. One of the expressions I was often told as a child was 'Sticks and stones may break my bones, but words will never hurt me.' That is an absolute lie. Words do hurt, and if we're to have successful relationships we need to take care with them.

We need to recognize that under threat we often retreat to our earliest defences: we feel childlike. As odd as it sounds, when partners are in conflict we can learn how best to resolve it through child psychology. We now know when we bring up children that we need to criticize the action not the person; we take time out if we're furious with our child, we self-soothe and come back when calmer. We make sure we give more positive feedback than negative: we know it nurtures their self-esteem and develops the connection between parent and child. If we're parents and behave in this way it is helpful to understand that these behaviours have the same impact between adults.

New Ways of Finding Love and Dating

As we saw with Jackson and Robbie, how we date is changing. The traditional route of meeting through friends, work and university is still current but waning. Social networks and apps are growing: about 22 per cent of straight couples and 67 per cent of gay couples now meet online; for young people, 18- to 24-year-olds (single or otherwise), dating online has tripled. It is important to recognize that the purpose of dating websites and apps is different for different people. Some are looking for love in a longer-term relationship, while others want to date and see it as fun entertainment, even a recreational activity, for which the app is a hook-up tool. Untold heartache and distress come when those aims collide. It is worth making the point that apps such as Tinder were designed as games, for fun, and if they want people to stay on them, surely it aims to keep them single.

Nevertheless, apps have extended everyone's choices, enabling men and women, who use them equally, to meet someone who could otherwise never have crossed their path, giving at times confidence and fun, particularly for those who may feel isolated working from home. For those who move around the globe, it offers a wide group of connections.

The research on this is relatively new, and not extensive. Zygmunt Bauman, the sociologist and philosopher, wrote about the term 'liquid love' in which he argued 'The twin forces of individualization and social change have liquefied' the solidity and security once provided by romantic partnerships and family structures. This concept was taken and further researched and it was found that the view of dating apps is too negative: there are positives in increasing people's connectivity. The argument against them, which I hear anecdotally, is that the endless series of choices when finding a partner is unravelling tight bonds, recognizing that, with so much choice, partnerships don't last and therefore people don't invest time in them. It becomes a vicious circle. Additionally, other commentators have argued that, as much as it might empower women sexually, particularly with apps such as Bumble, where the woman is to make the first move, one of the biggest downsides of apps is that there can be cognitive overload: we can't make a choice at all as there are too many options. Or because we hope the next choice will be better.

There is a potentially damaging side to matching through photograph-based profiles. It heightens the importance of looks as the first hook, increasing the need to be seen as beautiful or handsome. In those who attract many likes, it can increase vanity dating, and the need to keep looking good to massage their ego. Conversely, for those who don't receive many likes, it is concrete evidence for them to use against themselves, wounding their self-esteem.

Interestingly, when people were asked if they'd prefer to find love via an app or face to face, 61 per cent said they'd prefer the in-person encounter while 38 per cent didn't have a preference.

Modern Adultery

According to Dr Kenneth Paul Rosenberg, the psychiatrist and author of *Infidelity: Why Men and Women Cheat*, the landscape for adultery has altered radically. The modern adulterer is more complex and less predictable than the cartoon image. Adultery has increased in all brackets across the generations in the Western world, and it is women like Isabel who have joined the fray.

For twenty years the number of men having affairs has been the same, but the female statistics have increased by nearly 50 per cent: in 1993 it was 10 per cent of women; now between 15 and 19 per cent admit to having an affair. I can't help wondering how big the number would be if everyone told the truth. Those women are likely to be high earners and aged between forty and sixty. It is women moving out of the home into the workplace that has offered them the opportunity and financial freedom to break the traditional rules of fidelity.

Earlier, we read about Jackson's encounter with Suki, who ultimately was unfaithful. A survey into millennials shows that young women's behaviour is similar to what is traditionally thought of as male. Their focus is on sexual arousal and satisfaction, rather than what is thought of as the more gender-typical stance of seeking desire for emotional connection.

Adultery among the over-sixties has also increased since 1991, by at least 10 per cent for women and 14 per cent among men, a phenomenon due to living longer – perhaps they've been married for decades and are bored – being healthier and gaining the benefits of drugs that prevent impotence. From recent surveys many of those having affairs today are happily married. More than a third of women and half of men having affairs say they are perfectly happy with their long-term relationships.

Rosenberg adds, 'The more opportunity we are given to have affairs, the more likely it is we will have them. For where biology and opportunity meet, sexual straying is increased.' Despite the cultural norm of fidelity in marriage, we are wired to mate: it is in our biology to seek genetic diversity for the human species. It may be that for those who can no longer procreate their drive is to seek excitement, pleasure and new versions of themselves.

Modern life has brought with it a new context, which inevitably changes how we view fidelity, love and sex: financial independence, physical health, being in the workplace, the decline of social stigma, all aided and abetted by smartphones, which enable much wider access to hook-ups, and instant gratification of sex and intimacy. These are all an invitation to roam outside marriage. Yet the consequences may have a greater impact than the meaning of the fling/affair. The research varies, but some say 50 per cent of marriages end following adultery, others 25–30 per cent.

Does Love Matter?

The most convincing evidence I've seen is the Harvard Longitudinal Study of Adult Development, which tracked the lives of 724 men, from teenagers, year after year for seventy-five years. Yes, the researchers focused on men: it was seventy-five years ago, when women were not seen as of interest. They have gone on to research their wives and more than two thousand children. It asked about their work, their home lives, and their health. It was reported by the director of the study, Robert Waldinger, that it is 'the quality of our close relationships that matters . . . with family, friends and our community'. High-conflict marriages are very bad for us, truly detrimental to our health, worse than divorce.

Living in close, loving relationships protects us. This isn't about not having disagreements as a couple but about being able reliably to trust the other.

Interestingly, those in the most satisfied relationships at fifty were predictive of those who would grow into happy, healthy octogenarians or older. It showed those who were most happily partnered in their eighties were happy even if they were in pain. For those in unhappy relationships, their physical pain was intensified by the additional emotional pain. The study demonstrated that those in good relationships in their eighties had sharper memories for longer. Conversely, there was marked earlier memory decline if they were not.

As Confucius wisely said, love is difficult. It can be our greatest source of pain and it can literally drive us mad. Nevertheless, as we change, and our love changes, we will fare better if we do the work love requires. For our deepest source of happiness is found when we are loved and love.

Work

'Love and work, work and love, that's all there is.'

Sigmund Freud

Caz

First Job

Caz came to see me, reluctantly, because his life had stalled. He had been jobless for the last ten months. Caz was twenty-four years old, the youngest of four brothers, two of whom were step-brothers. He was tall and looked as if he should be very thin but in fact had quite a tummy. His pale skin reflected the fact that he hadn't set foot outside his rented room in east London for months, and when he spoke he blushed. The hot spot on his unshaven face throbbed, showing more life than the rest of him, as he loped in twenty minutes late for his 2 p.m. appointment. He told me his alarm hadn't woken him, and he'd got lost walking from the tube. His chaotic disorganization played out in every aspect of his life: he was 'completely lost'.

Caz was born just outside Manchester. When he was eight years old his father had gone to live in Spain, and he had very little contact with him or his step-brothers at that time. His father's lack of financial contribution to his children matched his lack of emotional commitment, which I could tell had left its mark on Caz. He sealed off that part of himself, sharply dismissing my questions. Caz's mum, on the other hand, was the pivotal person in his life, warm and reliable. He knew, with a certainty in his core, that she loved him. She worked long hours as a secretary at the Co-op, being a single mum. I could clearly picture the tough time she'd had juggling parenting and work. I silently sent her a nod of respect and admiration.

My need to gain clarity of the work we had to do was thwarted by Caz's non-appearance. I had met him only twice out of five booked appointments, and I felt as if I was making all the effort to keep us on track. I could feel myself withdraw as my annoyance increased. When we spoke on the telephone, Caz having missed another appointment, I heard the shame in his voice as he apologized for the umpteenth time. Surprisingly, my frustration alchemized into determination. I wanted to fight for the relationship and fight for the part of him that didn't know how to do this for himself. I told him not to give himself such a hard time: this was part of his problem. Our job together was to find a way to work with it. I could sense him breathe more freely, as he chuckled, saying, 'The proof is in the pudding and this is the pudding.'

I needed to hear in detail the extent of Caz's difficulties: what happened on a daily basis? I wanted to help him unravel his confused thoughts, work out what the impact of his father's departure had been, and understand whether the coping mechanisms he'd developed then were holding him back now. I wanted to help him think about what he was interested in, and how that might inform his future direction.

I heard Caz was at a particularly low ebb. There'd been times when he'd functioned more effectively, but those months when he'd tried getting a job and failed had taken their toll. He had sent out hundreds of applications and had received barely an acknowledgement. This fed into the battle being played out inside his head: New Year's resolutions to stop drinking, endless to-do lists, and promises to himself that he would start a new routine. But his self-discipline evaporated after a few days, as greyness descended, 'and the internet completely sucks me in'. He wanted to unravel his compulsion to do things knowing they harmed him – he sought activities 'that kill me but make me feel alive'. The treat of partying and drugs promised pleasure he couldn't resist. This would set up a hugely negative cycle, where he felt so low post-drugs and -alcohol that he couldn't move at all or do the smallest of tasks. Consequently, his belief that he could get work done would suffer another blow.

I was aware that as Caz verbalized his negative patterns his voice flattened and he seemed to swallow his words, which reinforced his criticism of himself. He shifted around uncomfortably in the chair, as if he wanted to run away from himself. I wanted to harness his naturally creative self – I'd seen sparks of it by doing a visualization with him. I asked him to close his eyes and breathe in, to move his attention internally and visualize a place in which he felt safe. His ability to switch out of the present and into his safe place was remarkably quick, as if this was where he'd prefer to live.

Within minutes his heart rate slowed, and the tone of his voice expanded as he depicted a beach in the West of Ireland, evoking the wind, the sea and its barren landscape. He stayed there for quite a while, drinking in the calm. I asked him what was happening inside him and he described the peace he felt, being alone, being in nature and having time. Reluctantly he came back into our room and was able to tell me how that calm was the reverse of his life. How deep anxiety permeated every moment of his day and could spin him into a sense of feeling outside his body. He feared anything and everything. His eyes were pinned to the floor and I gently commented on how lonely that must be. He didn't look up or speak. I could see the heat of suppressed emotion moving up his neck to his cheek. The connection I intuited he needed was also what he most feared. I invited him to breathe deeply and let his emotions flow through his body. As he looked up, his face was clearer, as if he felt more grounded. He gave me a tentative smile.

We spent the whole of one session examining what had actually happened to him since he'd left university. He had loved his university life, unlike school, which he'd hated. He'd read biological anthropology and been fascinated by it and, more importantly, had had tutors who believed in him while helping him organize his work. They inspired confidence in him, as did his friends: 'I was lucky as lots of people find it difficult. I was with a great group of people, eleven of us in halls and we hit it off. It was the best three years of my life – every day was good.'

When he left university, he'd assumed London would be a continuation of that happiness. He was shocked by how totally unprepared he was. He had found life there alien and lonely. When he did manage to meet up with friends, he told me that he would be very obviously upset, not speaking much, perfunctory nods, yet no one seemed to notice he was not okay and they talked over his distress. It made him feel even lonelier than if he'd been on his own. I could feel his anguish in their lack of acknowledgement, as if his suffering didn't matter, almost as if he was invisible – all of which was intensified by being in this vast city.

Pragmatically I reflected on how the transition between university and employment is often unrecognized. The safety of university, after school, in having a clear set of hoops to get through, a set timetable while living in a familiar place, the easy proximity of friends in the Common Room or Student Union, local pubs and clubs making social life accessible. The move to big cities, London in particular, meant dates had to be made with friends who often lived long distances apart, which was stressful and required organization and confidence, the two qualities Caz didn't have.

Similarly, when Caz was looking for a job, he felt ignorant and scared because he didn't know how the world worked, what the different industries were and what made them tick. He got his first job relatively easily, working for a recruitment agency. 'I loathed it with a deep and burning passion. I hated the sharkish attitude, the sink or swim – I had to be an asshole to be successful there. A manager even said to me, "You aren't enough of an asshole," and I left two days later.'

That first experience had burst his bubble of innocence. The thought of looking for a new job had terrified him, and led him to want to escape, unable to stand the lack of freedom. He went travelling for quite a few months, but when he returned he had to face the same difficulties, and his confidence was broken further. Caz reflected on where he was now, scratching his head. The discomfort he felt was forcing him to understand that he was no longer a child: he was going to have to do things he didn't like. Caz railed against the reality that he would only have three weeks' holiday a year, saying, 'It should be illegal.' He even found it hard to accept that he had to work in a shoe shop to pay his bills, which didn't match his vision that work would be fulfilling and meaningful.

Caz's difficulty in showing up to see me didn't abate; neither did my frustration with him. But we disjointedly continued, doing our best when we met. As Caz talked, I saw that having been told off as a child for being 'scatty', 'disorganized' and 'stupid' was a tape that continually played loudly in his mind. We looked more closely at his 'uselessness', and it became clear that he had, in my terms, a wiring problem. A likely diagnosis was ADHD, although I realized that taking drugs can create similar symptoms. He went away and looked it up online at MedicineNet. When he returned the following week, he showed me a printed version of it, as if he'd won first prize:

Adults with ADHD may have difficulty following directions, remembering information, concentrating, organizing tasks or completing work within time limits. If these difficulties are not managed appropriately, they can cause associated behavioural, emotional, social, vocational and academic problems.

Caz read out the accompanying list of traits and behaviours. It was as if a light came on in him: he could see he had many of the traits. We spoke pragmatically about how shouting at himself for this was like beating himself up for being left-handed or tall: it was part of him, and needed to be befriended. We could also develop systems that would help him organize himself better. Not his endless lists, which overwhelmed him: instead, using a few consistent behaviours every day would give him the clarity of mind to get tasks done, and build his confidence in his competence. He was reluctant to work out what those behaviours might be, and we tussled for a while. I asked him what was really going on. He paused, tapped his front teeth, which I knew meant he was in touch with something difficult, and said, 'I'm just not there. If I try my best and fail, that's terrifying.' We let his words land and knew he'd managed to voice an internal block to his functioning: it was unconscious, but was telling him powerfully how devastating trying his utmost and then failing might be. Less risky not to try at all.

In the next weeks we worked on building that safe place inside him, based on the Irish beach he had envisaged earlier. In order to develop a core part of him that could help steady the terrified version that had to face the world, I told Caz of the picture that emerged in my mind when I thought of him, of a horse, rearing and snorting, in a field where fireworks were exploding. It needed someone to come along and be kind to it, take it into a quiet field, soothe its flanks, give it water.

The metaphor clarified the cruelty of his own behaviour towards himself. It took time, but gradually Caz was able to incorporate a kinder voice that was like a mentor's. A voice that helped turn down the volume of his fears, told him to play his guitar, to do a breathing exercise, suggesting he eat regularly, rather than 'forgetting to eat and then having a blow-out'. Sometimes he just told the critical voice to shut up. He'd also listened to a speech from an Admiral McRaven, an American, which had gone viral: 'If you make your bed every morning, you will have accomplished the first task of the day. It will give you a small sense of pride, and it will encourage you to do another task, and another . . .' The simplicity of it worked for Caz and became part of his core behaviours.

We had a session that was lighter, with laughter, when Caz described in vivid detail the Steve Jobs character he envisaged he should be. He'd have iron discipline, an obsessive work rate that spat out results like a machine. He put on the voice that matched this character and sat appropriately upright in his chair, 'ready for action'. As much as we laughed together, it was illuminating to see how ambitious he really was, and I told him we needed to find a way to harness this ambition for himself, and for him to internalize some of the tenderness I felt towards his disorganized self, which got in his way. He looked at me briefly: I could see my words had reached him. As he turned away, I felt as if he was envisaging a more rounded version of himself.

The Steve Jobs character inevitably led us to explore his need for a male role model and the absence of his father, the difficulty being that Caz couldn't access any feelings he had for his dad. It was as if they had been wrapped in an armoured coat that pinged off an electric current, 'Do Not Touch', when we came close. Caz would try to talk about him and could retrieve a few early memories, like playing football with him in the garden, but as soon as he talked about his dad leaving, he cut off. And within a few minutes he had changed the subject. It let us both know that there was a great deal of hurt beneath that protection, which was something we could hopefully get to in time.

I wondered whether the escalation of fear and low self-worth that had built up in Caz to crisis point, when he first saw me, was actually ADHD, as I'd suggested. Or a reaction to events, the fundamental one being the departure of his father. In some ways it was immaterial: the diagnosis of ADHD had helped him be more accepting. But the thought gave me a focus, and as our relationship grew stronger, I encouraged Caz to go deeper. I felt there were a lot of boxes in his mind that needed to be unpacked to give him clarity as to who he was, who he really loved and trusted, what he believed and what he felt beneath his ever-circulating anxiety.

I heard more about his mother, whom he loved deeply. He could tell her anything. Her parenting position was that he had to learn for himself, from his own mistakes, and she wouldn't help him make decisions, which infuriated him, though he respected her for it. Their recurring fight was about screen time. She'd hated him playing Nintendo incessantly as a teenager, and then being on his iPhone as he got older. It was a fight she never won: his relationship with his phone was stronger and more faithful than his adherence to her vehement wishes. Often, he couldn't afford his room in east London, and would sublet it, go home to Manchester. It heightened the tension between them, for she was tired from work, worried about his lack of success in the job market, and he was angry with her for 'badgering him', simply because she was an easy target. As a mother, I felt for her.

One of Caz's step-brothers was a key person in his life: they regularly sent each other links to stupid jokes and had an unvoiced commitment to FaceTime each other at length on Sundays, when they mainly talked about sport. But the message beneath was of love.

Caz's sense of chaos quietened; there was a clarity that came from exploring himself further. It opened up a question in him of what was the point of having ambition *now*. 'I wonder whether I need to have a real work plan yet. I'm likely to be working well into my seventies, whereas my dad stopped working in his fifties. Why would I start now?' He knew he needed to earn money doing something other than his temporary job: working in a shop was seriously depressing him. Some of his friends were getting jobs, some were even doing well, earning good money, liking their jobs, and Caz feared he was 'missing the boat'. He could easily fall into regret for being so 'naive' when he'd returned to Manchester, for initially turning some jobs down, then not really looking very hard. He thrashed out the argument between travelling and getting life experience, or sticking with it and finding a job. He decided to stay for now, possibly travel later, which lessened the sense of being imprisoned in work for the rest of his life. He used his anger to fire him up, telling me it was 'now or never'.

Finally, Caz succeeded in getting a job. The tide had turned after he worked in a hospital for five months, moving stuff around, doing anything and everything. He liked his boss, a tough woman, who was straight with him and had a sense of humour. Being around people was good for his mood. A few months later he got a paid two-month internship, doing digital marketing for a digital magazine. It was a draconian office where he couldn't even go out to buy paracetamol without being threatened with the sack, and at the end of each day he felt subdued, almost like he wasn't a person. But it gave him structure: he knew that all he had to do was get up, make his bed, eat breakfast and get to work. The experience of knowing he could manage going to work every day helped him when the job ended: a few weeks later, he got a two-days-a-week job creating digital content for a start-up company.

Caz came in smiling. Grinning, even. The company had taken him on full time. He described the work: 'It's non-stop content, and because it's a start-up there are cross-over roles, marketing, anywhere I can help out. I like it because I feel I'm in the place things happen, and I can do my job, although I do feel utterly wiped out by the end of the week. My colleagues are good to me and that makes a huge difference.' I felt as if he'd won an Oscar. The internal battle he'd had to fight, and the external job market he'd had to overcome to land his first full-time paid position, had been much tougher than I'd known. I later learned that his story was very common and felt angry that schools and universities don't do more to prepare their students for the job market. It seems completely mad that for one of the biggest steps they will take they are given almost no preparation, knowledge or skills.

As we were having our last session I was interested to see how Caz had changed from our first meeting. He was twenty-five now, and still had that slightly wafty air, but when he spoke his voice was stronger. He looked me in the eye, and I could feel our contact, his presence connecting to mine. It was hard work for him to keep himself on track, and it took real discipline, but the pay-off was this energy, his sense of engagement with people and his own life. We hadn't fully dealt with the impact of his father's abandonment – I guess he'd sensed he couldn't cope with that while he needed to build his strength and confidence.

He had settled some questions in his mind, the important one being a clearer picture of what he was aiming for. He wanted by his mid-thirties to be 'running my own show, whatever that is. I know not to be ashamed if it doesn't happen. Life is a rollercoaster, and I want to learn from my mistakes. I used to feel such a failure but now I know it isn't me being a failure. I want to enjoy the unexpected, the richness of that, and stop worrying so much. I have a picture of me living in the country, in a small place with a wife and children. It sounds simple and even naive but that is what I know I want.'

Rachel

Back from Maternity Leave

It was halfway through our first session, when Rachel looked up from picking at her reddened cuticle, that I managed to get past her anxiety and glimpse the shining woman beneath. She was talking about her love for her baby boy, Daniel. Following his birth, she had trusted her instincts, they had both thrived and 'all that indecision that plagued me fell away. I was completely happy. I feel like the grown-up as a mother, and I'm doing a really good job. I want to translate that into the rest of my life.' She had come to see me because she had to make a decision over the next few months about going back to work, and the spectres of fear and lack of self-belief had begun to haunt her again.

I looked across the room at this pale, worried face, surrounded by her long luxuriant red hair that bounced around on her broad shoulders. Her build was tall and strong-looking, in contrast to the tight worry in her startled eyes. I wanted to say over and over, 'You are enough. You can. Breathe, slow down,' but there wasn't enough trust in our relationship for her to take that in yet. For now, I acknowledged how distressing this must be for her. I asked her to tell me what was going on in her mind.

I learned that Rachel had been brought up in Leeds by parents who had divorced when she was thirty-one. Her mother had wanted education to give Rachel and her younger sister, Belinda, the opportunities in life she'd never had. Rachel had had great success at school, and felt she'd got addicted to the praise of doing well academically. Yet despite her consistently high marks, her brilliant exam results still surprised her. At university, she would panic about an essay – 'The anxious monster would take over, giving me negative messages that said I can't do it.' She would seek her tutor's reassurance, and he would laugh at her, saying it was the best essay he'd read, which served to illustrate her lack of trust in her own judgement but failed to give her self-belief.

After university, she had fallen into management consultancy through an internship. There had been times at work she'd felt at her best, thriving on the pressure, knowing she was capable, and delivering what was required. It took a number of sessions to uncover that Rachel felt ambivalent about going back to this field, her sense of what she should do overriding her truth. This would be a recurring theme in our work.

Unlocking her ambivalence, Rachel questioned whether management consultancy suited her personality. Working in the macho world of cocksure men, who seemed better at putting on a show, undermined her. Rachel knew she was a perfectionist, who needed time to think and to process information. When under pressure she could get trapped in a loop 'where the ground splinters beneath my feet, my confidence goes and often one small criticism can tip me into not sleeping, and I feel I fall off the precipice'. She saw anxiety as that monster, a very physical beast she had to wrestle to the ground.

A particular project Rachel had worked on before she'd got pregnant had scarred her. She'd been engulfed by fear and had had to tell her boss that she couldn't continue. On reflection, Rachel realized her fear had been unfounded, for she had done most of the work, which, when finished by her colleague, had been very good. The memory of how painful that had been burned into her, the words choking in her throat as she said, 'I'm scared of getting too near the flame.'

The alternative she was instinctively drawn to, and had been

thinking about for a long time, was working in a charity to protect the environment. The activism, wanting to fight for a greener
planet, was intensified by the birth of Daniel. It would mean a big
pay cut. She imagined she could, over time, work this out with
Toby, her husband, but her mother was utterly dismissive of such
an option, telling her that she was brilliant as a consultant, that she
should just bite the bullet and go back.

Rachel's other preoccupation was with herself as a mother.
When she thought about it, she leaned forward and sighed, a tight
caught-in-a-bind sigh. If she could afford to stay home she would –
although it wasn't quite that simple: she had an ambitious feminist
voice too. She didn't want to be 'that woman who had started her
career successfully and then ended up in her forties in a crap job
because she had taken fifteen years out of the workplace to bring
up her children'. Rachel's dilemma was no different from the universal question that has challenged women for decades: how to
square work ambition and family.

It seemed to me that Rachel represented a generation of women
who almost knew too much, and the information they were juggling in their brains was making them crazy. They had reams of
knowledge about the importance of child development and parenting, which meant the natural guilt of parenting had even
higher stakes. I felt the feminist voices of her generation were less
'Hit the barricades for our rights,' and more 'We must fulfil our
potential: we are the next leaders.' And 'I need to be the perfect
parent with the perfect child.' There was pressure from her peers,
who all compared themselves and said they weren't competing
but, boy, were they competitive.

We both agreed vehemently the corrosive damage that comparing can do, particularly through social media. It wasn't a cry to
'have it all' but more 'How can I juggle and give both enough?'
For Rachel, with her brain the size of a planet, those imperatives
were limitless, in technicolour, clashing, and locking her mind. I
could feel her wanting to run very fast from her anxiety, and
escape it, but there was nowhere to run. I felt we would make

progress if we could distil her truth into a few simple priorities. Find ways to shut out the outside noise. Quieten the commands and counter-commands that were fizzing in her head.

Becoming a mother had been no easy process. Rachel had been through infertility treatment to get pregnant, finally conceiving Daniel after six years. When she described the dark cloud she had lived under for those years it was a bleak picture: grieving what she didn't have, her despair and hopelessness as her and Toby's hope had faded, and losing touch with friends who had children or were pregnant. The IVF treatments had put immense financial pressure on them both. The whole experience had been gruelling and terrifying. Toby had tried to be patient but they'd had some terrible arguments that made her shiver in retrospect. 'It broke me – it broke us both, financially and emotionally.'

I was still with her feeling of brokenness when she switched tack, her head to one side, brushing her fingers through her hair, as she acknowledged they had weathered 'the repeated gut-punches of loss' enough to keep working, keep their marriage intact and succeed in having a baby. Her eyes fired as she said quietly, 'I was brave.' I cheered equally quietly, hearing her speak up for herself. She gave me one of her rare joyous smiles. A moment of meeting.

What unfolded subsequently was how having a baby had changed her perspective on what she valued in life, and what gave it meaning. There was a tug to go back to the familiar, but her profound love for Daniel overpowered it. Rachel had found a side of herself as a mother she had never known before and didn't want to lose. We both acknowledged that her priorities had changed, and this was an opportunity for a proper transition, to give herself time finally to get to know herself, listen to herself, her different voices, and find out what fitted for the person she was now. 'I wish I could stop wanting to be normal – I don't even know anyone who is normal. It's a futile pursuit, but one that uses up vast amounts of my brain.'

I felt tenderness towards the parts of her that had been silenced by fear of failure and the need to please. I wanted her to know that she was enough. I wanted to create a space between us where she could give herself permission to listen to all the versions of herself, and all that was going on inside that creative, and clearly brilliant, mind.

Rachel came in one morning, dressed in her usual colourful array of floaty top and maxi skirt, her feet encased in Grecian sandals. I could see from how she turned away from me that she felt uncomfortable. She said, 'I'm thirty-eight years old. I wonder if there's any point in this. I feel guilty I'm being indulgent.' She was in the grip of self-doubt. I wanted to know what that felt like: what messages were going on beneath her guilt? She was holding her breath, felt kicked in her stomach, and wanted to run.

We did a visualization, which initially gave us an image of a black ache, which was weighing heavy in her head, and eventually became a layer of black tarpaulin, which was in place for protection. The other side of protection was suffocation. It let us know that she wanted to escape, run away to her imagined sunny uplands, where she would be at peace and all would be well. It felt significant to see how deeply wired in her was her drive to escape. She felt happier when she saw that below the black lay some blue: it connected her to blue sky and trees, which she absolutely loved. She often found herself looking up at the sky for sustenance. It raised the question of how she could bring nature into her life and its accompanying happiness into her everyday world.

Perhaps it was the first clue as to where she should look for work. We could see that she had an energized creative mind, which sought intensity and tough projects. It could surge and leap into action: perhaps she could find meaning by doing something in the environment. The other part of it was that she didn't have the tools to calibrate herself when she got frazzled with intense levels of stress, and feared that a blade was about to fall, like a guillotine, on her neck. We both knew that finding gears to help slow herself down was key – by developing a regular practice of breathing, meditation and yoga, or any other activity that helped reduce the overwhelming speed of her thoughts, which crashed and burned her. It became clear to us both that, for Rachel, self-care was not an optional extra.

I realized, with a start, that when we had finished our session I'd said goodbye to Rachel with an endearment I would have given my own daughter. With my supervisor, I discussed when it was helpful to allow myself to feel maternal to the young child in her. Rachel needed my empathetic attention, but when did I step over the boundary so that I was no longer her therapist but meeting my need to mother her? It helped me when I acknowledged I was angry with Rachel's mother because she seemed incapable of listening to her. Her attitude was either that Rachel agreed with her vision or that she was wrong. It not only disempowered Rachel from listening to herself but blocked her belief in herself. It felt to me that the blade Rachel feared was the swipe of her mother's words, which cut her off from her own mind. The work for Rachel was to find ways to protect herself from continually hoping that her mother would finally listen and respond sensitively: 'Feels like I'm speaking a different language . . . drives me nuts. I think sometimes she might get it, I'm always hopeful, and still I get upset when she doesn't – I have to stop asking for it, it's never going to happen . . . It feels lonely.'

Beneath the loneliness we needed to access how furious she felt. Her rage often turned against herself because she couldn't give herself permission to voice it.

Rachel had spoken to Toby, and surprised herself, going on a rant about how much she hated her mother. 'I properly hate her. Sometimes I feel so angry because of her complete lack of ability to see me as I am. She's a bully. She makes me panic. When I think I'm about to get a blast from her, I have to go and find a hard hat and hide.' Even as she repeated it to me, she looked up at the ceiling to check that the sky wasn't going to fall in on her. We unpicked her hate. She hated that her mother was blind to whole aspects of her, could see only what she approved of. She hated that her mother saw the world in black and white: for Rachel it was a million shades of grey. Above all, she hated how hurt and disempowered she felt after seeing her mum.

She knew she needed to have as good a relationship as possible with the mother she had and find ways to grieve for the mother she dreamed of, who was never going to appear. My experience is that daughters often cut contact with mothers when they find this too hard to negotiate. But Rachel and I knew that that would take even more psychological energy. We acknowledged her mother's attitude came from love, her disquiet from witnessing her child suffering and being unable to bear it, thus needing to come in with a fix, which had been simple when Rachel was young. But as the parent to an adult child, she couldn't fix anything. Instead she could be a sound and supportive listening ear, while putting aside her own assumptions and views, to fully hear those of her daughter. It would mean, at times, saying what her worries were, or even offering her suggestions, but only after she had taken on board her daughter's position. It was painful to Rachel, having a picture of the mother she wanted, but it was also clarifying. It helped her see her reality, not the wishful thinking of the child in her. I quietly commented that perhaps she could use this image to support herself when she was with her mother, to help protect her from disappointment.

Rachel's cycle of turbulence continued for a number of weeks, leading into months. Following her exploration of possible jobs, she described it as opening too many windows on her laptop: she didn't have the tools to sift through them and sort out which ones she needed and which ones she didn't. The whirlwind of research was like the spiralling wheel on her computer, which froze her system. She believed she could never change, and it tipped her into troughs of despair. Hearing her say, 'I don't know how to deal with myself, my anxiety. I hate it. I want to hit it and make it go away, cut it out, be quite violent towards it,' I felt my heart lurch as I looked into the face of this talented young woman, using words as weapons of self-harm. It was hard to sit with it, but fortunately I had enough awareness to stop myself jumping in too soon with an injunction to stop her attacking herself. Rachel needed me to hear this voice in her, which had never been properly attended to. Her plaintive cry that no one could help her felt as if it had been in her since she was tiny. Agreeing that she felt as if she had finally spoken for her six-year-old self, and in doing so had released their buried poison, I made a *phew* sound, and wondered what she needed now: I wanted to move with kindness towards that six-year-old child.

Tears came down her face, and she started to breathe more deeply. She felt profoundly sad and, for the first time, some compassion for herself, saying simply, 'It's been horrible.' That seemed to cover a world of self-recrimination but gave us some hope. I acknowledged how hard this process was, falling into holes she had hoped the birth of her son meant she would never revisit. Now she needed to support herself to stay in the discomfort of not knowing, while exploring this untouched new internal territory.

In many sessions Rachel mentioned her husband, Toby, with love and affection, saying how much he'd revelled in seeing her and Daniel thrive together. Toby was a food engineer, travelling all over the country, sometimes five days a week. She felt his regular absence when doing his job more keenly than normal. She was reluctant to say it, bending inwards to contract the feeling she felt she shouldn't have. Rachel felt she should be grown up and cope better, but the truth was she felt lonely. Her NCT friends had begun to go back to work, and her sister, who was single, was preoccupied with her job at the UN. The tearing at her nails increased as Rachel spoke, in what felt like a preferable pain to the one of isolation.

When Toby came home from a tiring week, she understood he didn't have the energy to help unlock her stuckness, and certainly not to hear her self-hate: he wanted to have time with Daniel and peace. It meant she put on a show of happiness for him, which probably wasn't very convincing, and the space between them grew. We talked, knowing this is a familiar tension in all couples with a young baby. I could hear Rachel's silent scream for love, which perhaps was being offered to her but she couldn't feel it. We finally agreed she needed to talk to Toby more honestly, and as a couple they could explore ways that might help them.

Toby came up with a genius idea: swimming in the freshwater pond early in the morning. He'd read an article about it in the paper, and believed it would do something special for Rachel, feeding her love of nature: this would literally immerse her in it. The first time, baby Daniel woke them early, and as they walked to the pond, they found a new beauty in winter. Rachel gingerly stepped into the freezing water, then jumped – the shock of the cold forced whooping and shouting from her, and she found herself giggling in a way she hadn't for a long time. The intensity of the cold slowed her down: she just had to breathe and swim but felt the thrill of being alive. The exhilaration stayed with her for days, and she knew she had found something that would help her step into her new life.

As the months passed, she continued to swim in the freezing temperatures and her sense of bravery grew in her, like a pillar of strength, deepened by her fellow swimmers, who became an important source of friendship.

An additional transition was that Daniel had naturally withdrawn from breastfeeding and she felt as if her magic, the unique intimacy of breastfeeding, which had always soothed him, had been taken from her. For the first time she felt incompetent as his mother. She sobbed, apologizing for the tears, wiping them away with tissues pulled angrily from the box, pressing them into her eyes as if she wanted to hide from them, but every time she spoke, more tears came. She described the sadness she felt that their joyous time of absolute togetherness was over. But in a little while her confidence was restored when she found that singing Spanish songs (who knew?) calmed him, that pressing gently into his acupuncture points soothed him, as did massaging his back after his bath. It was the first of thousands of steps she would need to take as his mother, of loosening her hold on him with love, yet being open and present to his needs.

They went on holiday as a family, walking and camping in the Peak District. Rachel and Toby had time to talk, as well as time just to be. She felt close to Toby again, and I was touched as I felt the warmth of her love for him. Time without telephones, outside noise and in nature healed them. Prior to going, Rachel had done a vast amount of research about potential jobs in the environment sector. She had also been in contact with various colleagues, and her old boss, to see what was available. She had investigated 'highly sensitive people', reading books and listening to podcasts. It helped her see herself with more compassion: she wasn't the only person who had this difficulty.

Walking and talking gave Rachel the clarity she needed. She would go back to work in management consultancy three days a week, focusing on a specific project. The decision had not been an easy one to make, and she was sad not to be stepping into a new profession. Through discussion, she knew her priority was Daniel and that she didn't want to work full time. Working in the third sector part time would not pay her enough; consulting would. She was going to look into volunteering a few times a month for an eco organization, to have a taste of that world. It was hard to sit on her ambition, frustrating not to make progress in a new direction, but she eventually consoled herself with the idea of 'The 100-Year Life': there were still many careers ahead of her.

Rachel felt calmer now the decision about her job had been made. She began to see she could trust herself and Toby. It gave us the opportunity to explore the roots of her anxiety. As a child, much of the turbulence in her family life had been unvoiced. She had tried to interpret the silence, picturing scenarios in order to exert a feeling of control. Sometimes she had been right, which gave her a false sense of her power to control the future. Her brain could be an exhausting kind of superpower. This was a significant realization.

It further helped her to see that her mother and father, in their different ways, had a fixed view of her. To protect herself, she had put up a wall to defend herself against their judgement. She talked about their history and upbringing, which had not been straight-forward. Her compassion for them grew and helped her to be less angry, particularly with her mother, who exerted most emotional power. She worked towards accepting them for who they were, and what they were capable of. She realized it would help to stay in the present: her mother loved being useful, and since she lived nearby, Rachel could be appreciative of that. Her father lived in Scotland, so visits were rare. He was a joker, and very good at playing with Daniel, if only for short bursts. Keeping her relation-ship with them simple would be critical going forward, shifting the dynamic to one of equals, and she would stop asking for their advice, which was always a disaster.

There were months when we needed to revisit Rachel's rela-tionship with her mother and father. She practised calming herself before she saw her mother, whom she saw much more, consciously quietening her push to blaze with fury. She expressed the heat in safer territory with me. After many discussions, she made a fun-damental shift in her attitude to them. Finally, she was released from the burden of their interactions, the weight of expectation, longing and then disappointment, which allowed her to feel closer, even loved and loving.

It seems a miracle to me that our brains really are plastic: we can change. However tight the knot of our perceptions and beliefs, if we put our mind to shifting it, bearing the discomfort, even pain, of it, and persist, something inevitably changes. Change doesn't remove the scars of the past relationship or, on high-octane family occasions like Christmas, stop old feelings being reignited, but it does give new possibilities for the future relationship.

We had some good weeks, Rachel growing stronger. She went back to work, which rocked her at times, but after the first month she settled in. Her perspective had changed: she didn't get as wound up about work, and when she felt the anxiety build, she would go for a walk around the block, then return and do the task, rather than ruminating on how to perfect it. Finally, her feeling matched her thinking, and loving her son had shifted her unrealistic expectations of herself at work. People have to want to get better: they need to be willing to fight and endure the pain of change. Rachel was a living embodiment of that.

Our sessions came to a natural end. Rachel was back at work and was quietly proud of herself, smiling with her head down. It wasn't her dream, but it paid the bills and it was interesting enough. Work and love of family would never sit in perfect balance. There would always be a tension. Her developing awareness of herself, and tools to self-soothe, enabled her to learn to manage that tension, not be spun out of control by it. We laughed that, as humans, we often look after our cars better than our minds, checking them in for regular services. She said, 'I need to drop out to drop back.'

Heinrich

Life after Work

I could see from the Skype screen that Heinrich looked younger than his sixty-five years. With a neatly trimmed grey beard and shaved head, he was elegantly attired in a tweed waistcoat and bow-tie. He wore rimless spectacles over smiling eyes that matched the grin on his face. I don't see happy people for counselling, pain is my familiar territory, and I found myself discombobulated by his good cheer, and wondered whether we would get to the depth of his experience.

We had made contact with each other because I had let it be known through colleagues that I was looking to work with someone who had retired, and Heinrich had responded. I framed our relationship as a therapeutic conversation rather than therapy: he hadn't come to me because he was suffering. I told him I would respect the usual ground rules of therapy, but perhaps we would both need to be alive to when he felt uncomfortable in opening up to me or not.

Heinrich surprised me by saying that he wasn't fearful of that, he wanted to find out what was going on inside him at a deeper level. He'd talked to his wife and friends but didn't feel he really knew what this big change meant for him.

Heinrich had worked in Heidelberg, where he still lived, as a forensic pathologist for the last twenty-five years. My ignorance of what this job entailed, then my instinctive revulsion that it meant cutting up dead bodies for samples of their tissue, meant dark images flooded my brain and stopped me listening. He picked up on my response: he was used to it, most people reacted in the same way, with fascination and disgust. Heinrich described briefly what he did. At the beginning he had performed post-mortems for unnatural deaths, which often became criminal cases, but over time, he had worked in a forensic-science institute where he had led a growing team on different projects, many of which were innovative. What had been difficult for him was that the institute had decided his retirement for him. He was initially pushed to one side as an adviser, then told he had to retire at sixty-five. Heinrich would have preferred a slower end, working part time, then gradually fading out. He felt obsolete: one day he was there, the next he was not.

I didn't pick up any resentment in Heinrich's tone, more an open question as to who he was now. Before, he had had a purpose, he had been needed, and his work had brought him status. Now he was at home all day, with no job title, and part of him felt he was on the last downhill run. He found it difficult to say the word 'retired': it brought images of aged old men with stooped backs and walking sticks, which he quietly admitted scared him.

He had imagined he would immediately start taking seriously the hobbies and interests he'd had before he retired, but he discovered it was not that simple. He spoke slowly, as if he was unwrapping the parcels in his mind that had come through the post to see what was beneath. To his surprise he couldn't replace one thing with another: he hadn't been able to start doing his photography or drawing immediately, which was what he had planned. The only structure that he had started from day one, and maintained, was to go on the rowing machine three times and cycle twice a week. They were pegs of structure that lifted his mood, kept him fit, but also enabled him to manage the not-knowing. Although part of him felt like he was on holiday, which came out with a giggle, another part felt ambivalent. He couldn't motivate himself to seize these new opportunities, however much he told himself to get going.

I explained that as human beings we have a natural resistance to change: our systems are wired to maintain our habits and seek regularity. Even if it is change we choose, the level of resistance will equal the size of the change, meaning a very big change will bring a proportionate amount of resistance. There was a pause as he realized that before he could start something new he had to let go of his previous self, and right now he wasn't ready to do that. He was afraid if he actually let go he would feel empty inside. I said that perhaps he needed to feel that emptiness in order to let go. It had a pace of its own, which he sounded as if he was respecting, although it was slower than he'd hoped, telling me, 'I want to use this opportunity to become a different self, rather than become an older version of my earlier experience.'

I asked Heinrich whether he was angry, which, in retrospect, was more a reflection of what I would have felt than what he was saying. He wasn't angry, he was confused. He believed it was right that he should retire, to make space for the next generation: it needed new theories and research from younger people, with a new perspective and energy. He just hadn't liked the speed of it. He added that he hadn't been depressed as yet, though part of him was waiting for depression to descend. Mainly he felt neutral, not very happy but not unhappy.

I could hear the smile in Heinrich's voice as he told me that his friends who had retired seemed to have jumped straight into other jobs, commercial or voluntary, and were endlessly telling him how busy they were. Busier than when they had worked. That wasn't the case for him. After his teenage children had gone to school, he had a leisurely breakfast, his favourite part of the day, reading the paper, drinking coffee. He did things that amused him, and certainly many more domestic chores than he'd done before, but very little that was interesting. As he spoke, he realized anew what he had known but not voiced in a while: his job had been endlessly fascinating. It had led him through his day; he'd needed to prioritize. It was never a question of what to do and, more importantly, it had given his life meaning. He didn't underestimate the value of being a husband and father, but society certainly didn't value that as much.

When he told people he'd retired they were much less interested in him, and he found he wasn't that interested in their work. He'd gone to the barber recently, and when he told him he'd retired, he'd been asked, 'What did you used to do?' almost as if he wasn't a person until he had the label of his past profession. I wondered if it was to do with our natural survival mechanism: do we need to know where this person worked to measure them against our own pecking order? Or perhaps we find it awkward not having a pre-determined list of questions to ask about work, such as 'Do you like your job?' Are we stumped by the word 'retirement'? It seemed a word that hit a brick wall, or perhaps a gravestone. We agreed there were no role models of people in retirement to whom we could look up. The role models in old age who were celebrated were those who never stopped working, like the Queen, Ruth Bader Ginsburg or David Attenborough.

The big question was 'Now what?' He was in limbo, knowing he wanted to step into a new sense of self. What emerged for us both was the fact that he couldn't force it. He didn't want to. He was curious to see 'what a new me might look like'. He was wondering whether we measure our self-worth nowadays by busyness – or was it fear of the abyss of the big emptiness? He found the most difficult thing about retirement was controlling his fear of the negative. He wanted to make a positive one – finding a new fulfilment, a new version of himself. I felt it showed a real level of confidence that Heinrich could trust this new self to develop over time, not wrench himself into frantic activity to present himself to the world in a way that would meet its value system. But to sit with the discomfort of not knowing, the 'fertile void', is the necessary stage before a new beginning, but it is often short-circuited, which means that the potential growth and thereby satisfaction in the new phase is diminished.

I could tell by the tone of Heinrich's voice, for he spoke with less vehemence, that a sensitive area of change was the recalibration of the relationship he had with his wife. She was twelve years younger than him, and worked in television as a director, which meant she was away a lot. He had a pension, but it was considerably less than he had earned, so she was now the main breadwinner. He found he had to ask her to pay particular bills, or even ask her for money, which they both found uncomfortable. Sometimes she questioned the amount she had to pay, which certainly hit a nerve in him. He also did much more of the domestic work, cooking and cleaning, and there had been a particularly tense interchange when she'd asked him irritably why he hadn't fixed a broken shelf. It highlighted the new order: she felt, although never stated, that he was twiddling his thumbs at home while she was doing all the work.

Heinrich was riled and let her know he was in charge of his time: he most certainly was not her new domestic staff. He sounded as if he was on steadier ground when he said there was a big difference between talking through a disagreement and fighting. Fighting meant shouting and not listening. Talking from different positions, even if they were both angry, was vital. They knew how to sort out disagreements fairly rapidly, and even though they felt frustrated with each other, they could at times challenge each other to be their better selves. He didn't talk in depth about his relationship, but I gathered they'd been married for twenty years, and their partnership was embedded with the two vital ingredients: will, and the desire to keep the relationship alive.

Over the weeks that we spoke Heinrich noticed that his interest in the field of pathology had gradually dwindled. He was no longer reading papers, or following cases and, to our mutual surprise, he had turned down a supervisory role, of a few days a month, when it was offered, something he would have jumped at previously. His old skin was beginning to fall away. His children drew his energy. Being at home to greet them at 4 p.m. became an important point in his day: they didn't necessarily talk to him – there seemed to be a party going on in their phone, which he couldn't compete with. But I could hear happiness in his voice, from his heightened tone: they all enjoyed the presence of each other, the availability to stop and chat if they wanted to.

He loved cooking them supper, and discovered a new interest in food, trying out new recipes, reading articles. When they brought friends home he heard about new music, films and their opinions, which challenged his own but kept him connected to them. He took immense pleasure in having time for them, time when he wasn't exhausted or preoccupied with a work problem. I felt he was describing the precious gift he was able to accept: being with his children through the last years of their puberty. The slower pace of his life enabled him to savour the time in a way that was entirely new to him, and exciting.

Heinrich had started going to philosophy classes, and visited art exhibitions, enjoying the free time he had to listen to the talks from the curator. The visits fed his soul and gave him new perspectives with which to look at life. He understood, without needing to verbalize it, that what we put into our mind is as important as what we put into our mouth for health and well-being. Often he had coffee with other visitors and, with the keen eye for detail he'd used for work, became focused on them. Heinrich's now familiar deprecating humour emerged as he described observing their group behaviour, including his own. He could see there was a constant scoring going on, and a kind of drifting towards people of the same tribe. It would start with platitudes about the talk, then quickly move to what their job had been – work was the status badge – as well as family. Having successful children and numbering their grandchildren were further badges of honour, moving closer towards those who were of the same

education, intellectual and class level, in what he called a sublim-
inal Darwinian response of the survival of the fittest – pulling
together to win.

I was interested to discover whether there was a parallel relationship with leaving work to the death of someone we loved. At
many levels it can't be compared – it even seems trite to try. But
when I was talking to Heinrich I learned from him that part of
what supported him to leave without massive turmoil was that he
had no regrets about what he had done. He was proud of what
he'd achieved. He had even been given an honour when he left, in
recognition of his contribution to the field. I was interested that he
was slow to mention it, which also demonstrated to me that his
sense of self was not only rooted in his work. He was able to hold
inside himself the substance of the work he had done, and it continued to feed his confidence, although it was no longer present on
a daily basis.

It seemed to me that those who have been dissatisfied with their
work are similar to those who had a difficult relationship to a person who died: it is hard to hold on to the good things because
the unfinished business blocks them from letting go. Although
Heinrich would have preferred a slower ending, he wasn't fired. It
most certainly wasn't personal. Most importantly, he had enough
money: he wasn't thrown into the terrifying territory of inability
to pay the bills. He could hold his head high, it was the established
age of retirement, and he had the capacity to come to terms with it.
Someone who is sacked peremptorily, like a sudden and unexpected death, is often preoccupied with how it happened, what was
said. Who is to blame? Their anger and energy are used up trying
to make sense of what is often impossible to make sense of. Shards
of broken glass from the act stick into their confidence. Heinrich
was freed from those ruminations, while the love he could rely on
at home, and his network of friends, gave him secure foundations
he could stand on while his internal self was scrambling to
adjust. We know the single biggest factor in a person's ability to
rebuild their life, following bereavement, is the love of others.

We discussed the metaphor that Heinrich was sitting in the middle of a see-saw: he could tip downwards or up. It seemed to us both he needed to sit in the precarious middle until he knew what his next steps were. If he was to succeed in getting there, he needed to be clear as to where he was heading. He needed to remind himself regularly to enjoy each day and be grateful for what he had. Take mini steps in new directions by trying out fresh ideas. Sitting in the middle would free Heinrich to pivot in the new direction his life would take.

His youngest son succeeded in gaining a place at an international college, which meant he was leaving home a year earlier than they had expected. I could hear the pride in Heinrich's voice – he was happy for his son – but he became more tentative when the reality of 'the sad and empty house' came close. His son was a noisy child, and Heinrich was daunted by the silence he foresaw. In some ways this ending felt as big as retiring. Heinrich had begun to feel calm and adjusted to not working, and now he was facing a new transition.

As he spoke I recognized the coping mechanisms Heinrich had used before coming into play. He allowed himself to feel his anxiety, his sadness and the difficulty of not knowing. He also engaged his thinking. The two systems of feeling and thinking were aligned and supported him to allow this new transition to process through his system and his life. He knew that, with even more time being freed up, he didn't want to become old and passive. One of his next steps would be to build a new network of like-minded friends – to find new ways of being alive and having purpose.

Heinrich had been on holiday with his family and, through discussions with them all, had formulated a clear plan for the future. With their youngest son going off to college the next year, he and his wife had decided to move to a smaller house outside Heidelberg, within commuting distance of the city for his wife, who had eight more years to work. It would release capital and be less expensive to run. Heinrich said, with some excitement, 'It is going to be a period of fundamental change,' in the way they were going to live. He would have to be very active in making it happen, selling their family home, buying a new house and building an entirely different life.

His parting remark in our last session summed it up: 'For me it becomes a process of feeling, thinking, but not of a replacement from my working life to a pensioner in a different part of the country. It feels more like a process of accepting that work cannot be replaced. It's not a matter of this or that. It is for me more a matter of letting go – letting go of my old working life and accepting that it's gone. And what now? I don't know. But I notice that I am very curious to see what will happen. It's not a new project that we move to a new house. A project means work, with a goal, a beginning and an end. It is more a process of letting go and seeing what happens.' Heinrich was clear that leaving his job was by no means a matter of finding new ways to fill his time but of discovering new ways to find himself.

Cindy

Fired, and Love Uncertainty

The way in which a new client contacts me can give me a surprising amount of information. Cindy, a thirty-one-year-old American living in San Francisco, had listened to a podcast I'd recorded, was curious to know more and followed my trail of interviews online. She learned I was doing a book on transitions and sent me a message, via Facebook, telling me she was a perfect candidate for a case study. Would I meet her?

Before I'd seen her or heard her voice, Cindy's approach told me she was someone who looked for what she wanted, and when she believed she'd found it, she had the confidence to ask. Cindy was also someone who would jump into a situation without knowing much about it.

When I meet someone for the first time I assimilate information, as we all do, from their eyes, body language, clothes and attitude, as well as their words. When I saw Cindy, I thought, Wow. She was stunning. My second thought was that I could be held hostage to her beauty and miss the tangle of ugly processes hidden beneath her olive skin and tanzanite eyes. I would need to build up a clearer picture of her over a number of weeks so that I wasn't limited to that first impression.

In our initial assessment session on Skype, Cindy told me she worked in the tech industry. As a start-up entrepreneur, she had built a location-based mobile app with funding from an investor. The reason she wanted counselling was because, in her work and love life, she was at a crossroads. Her investor wanted her to find a buyer for the app. Her ex-fiancé, Elliott, wanted to go out with her again, after a year apart. He was bringing gifts and promises of love. As Cindy was speaking I noticed her narrative was one of hope. I had the impression she would look for the upside of any situation. Her athletic frame shouted chia seeds, smoothies for breakfast, and an intense fitness regime, energy zinging across the screen at me. She smiled constantly, her smile not always matching the worry in her eyes or the quaver in her voice as she tried to swallow her distress.

Cindy had been brought up to believe anything was possible. As a young, intelligent woman in the twenty-first century, the world was her oyster. She had worked hard and jumped every hurdle to give herself the best chance in life. She believed she had found it, for she loved her first job. Cindy had worked for an estate agent, felt passionate about property, clients and the business as a whole. That excitement came to a shuddering halt two years later, as the crash hit and she was made redundant. Property as a career had to be put aside for now, and over the next several months she had applied for hundreds of jobs in every industry, with no success. She was broke, living at home, with no likelihood of finding a job.

Following the model of her step-father's success as a businessman, she decided to be her own boss, and with a friend started a local online organic-food business. Despite two years of hard work, the company went under. Its collapse upset her, but the experience gave Cindy a taste for entrepreneurial endeavours. Her parents had told her to keep the faith: the business failure was not her failure. Her mother reminded her that her grandmother had been an entrepreneur as well so it was in her blood. Her parents were wealthy, and usually espoused the belief that their children had to make their own way in life, but this time they wanted her to try again and would back her, but only on condition she remained in Arkansas. Cindy felt suffocated by their control, which gave rise to a surge of energy to get away from home and give herself new opportunities. The tech industry was one of the few that was growing: she made the decision to get herself to the centre of it, San Francisco, and sold everything she owned.

Cindy arrived in San Francisco from Arkansas with no money and no contacts. A place she had never been to before, a city as different from her home town as New York is from New Orleans. Living in terrible accommodation, infested by cockroaches, with a landlord who wouldn't fix anything, working in cafés and restaurants, Cindy put herself in front of anyone she could find, asking for the opportunity to work and learn. After various jobs, she had the idea for the location-based app, and miraculously found an investor who said he believed in her. Cindy told me the app had been her 'heart and soul' for the last few years, but her investor wanted to sell it far sooner than she had envisaged. She'd had five potential buyers, with whom she had gone through a process of negotiation trying to come up with plans to buy it back from her investor, but they had all fallen through. She followed her bouncy sentence with a short gulp of air, which felt like fear.

I was aware of an underlying difference between us; I wasn't sure if it was informed by age, culture or experience, but my instinct was to go for the dark and hers for the light. I could feel myself wanting to focus on her fear, all of the difficulties she'd had to face, the intensity of not knowing what would happen despite her hard work. In doing that I might crush her capacity to surf the disappointments and keep going with hope, which was, after all, her natural coping mechanism. I managed it for a while, but when she told me she felt disappointed in her investor, I thought, Disappointment? Really? He had promised her equity, reneged on it, promised a good salary, reduced it. She had built a growing business with her work, her contacts, and her reputation on the line, and out of the blue he had shortened her timeline for an exit by three years.

Wasn't she angry? I asked. I felt angry and it wasn't my job on the line. She told me she wasn't sure, maybe a little bit, but more she felt let down. Then she moved quickly to her learning, that it had taken her a long time, but she had overcome her fear of the unknown, and now pursued the best opportunities, which made each day the best day. I needed to rein in my feelings, acknowledge the challenge she faced and support her optimism.

The other issue Cindy wanted to explore with me was whether to restart her relationship with Elliott. He had been her best friend for a few years post-college and they'd had a lot of fun together. After a particularly good party they had started dating and became engaged. With me, she focused on the break-up. Two significant aspects had left her carrying 'a ton of hurt'. Elliott's mother didn't think Cindy was good enough for her favourite son. She had created havoc from the minute they were engaged, threatening to boycott the wedding, refusing to pay for any of it, and leaving long, furious, sometimes menacing voice messages on Elliott's telephone. She was 'the angriest woman on the planet', but Cindy believed she could have withstood her fury and had a small, private wedding, but Elliott didn't stand up to his mother. He 'retreated into his cave' and the wedding was cancelled.

As far as I could understand it, they had never gained a mutual consensus of the subsequent events: she felt they had cancelled the wedding celebrations, with the expectation they would still marry. Elliott's version was they ended their engagement.

The far greater wound was Cindy's abortion. Again, she believed she'd said she wanted to keep the baby, but Elliott's 'silence was deafening'. Without a secure job, or relationship, and being young, she felt she couldn't go through with it. She covered her face with her hands, as she stutteringly told me she had assumed, once it was done, it was a sacrifice that would be painful, but she had had no idea she would never settle with it. She cried deep sobs, regretting the decision now and, she felt, for ever. Following her tears, there was a long silence as the pain subsided and the clarity of her thoughts could surface. Her tanzanite eyes pinned me with her regret, as she told me that most days she imagined the baby as a person, and prayed for it, prayed to be forgiven for her decision. Ending on a positive note, she was grateful to have had such a searing experience to learn from.

I felt profoundly moved and could hear how the two voices in her could never be aligned: her pragmatic voice that it had not been the right time for a baby, and the voice from her heart, which grieved for the future of which her decision had robbed her, leaving her with images of a child she would never know and always miss.

Ideally, we would have explored together what was important for her going forward with Elliott, but I found myself asking direct questions, pushing her to protect herself when I wasn't entirely confident she would. Could they find a way of building trust by talking more openly and fully? Would Elliott be able to stay on her side when faced with difficulty? How would they deal with his mother? What did they both believe in? What were their dreams? Who did she find herself to be when she was with him?

She told me she loved him. She could be herself with him, and he'd apologized for how he'd been. They had both cried about the baby. She did want to make sure she wasn't repeating a cycle and going back to him for fear of being alone, but she could picture them growing old together. In the year since her break-up she had tried dating, gone on Tinder and Bumble, but found it a brutalizing experience. She felt either bored or, worse, disrespected by the men who aggressively wanted sex. Their outlook on life was markedly different from hers, which she found alienating. She hadn't met anyone with Elliott's qualities – no one was as much fun, as clever or as attractive. I could see her heart had decided for her. My scepticism remained but I wasn't her mother: I was her therapist. My role was to raise awareness of potential difficulties, not to influence her life choices.

Over the next weeks Cindy was brutally ousted from the business. Her work partner, Todd, whom she had trusted completely, had gone behind her back and bought the business from the investor. The promises of severance pay and moving costs were withdrawn. She was given nothing. Worse, her name was tied to some of the company's debts and she was being hassled by debt collectors. Cindy was broke. She couldn't pay her rent, and had to move into a friend's apartment; she slept on their sofa. She looked pale and shaken. She was shocked by the speed of her exit but was determinedly smiling at me.

Her investor, who I called The Tosser in my head, would call her in the middle of the night, battering her with questions, demanding charts and financial statements. Cindy would wake in the early hours in a cold sweat of fear. At times her anxiety escalated to panic attacks. I tentatively suggested her reflexive response was 'to be fine' although I wasn't sure she could be, given all that was happening. Cindy told me, 'I feel sad and disappointed. In a way it's a relief. I'm happy there is an end.' The pressure of the last six months had been overwhelming.

Cindy had a point: as a first response 'being fine' is a pretty good one because it kept her sane while the storm was whirring. But if that was where she remained, it was unhelpful. The extent that she cut off the pain of her loss would also cut her capacity to feel joy. We cannot shut out one feeling without shutting out our overall capacity to feel. It meant she'd have to narrow her bandwidth of emotion to stay there, which could potentially suck away her ability to engage fully with life. But these was early days, and I just needed to check what she did to help soothe herself. Cindy had started painting and writing creatively, outlets for her swirling thoughts and emotions. Watching funny TV calmed her. Running always helped, particularly when she hadn't slept. But the thing that worked best was being with friends, downloading her feelings, and letting them make her laugh.

Clients in crisis tend to stay on my mind, and when I thought of her afterwards, I smiled at how the culture of self-care is embedded in the life of millennials. How great is that? To a contemporary of mine in their thirties, the idea of having a toolkit of self-care options that they used when desperate was unthinkable. Their tried and tested calmer was a great deal of alcohol.

I need not have worried about Cindy avoiding the process of loss. Over the next few weeks, her initial disappointment turned to fury, when she was sent threatening lawyers' emails and uncovered Todd's full betrayal. She felt hurt most by other close working associates, who went with the new business. The behaviour of one in particular, who had called Cindy 'my sister', she found especially galling. She'd suggested they pray together and kept sending upbeat quotes. If she'd been straight, and acknowledged she'd chosen Todd because she needed the money, and apologized knowing it must have been tough for Cindy, the friendship might have survived. But her sanctimonious messages were intolerable.

This was a significant loss, and the work for Cindy was no different from grieving. It would be a process of supporting her to express her feelings and help her adjust to this new unwanted reality. It was important to understand what had happened. Cindy needed a narrative she could make sense of, the beginning, middle and end, which would enable her cognitively to come to terms with it. Next steps would be influenced and informed by that understanding.

Cruelly, and it frequently happens in grief, Cindy's anger swiftly moved from being directed at her investor and Todd to herself. She felt furious that she had not looked out for herself more. She castigated herself: she had not pushed for a contract. 'I did everything for that business, and now I leave empty-handed. It feels like they've stolen it from me.' She wished she'd left earlier, given less. She knew that if she had been advising a friend, she would have encouraged them to leave when the danger signals first appeared. I was interested that she had been warned early on not to trust her investor, and there were questions about Todd too, but she had gone ahead. Cindy looked surprised. 'Oh, I don't know why I do that,' she said, twisting the ring on her finger, as she tried to unravel the question in her mind. 'I want to give people the benefit of the doubt . . . At what point do you become ruthless if you don't give them the benefit of the doubt?'

I could see her dilemma: she didn't want to lose her trust in people, become that bitter, tight-lipped paperclip of a woman. At the same time, blind trust had injured her. Where is the line of wisdom in that tension of trust and mistrust? It wasn't solely her judgement of people that had kept Cindy hooked. Her drive to make the business succeed, which, to be fair, was the only opportunity available to her, overrode her instincts: she hoped her hard work and some luck could swing it in her direction. I'd noticed it in other people, the blindness that comes with the will and almost addictive ambition to succeed.

For all its complexity, I could see Cindy was robust enough to let herself roll with the turmoil that ensued. When she suffered, it went deep. 'My world, my home, my pay cheque, gone. All the lessons I didn't want to learn, not to mention years of my life going to someone I don't respect. It's so painful.' She still couldn't sleep, waiting with icy fear, then with raging circular thoughts against the line-up of people who'd betrayed her. Like the self-harm of an ex-girlfriend following their boyfriend on Instagram, she would give herself hits of pain by following the app on social media. Her health regime went out of the window, and big dinners with Elliott, who was still wooing her, left her feeling heavy. Dealing with the lawyers and the death-throes of the business induced either tears or panic.

One morning she woke and her phone had been cut off. Fear crashed through her. She had no money – she wasn't even sure she had enough money to eat. Despite that, when her old company tried to bribe her to sign an NDA she refused. They couldn't buy her silence or morals. She wanted to use her experience as a case study of what not to do. She wanted their behaviour out in the world, big-time.

While Cindy allowed herself to feel the pain, she had times of
confidence and hope. There were two potential job offers with big
companies, which would answer her career question and dire
money problems. She was through to the fifth round of interviews
and could feel that her experience and knowledge were valuable
assets; she had no money, but she had learned a huge amount. Elliott reiterated his desire for them to get back together, and she
agreed to move in with him.

As she talked about him she cradled her drink against her cheek,
the warmth of his attention shining in her face. She hadn't known
fully how scared she'd been until she was no longer alone. Often
we don't know what we have been missing until we have it. He
kept telling her how much he loved her, that he was hers. Whenever she wanted they could marry, have a baby. He cried with his
love for her, and she saw an openness in him she hadn't seen before.
But she didn't want to repeat her mistakes. No jumping in this
time.

She wrote a document of conditions, laying out what she
expected from him: to talk more openly with her, to support her
with his mother, to find new ways of dealing with difficulty. He
agreed to them, repeating how much he loved her, stating he
didn't believe in divorce. At one level it felt humiliating to return
to his apartment, the one she'd left following the breaking off of
their engagement. She was back where she'd started, with even
less. But she felt safe. She was happy with Elliott.

Over the next two months Cindy's hopes were crushed again.
She didn't get either of the jobs. The interviewers wouldn't give
her any feedback, which sent her mind into a swirl of imagining
negative reasons. But a friend had said, 'You are the same person.
You have all the skills you had before. Use them.' Cindy's innate
resilience bounced back. She was a grafter. She hit her contacts
and people she didn't know, scouting for any lead to a job. When
she talked about it, I could feel in my body the force of her energy,
how compelling she was. Her confidence in herself instinctively
inspired my belief in her – I could imagine offering her a job in a

matter of minutes. The image that popped up in my head was that poster 'GIRL POWER' with rays of energy sparkling around it.

Within a couple of weeks, she had managed to get some consulting work with two clients, which rapidly grew to six. She worked long hours, wanting to over-deliver to ensure she kept them happy. It meant she had enough money to keep the lights on. Phew. It seemed to me Cindy was a poster girl for the frequently quoted Epictetus: 'It's not what happens to you but how you react to it that matters.' Her innate hope, combined with determination and work ethic, meant that when she was knocked down, she wasn't floored: she got up.

The far greater setback was when Elliott's apartment came up for lease renewal. Cindy suggested they sign for it together, and he said no. He wanted her to move out.

It was a complete shock. 'I can't even express to you how disappointing it was. It just took my breath away.' She'd believed they'd been doing very well and were getting back to their steady closeness. Cindy asked him about his declarations of marriage and babies, and he faded. He couldn't fully answer her. When she brought it up again he would cry and cry, 'But nothing would come out of his mouth.' She really didn't know what had happened. From that point she felt him slowly withdraw. Sex, which had been frequent and their key way of communicating, stopped. The cold chasm of being in bed together, but worlds apart, chilled her. Luckily, through her network of friends, she found a low-rent apartment for three months and moved out.

When I asked for clarity as to whether they had broken up, Cindy told me they hadn't had 'the conversation'. She didn't want to give him an ultimatum. I stated – the blindingly obvious – they both avoided having important conversations. She said she had tried but got nowhere. Cindy felt that once she had the space after she'd moved out they could speak more openly. I pushed a bit more, suggesting he was treating her like a lodger, not a girlfriend. I was worried their mutual politeness covered up their value to each other, and that avoiding their difficulties didn't reduce their significance.

Cindy didn't argue. She agreed that their relationship was unlikely to recover – she'd suffered too much with him. 'But,' she said, and this was a big but, 'I love him deeply. I think he's an amazing human. I secretly hope there is a turn-around.' Cindy was crying and she was scared. She tidied away her tears with a thumb, sweeping them from under her eyes.

I could feel her sadness in my chest. Instinctively I wanted to soothe her and left the space to allow her to cry. As she was crying she told me, 'I long for a little bit of peace. I know peace comes from within, and I have a lot to be grateful for, but this has been so hard. I'm ready to be productive and get back on my feet . . . I still love him a lot but I'm not scared of being alone. I know I can be with someone and feel alone . . .' Cindy was in the epicentre of not knowing. She wanted their relationship to continue, but from Elliott's behaviour she knew it was unlikely, yet nothing was clear. Her underlying attitude was that of a survivor: hope kept her afloat, picked her up when she crashed.

I was biased against Elliott. But couple relationships have their own weather, their natural pull and push – I couldn't gauge their relationship through Cindy alone. My role was to support her in this uncomfortable land of not knowing. As a couple, they had to find their own resolution.

Once Cindy had moved out she was surprised by how much calmer she felt. Living with Elliott, with all their unvoiced tensions, had blocked any processing within herself. She talked to me about her father, who was quite a remote figure. Her mother had done the parenting and shown her love. Her father knew very little about her life. He seemed to live in his own world, distant from everyone else. She had a sense of searching for her dad, her norm. We wondered how that shaped her relationship with men. Cindy could see a parallel with Elliott: she was recreating that absence, and the holding on, hoping for connection. When I invited her to go further, she blocked me. She didn't want to delve into her unconscious processes. She was happy to learn from what she cognitively knew, but deep therapy was not for her.

On the other hand she conjured up her mother vividly: a powerful, loving mother, who put a lot of pressure on Cindy to either marry Elliott or come home. Telling her how many of her school friends were getting married: it was Planet Wedding that summer in Arkansas. She didn't like Cindy going against convention and sent her ads for local jobs and suggestions for a new boyfriend at home. Cindy held firm. She felt her mother's love, but she did not want to be controlled by her. One of the reasons she'd gone to San Francisco was to break free from the norms of the South. She wanted to be an independent woman, forge her own life.

A month later I wasn't surprised when Cindy told me she felt our work was complete. Her relationship with Elliott had improved. They still hadn't had 'the conversation' but they spoke every day, dated a few nights a week, and had reignited their love-making. Cindy looked happy. She felt much more at peace. Her money worries were gone for now, and she wanted to enjoy being with Elliott without forcing marriage: their engagement had burned them both. She reminded me, somewhat vehemently, that one out of two marriages failed. The relationship was fulfilling and she felt she was building herself up again. Her self-respect had grown, and through her self-care practices she felt she was healing – finally. She wanted to trust and enjoy their togetherness. She didn't need the next step yet . . . if ever.

Reflections on Work

Working is good for us. We have to work to pay the bills, and we are meant to work, to produce. For some people their work defines them: it is who they are. For others a job is about putting food on the table. Shockingly, according to the Joseph Rowntree Foundation, workers in poverty hit 4 million in the UK in 2017, meaning about one in eight in the economy are now classified as working poor. Yet according to a recent survey, the majority of people like or love their job, while only 10 per cent dislike theirs.

Work is central to our lives. It takes up the bulk of most people's waking hours, forging their sense of purpose, meaning and identity in countless conscious and unconscious ways. For many people work is where their optimal selves thrive: they have potency and a sense of growth from seeing the impact of their labour, having a direction to travel and a team to work with. When our personal life can feel complex, or painful and uncontrollable, our work can sometimes be the saviour and fill the holes that other areas of our life cannot. For the 10 per cent who dislike their job (6 per cent actively hate it), work can be the place where they feel out of control, controlled, demeaned or just plain bored. Having no autonomy or a bad boss are among the key factors in people disliking or hating their jobs. Ideally, to have a sense of wellbeing we need every piece of the pie that makes up our life to be going well: our relationships, our health and our work. They are interconnected and shape each other. Research is clear, though, that those who don't work fare worse on every measure.

Statistics: UK YouGov Survey 2017

When asked how much they like their job:

45% like their job

17% love their job

20% neither like nor dislike their job

10% dislike their job

67% of middle class asked like or love their job

55% of working class like or love their job

Women more likely than men to say they like/love their jobs:
    68% vs 58%

When asked if they would rather have a job they hate that pays well or a job they love that pays poorly, 64% said they'd rather have a job they love that pays poorly

The culture and climate of the working environment in the UK have seen exponential change in the last fifty years, with even greater speed in the last decade. The big shifts have been that 48 per cent of the workforce is now female and the move from a manufacturing-based economy to service industries. The standard of living has been on the rise: with the stability of peace, household incomes have doubled, home ownership has grown inexorably, and people are living longer than ever. Despite the increase in debt, it seems people are far better off, and in this climate their attitude to work is changing, from one that is all about earning money as the only definition of success, to one in which work provides them with meaning in their life. The YouGov research indicates 64 per cent of the population would prefer to be paid less in a job they love, while only 18 per cent would prefer a well-paid job they hated.

The new expectation of work from Generations X and Y is that they should flourish in it, an environment in which they and their companies work for the greater good, a source of inspiration when people believe that what they do matters. They are seeking to have a balanced home and work life with flexible working. As the institution of religion has fallen away it seems to me that work has begun to fill the void that faith left. It is the place we gather together to belong, to share goals and beliefs. It brings to mind Abraham Maslow's Hierarchy of Needs: now that our basic needs are met for the majority – food, clothing and a roof over our heads at the baseline of the hierarchy – we are now looking for growth and passion through the workplace.

According to the report from the Oxford Martin Commission for Future Generations, 47 per cent of existing jobs are at risk globally of being lost to automation; other research shows it to be 30 per cent by 2030 in the UK. Due to the fourth industrial revolution of the digital age, it is predicted that 40 per cent of the workforce will be in a gig economy by 2020. The importance of the demand for global political forces to think more long term in addressing the biggest challenges that shape our future cannot be underestimated: how can the younger generations thrive in the way we have taken for granted if they are not equipped with the skills and the environment to do so?

We can see in the case studies of Caz, Rachel, Heinrich and Cindy that a person's relationship with their work will be influenced by their beginnings: the luck of the draw in the lottery of life as to their social position, education and how they were parented. Their parents' role model was formative in giving them a direction to emulate or oppose. Never underestimate the importance of role models. Their unique areas of interest, combined with their natural ability and a good dose of luck, led them to their first jobs. Certainly, when they disliked their job, were fired or ambivalent as to what to do, it had a major impact on their wellbeing and quality of life. Success, although often judged externally by factors like money or power, can only truly be seen inside the skin of the person whose career it is.

When we are asked what we do, it sounds an innocent question, yet our response will allow others to make assumptions as to what kind of person we are, how high up we are, where we are in the 'survival of the fittest' scoreboard of life. It will influence their reaction to us, our sense of identity and even our self-esteem. There can be a pull and push between who we authentically believe we are and what that means for our work, and our need to be valued by others. It is worth taking the time to reflect and discuss with others one's own values and measures of success – and it is important to recognize that comparing oneself to others is a direct route to misery.

Retirement

Heinrich had a good relationship with his work. There was enough difficulty to keep him challenged and satisfied; he was still passionate about it, it gave him meaning, and he managed the balance between work and home. Research shows that passion can lead people to make work all-encompassing and lose that harmonious balance, damaging their home life. Heinrich was very much a man of his generation in that he had the stability and security of one job all his working life, and then he retired. He had the traditional Western three-stage life: education, work and retirement. It is unlikely that that will be so for the next generation.

For those whose value as a person has been entirely entwined with their work, it is terrifying to face the future without it. For them a common barrier to retiring is the deep need to leave a legacy, sometimes termed the Edifice Complex, fearing emptiness of life outside their job. The absence of work is likely to expose those areas of life that have been ignored, like friendships, their loved ones or the development of other interests and hobbies. Those who replace work relationships with new friendships fare better.

It is important to recognize what a huge transformation retirement is in a person's life, even for those who want to retire. They are losing the identification of being in an organization or system that is more powerful than the individual. They no longer have the daily sustenance of their work social life and networks, with their own language and chatter, their focus, structure, finances, responsibility and perceived status. They are, in effect, leaving everything they have known for their entire adult life. It is certainly a loss, which often goes unrecognized. It is thought of more mechanistically, as if it is just a normal part of life, treated rather jokily, without the acknowledgement of the psychological consequences. And there are many.

As with all aspects of life, there are no absolutes. Retirement means different things for different people at different times of their life. Retirement can be a real double-edged sword: it can have positive health benefits such as a lowering of stress, more time to spend on fitness, freeing up time to socialize. However, it can also have a negative impact on health and wellbeing: free time may lead to consuming more alcohol, a downward spiral of immobility and bad habits. Stress levels may have been so high that there is little possibility of reversing them, with long-term adverse effects already caused. Research from the Institute of Economic Affairs found retirement increases the chances of clinical depression by 40 per cent and at least one diagnosed physical illness by a whopping 60 per cent. Early retirement is even worse: overall studies have shown that it has a negative impact on health and higher mortality rates.

Health is a good reason, among many, to carry on working and finding what is now termed 'bridge employment'. Those who had interesting jobs they enjoyed would be more likely to want to continue working part time. Those who were forced into retiring may also look for temporary work in the hope of regaining control and status, but may struggle as their confidence has been hit by the forced retirement. Those who chose to retire younger, who want to continue to work, are more likely to succeed.

There are often differences between men and women who retire. Women, on the whole, are more concerned with marital quality than men: if their marriage is perceived to be enriching it will help their transition into retirement. However, men, whose sense of self is traditionally derived from work, may battle with retirement. Couples may suddenly find themselves spending a lot more time together than they have for many years, without the camouflaging noise of work and dependent children. The shift in dynamic may be interesting, but more likely it creates a massive upheaval: 'I didn't marry him to cook him lunch.' Clearly those couples who put in the emotional work required to find a new normal do well.

Research shows that for those who are divorced, and have not found a new partner, retirement is particularly difficult, because there is the absence of income and their ex-partner to build a new life together.

One of the ways a couple might develop a new chapter together is through grandchildren. The role of grandparent has become increasingly important with both parents working. Those being active grandparents find less need for other employment, as there is fulfilment, joy and pleasure in being with their grandchildren. In addition, it supports the success of their children's career. Many will be in the mid-life cycle of work, and being free of childcare concerns liberates them to accelerate their career progression. This is a win-win for the grandparents, who are giving their children a better work trajectory and in turn a better retirement: research has shown that mid-life career growth is an important factor in how well you retire.

The Quarter-life Crisis

At the other end of the spectrum there was Caz. He had enormous difficulty in finding a job he liked, a job that would pay him or job security. His experience is confirmed by recent research, which showed that nearly 80 per cent of those leaving university felt under pressure to succeed in career, relationships or money. For 61 per cent finding a job or career they were passionate about was the top reason for anxiety, even more than finding a life partner (47 per cent) or dealing with student debt (22 per cent). It is not surprising they feel anxious since the possibility of their first job being meaningful is low. First jobs are, in the main, repetitive and boring, without regular praise from the boss.

The shift into working life from university for young people correlates with a time of huge transformational development, which can be anxiety-producing, creating a weakened sense of identity and exposed vulnerability. American psychologist Jeffrey Jensen Arnett sees it as a new developmental phase, coining the term 'emerging adulthood' for the late teens to the late twenties, similar to 'teenagers', which was coined in the 1950s.

It is certainly true that the generation of parents and grandparents in the industrialized world, looking at their children now, find frustrating their equivocalness, their lack of commitment or simply their not knowing what to do when they compare it to themselves at that stage. It would help both the parents and their children to recognize and accept that times have changed. The context for their children being born, in the main, in peace, but after huge social change, affects them. They have also witnessed and been personally impacted by the economic crisis which has changed their outlook. The fact that young people have often been more protected and intensely parented than their parents delays their maturity, as does going to university which many more young people do. They often see their early to late twenties as a time of experimentation and exploration, a space for many possibilities, rather than fixed ideas. It is the age of instability, of feeling in between their adolescent selves and adulthood while exploring their identity, who they are, and what they want out of love and work. We need to shift our understanding to recognize that, for many young people, the watershed age of full adulthood is close to thirty. The decade leading up to it constitutes a search for their place in the adult world, for discovering their adult selves, for forming their new families of close friends and trying out different jobs.

Since the working life of young adults is likely to be extended to their seventies, it fits that they wouldn't want to tie themselves down too soon. Some leap into it; others have a number of false starts – leaving home and returning – while yet others feel they have barely begun. For some this is exciting, and their varied and rich experience of travelling abroad or doing further studying will reap rewards in the future. For a personality like Caz, and he undoubtedly represents large numbers of young people, this was a tough process. This whole phase is more difficult than is often recognized. Caz believed, as most young people do, he should have been more grown up than he actually felt. In fact his cycle of confusion, through lack of money, the absence of structure after school and university, left him feeling unhinged. Also, the loneliness of being in a big city and the fear he wouldn't find his place led him to worry that he would never find his safe centre.

One of Caz's complaints was how little support or guidance he was given in finding a job. There is no doubt that schools and universities need to support students more in finding relevant work and networking opportunities – for instance, through matching alumni contacts with current students. It seems the institution has done only half its job if its students leave with qualifications but not the least idea of what they intend to do with them. But students need to play their part before they leave too. Research shows

that students who identify work opportunities, find work place-
ments and take on the task of career exploration are more likely to
find themselves in a job that is well matched to their skills and
interests. Students who seek career guidance are also more likely
to have positive career situations. They need to access insight into
the 'working life' of industries and workplaces that interest them
before they have left their educational institution. Proactivity,
along with networking, is seen as the most important factor in
securing the best possible job upon leaving university.

Experimenting with an eye to testing and discovery is positive.
But falling into a job and staying there for security is risky. Decisions made over this period may influence the shape of a person's
whole life, in particular in relation to careers and relationships.
They need to be made with as much self-awareness and knowledge as possible, through long discussions and thought. I am
astonished at how often I hear people say, 'I did what my dad
wanted me to do'; 'I married him because I thought he was my
only chance'; 'I sleep-walked through my twenties'; 'I fell into this
job, didn't particularly like it and I've been here fifteen years and
still don't really like it.'

This ties in with later life, scarily, especially with women,
where their start on the career ladder has a clear and direct impact
on their career trajectory. A man's early entry point to a job is less
important than a woman's: if a man takes a low-level job early in
his career it has a less negative impact on his onward career path
(it is seen as experimenting, building a sense of self). However, a
woman's choice of initial job can have a more pronounced negative effect on career advancement. Although most women are
likely to get out of a low-level job at a similar speed to a male
counterpart, their onward route of promotion becomes slower
when they take time out to be mothers. This indicates that, for the
best career progression, a woman must enter at as high a level as
possible.

Some term the young people of today the 'jilted generation',
fearing they have been failed even before they began. Their

opportunities of work, home ownership and stability are fragile and therefore their progression into genuine adulthood is stalled. In real terms, it may mean their future holds a work life of longer hours for less money, retiring later, being taxed more and having lower social mobility. Commentators believe young people have been robbed of their future by their parents, the 'Baby Boomers', and by their politicians, the consequences of austerity politics, short-term wins over long-term gains and the recession. These young people have gone back to live with and rely on the Bank of Mum and Dad, not out of choice but dire need. In comparison those aged over fifty now own 75 per cent of the nation's wealth. They are Britain's richest consumer group and have flourished in the post-war world but they need to do more to protect the future of the generations coming after them. For young people, it is changing their outlook as to what is important, questioning their parents' belief in 'survival of the fittest'. They are wondering if their new life skill should be to base their life decisions on an emotional and ethical framework.

Careers for Generations X and Y are more turbulent than for their parents. Young people are recognizing they are likely to have multiple jobs, even multiple careers. There are many drivers to this change: globalization, technology and increased life expectancy. It can mean that some organizations no longer develop their talent, not believing they will reap the rewards of longer-term investment. Employers hold the power: in 2010 there were 118 applications for every job. Young people have a burden of expectation put on them, with diminished hope of success since they lack the stability of a business organization to rely on. Politically, much is made of the power of the individual, freedom of choice and breadth of possibility. What is ignored is our inborn need to belong to a tribe, to be part of an organization, where the individual is protected by the group, its purpose and territory. This is both frightening and, at times, untenable, and can lead them to give up even before they start.

Generations X and Y will need to navigate change in a way that the Baby Boomers never had to contemplate. Young people should be taught about the process of change as part of their university syllabus so they have a grasp of what it is like and what they can do to help themselves. It would help them to realize they aren't going mad: what they are experiencing is normal.

Oliver C. Robinson, a psychologist whose expertise is in people in the quarter-life crisis, offers advice in recognizing that young people's anxiety follows a four-stage pattern: feeling stuck, breaking through the fixed patterns, experiencing turbulent emotions and testing new experiences until they come out at the other end of the cycle, which often feels like growth. Resilience can be taught and the successes will be for those who learn to be resilient by developing their own set of tools to weather that change. Popular tools include talking to friends and parents, which can help stop their critical voice, creating a manageable structure, self-care for mind and body, and doing something for others. More ideas for what helps build resilience can be found in The 8 Pillars of Strength, page 281.

Losing Your Job

Cindy was well educated, and well loved. She had talent, drive, a big work ethic and resilience, all the components that lead to a successful work life. She lost her first job as the recession battered the USA. As many losing a job often will, she grieved as if for a death. It is the death of one's work identity. People are initially numb, the shock immobilizing their body and mind. Shame is a common and pervasive feeling when one loses one's job. It takes time for the reality of the loss to counter protective denial, and as one begins to experience and express hurt and anger the healing begins. Often the greatest challenge is the fear of 'not knowing'. It helps to connect with friends, talk, cry and talk more – to go out and have fun, laugh. Exercising and eating well help rebalance the body, which is switched on to alert code red. One of the most helpful assets to develop is positivity. Research shows optimism improves performance and success at work on many levels – the decisions we make, the opportunities we aim for, the relationships we form, even the trajectory of our career. The old adage, it isn't what happens to you but how you pick yourself up that matters, seems harsh, for the pessimist who already thinks he is going to fail (he might), but this is not a done deal: pessimists can learn to be more optimistic.

How someone is fired or made redundant has a big impact on their self-esteem and confidence going forward. People are fired without explanation, security being called while belongings are collected, their dismissal announced over a loudspeaker or in private by HR, not the boss. Sometimes it isn't the words or the explanation but how it is voiced that injures. It makes worse what is already difficult. The person is left ruminating and wounded, trying to make sense of what is often inexplicable. The more sudden and brutal, the greater the impact. If the end is communicated with humanity, compassion and respect, the person can leave holding themselves personally in high regard, while still being upset they have lost their job. For someone who has had previous traumatic losses or an insecure childhood, the effect is even more profound. It may be that they lack self-knowledge to equate these events from their history to their reactions in their adult work career. Having the chance to seek psychological support would be an important part of their capacity to build up their confidence.

Importantly, Cindy had always invested in her network of relationships, which is shown to be a key influence in success at work. Platforms such as LinkedIn's PartnerUp, and BranchOut offer networking opportunities that connect us on an unprecedented scale. Careers, as ever, can take off in directions due to happenstance rather than a carefully plotted plan. Those who hope their career will follow a simple, straightforward path are likely to be disappointed.

Cindy's chances of finding work were much higher than those of someone older. A person in their fifties has a 70–75 per cent chance of returning to work within two years of a job loss, which is bearable; for someone in their sixties it is substantially lower. Research shows that while looking for a job it is better to do something than nothing – volunteering, interning (there are internships for older people), taking on lower-paid work. It is crucial for those who are older to be willing to retrain. Employers are looking for people who have a broad set of skills that can be used anywhere. The upside of this flexibility is that those who would previously have faced barriers to traditional working environments now have the ability to be self-employed and work in non-traditional spaces and roles. The rise of online teaching and support companies allows them to retrain from home, learn new skills and nurture new-found talents.

Good-quality relationships are key to weathering the difficulty of losing one's job. Inevitably it is our closest relationships that become strained. Both members of a couple are frightened, facing financial challenges and an uncertain future. They may find their upset blocks them from being able to communicate openly, which is, of course, what they need to do. If they stop connecting, the space between them will grow. It can be filled with blame, guilt, shame, fury and rejection. A toxic mix in which emotions can feel like facts. Arguments, impatience and misunderstandings multiply. It is important the couple commits to actively overcoming these challenges. They can do this by making the time to talk and, most importantly, listen attentively to each other. Walking and talking is a positive way to do this: being outside calms them, moving their bodies in sync, while not being eyeballed, taking it in turns to talk and be listened to helps them connect. Keeping their skylines short, not projecting further than the forthcoming week is an important way to keep their anxiety manageable. Consciously choosing to do things they are good at and enjoy helps maintain their self-esteem. A big part of having confidence in interviews will come from feeling securely loved at home.

How a New Mother Manages Her Return to Work

When a baby is born, so is a mother. We know becoming a parent will change us. We also know we cannot predict what that change will look like. The external and internal change is seismic. This new baby turns our world upside down, with love, fear, exhaustion, joy, meaning – the full panoply of feelings. For Rachel, having her baby boy was a source of boundless love and joy, as well as utter exhaustion. Very importantly, she discovered in herself a confident, happy mother she could only have dreamed existed. For her the challenge was going back to work, and her relationship with her job. Being a working mother is tough.

The intractable conflict between being an involved, loving mother and finding meaningful, rewarding work is one that each parent seeks to resolve, and in the end rarely feels they have got right. Some mothers feel anxious at the thought of going back to work, not wanting to leave their baby and also feeling less confident professionally. The logistical difficulty of arranging travel to work and finding good, affordable childcare may mean that returning to the previous job is no longer a viable option.

Often the thought of working is worse than the reality. In 2014, there were almost as many women with children (74 per cent) who participated in the labour force as women with no children (75 per cent). Since women continue to do the majority of care for children and relatives, as well as the domestic work, they are at the front line of balancing the pressure of home and the workplace and, consequently, are the demographic that is most stressed. The attitude has been that if a woman is going to return to work full time, and do her previous job, whether it was a stellar career or not, she has to work as though she has no dependents. Yet working mothers are less likely to be promoted as they are seen to have responsibility for their children – which may partly account for why the percentage of women in senior leadership roles has remained low, rising to 22 per cent in 2018. Men at work with children are seen as being competent in handling work and balancing family life – because, on the whole, they aren't doing the balancing.

Some women are able to square the circle and others feel the pull between both worlds. They may feel guilty when work interferes with family life and when family interferes with work, the 'shit mother shit worker' syndrome. But the guilty-mother voice shouts louder. Guilt is rarely a big issue for men. And there are the millions of women, like Rachel, who love their babies and don't want to leave them. They do want to lean in, just not too much, and they have talent, drive and the will to work, but undersell themselves through lack of confidence: 54 per cent of women are working in jobs for which they are overqualified. Their answer is to go part time and find flexible working. Part-time women are paid less than part-time men, and there are twice as many women working part time as men. Rachel's situation illustrates the common problem with working part time: the opportunities for work that is interesting and well paid are rarer. Rachel knew indisputably that her son was her top priority, but it meant she had to make many compromises for her career. Women cannot have it all.

The *Harvard Business Review* summarized a recent study stating on the one hand, 'Maternity leaves are related to lower infant mortality and reduced maternal stress', and on the other, research 'reveals that the longer new mothers are away from paid work, the less likely they are to be promoted, move into management, or receive a pay raise once their leave is over. They are also at greater risk of being fired or demoted.'

There is a lot of work to be done by employers and government to enable both parents to work and parent. The reality of the different needs may never be entirely squared. Perhaps women can have more than they did. Rachel has kept her foot in the working world, which research shows will allow her to have more success when she wants to focus fully on her job. It is much harder for women going back into the workforce who have had long career breaks, although there are organizations and movements to instil confidence, train and upskill them to return.

Highly Sensitive People

Caz and Rachel were born highly sensitive, which meant they were less robust in dealing with the rollercoaster of life. For them, and those like them, any change is likely to raise their levels of anxiety and overwhelm them. Elaine Aron, an American research psychologist and author of *The Highly Sensitive Person*, believed some of the signs of being highly sensitive are reacting surprisingly intensely to events or conversations, having a vivid imagination and exotic dreams, and needing time alone every day to recalibrate. It may feel as though they have a layer of skin less than everyone else, yet it is more common than you may expect, being inherited by 15–20 per cent of the population. Aron found that highly sensitive people needed a four-fold approach: first, they needed self-knowledge, to know their triggers and what it means to them to be highly sensitive. Second, they needed to look at their past with this new information and reframe it to give themselves a clearer, more accurate perspective – this helps build self-esteem. She suggests healing as the third step, working at a deep level to heal the early wounds. I would suggest this is best done with a therapist: it is hard to achieve it alone. And, finally, they needed to develop the skills of how to manage being engaged in the world, and giving themselves time to reflect and restore alone.

Health

'The first wealth is health.'

Ralph Waldo Emerson

Geoffrey

Illness in the Family

Geoffrey's daughter had suggested he see me and contacted me on his behalf. Emma was worried that her father's recent cancer diagnosis and treatment had left him without his usual vigour and engagement with life: he spent hours in his sitting room alone, watching television or sleeping, often with the curtains drawn during the day. She wondered whether this was a sign of depression. His wife found it oppressive for she was sociable and outgoing. Since Geoffrey didn't necessarily want counselling, we met on an informal basis, which I termed 'befriending' – I offered to listen.

On first meeting Geoffrey, I saw a tall, slim man whose face was very pale and completely unlined, despite his seventy-five years. He had thick white hair that peaked above his forehead, with corresponding bushy eyebrows. Geoffrey was polite in that old-fashioned way, and he had a natural warmth.

Geoffrey told me about his diagnosis and treatment of breast cancer (rare in men) with a jaunty optimism. His consultant had told him he was as likely to die of old age as cancer. Was he scared following his cancer diagnosis? I was surprised by the positive spin he put on it: 'To be honest we all took a big gulp, bad enough being diagnosed, but there's no point in being worried about it, so I haven't been worried about it at all. Life is for living. Why make a fuss about it?'

There was a sheen to his response that meant I felt myself sliding away from him. I sensed he had a filter that didn't allow him to feel fear, worry or bad temper. It wasn't that he was consciously hiding those feelings, more that they'd been switched off. It was as if he had been shaped by the military discipline of his Edwardian parents to have 'no problems at all'. I was puzzled – here he was almost breezily telling me he wasn't worried, but that didn't fit the description his daughter had given me: silent and alone in a darkened room. I had only just met him and this wasn't therapy, but I clocked it and hoped I could address the mismatch.

Geoffrey described his treatment of six chemotherapy sessions and radiotherapy with a CyberKnife (non-invasive robotic surgery for cancer) in further positive terms, praising the excellence of every health professional he had encountered. He was happy to be part of a trial for a new treatment and felt fortunate to have been offered it. He had managed the chemo successfully, despite the cumulative nausea, which had hit him out of the blue the first time, but after that he was prepared for it. The radiotherapy was similarly straightforward. As he sat absolutely upright in his chair, looking me straight in the eye, I couldn't argue that his attitude of endurance – 'Keep going and don't make a fuss' – had worked well for him.

When I asked if his family were worried, his face softened. This was where he allowed himself to feel. 'It was a jolly hard time for Anne and the children. They must have wondered what the future held for them – I wondered about my future too, but didn't voice it to them. I didn't want to turn a bad situation into a worse one.'

When I suggested, much more for my benefit than his, that in a family one person suffering inevitably has an impact on everyone else, for a family is a connected network, he looked pained, and worried that he had not been supportive enough to his wife and daughters. I could see him tuck away this thought, promising himself to put it right in the future.

I was interested in his career and how he'd managed his retirement. The story he told me was one of organized success. He was the son of military parents, who'd lived and worked in India all their lives. From early childhood he had moved from north to south India regularly. He had witnessed his mother managing with stoicism his father's absence in Burma, not knowing if he was alive or dead. He had admired his father, though recognized that he was a man of his time and was overbearing to his mother. Geoffrey had been sent to England to be educated, and only saw his parents intermittently. As he spoke I was aware again of how much we, as children, learn from our parents' behaviour, far more than from what they say. How could he have survived if he hadn't learned to be entirely self-reliant, not let himself feel discomfort or ask for help?

Accompanied by his wife, Anne, Geoffrey had followed his parents' expatriate existence by working for a large oil company all over the world, moving twenty-seven times throughout his career, to East Africa, Indonesia, Singapore and South America. Shaped by his childhood, change was Geoffrey's natural modus operandi: he adapted quickly to new countries and people, as did his wife. They both relished change and the experience of new challenges and places.

On retiring he'd worked for other businesses, which didn't sound as if they'd been as satisfactory. The first didn't fit with his moral attitude and need for order: he found himself in conflict with the management, and was relieved to have to leave. His next job was in the UK, for the first time in his career, working for a small local company as a manager. For a number of years it had gone well, but then he came into conflict with the new CEO and agreed to leave.

I was fascinated by his story, and asked what it had been like leaving a hugely powerful organization that he'd been in all his life, and joining a smaller, more idiosyncratic company, his time with it ending in conflict. His response showed me how he could manage his own feelings and feel alive to those of his family: 'I can't see any point in letting things thwart me. If there's a block ahead in the road, I take a quick turn to the right and find a different route. If something upsets me, I will talk about it, but I won't show great emotion.' He went on to acknowledge that Anne had been worried when he retired, and again that softness came into his face as he felt concern for her. As we spoke he'd often nod towards his dog and chuckle. It was a large yellow Labrador that had clearly become a central focus of his and Anne's affection in retirement; they took turns to walk him at set times of the day. I saw how dogs could be a source of reliable comfort, always pleased to see their masters, not asking difficult questions or being moody, as well as forcing regular exercise outdoors.

Geoffrey's resourcefulness soon came into play, egged on by his wife (he smiled like a naughty boy as he mentioned her encouragement) to fill the gap of unemployment. He worked as a volunteer for a local charity, which meant he met lots of interesting people and enjoyed his usefulness. It had also given him an insight into how difficult the lives of vulnerable people were, in terms of health and quality, which let him recognize how fortunate he was. But he had been forced to stop volunteering while he was ill, and he missed it. He hoped he could get back to it soon.

We agreed to meet again, but I found it hard to see where I could be of any help. We concluded there was a generational divide: my view is that when feelings are not expressed, they are likely to hang around, and in some way interfere with one's psychological availability, and at times stability, and his was that he successfully marshalled his feelings into a place that didn't interfere with his equanimity. It seemed to me there was a mismatch between what the women around him perceived, and what he felt. They, like me, had projected their response to his retirement and illness on to him. It didn't fit. What was particularly interesting to me was his capacity to be open with those he loved. He welled up with emotion when he talked about his wife and daughters and had a sensitivity towards them that generated mutual love and affection. I'd picked up from his daughter's telephone call to me how much she adored him.

I received an email from Geoffrey a few weeks after our first meeting, telling me he'd had a fall, due to a stiff left leg that carried an old sports injury, and he had fractured his hip. Consequently, the doctor had told him he needed a new hip, which meant I could only meet him post-surgery as he was pretty immobile. Given that I was a befriender, I suggested we meet with his daughter Emma at his house. There might be mutual benefit in having an opportunity to talk together, with me facilitating and opening up some of her worries as to whether he was depressed for him to respond to.

When I met them a few months later, his wife, Anne, was in the desert, which they coined 'her edgy desert'. Geoffrey told me with pride that Anne sought adventure, the more danger and discomfort the better. She'd recently been kicked out of Egypt, which she held as a badge of honour. Impressive for a woman in her seventies. Emma had come to look after him, and I could see immediately the playful warmth of their relationship. Predictably Geoffrey's response to his new hip was stoic, never mentioning the pain, laughing as he described the banging and sawing he'd heard during his surgery, which had been under epidural. He insisted he was doing very well, and he couldn't wait to take his beloved dog for a walk.

I asked them about their differing perceptions of how Geoffrey had managed his retirement and illnesses. Emma was able to say how worried they had all been, thinking he was depressed sitting in his dark room. Anxious about the combination of losing his status and purpose from his job and then being ill, they had imagined every kind of bleak scenario, particularly when he was silent. Her words unlocked him. He was able to acknowledge that he had been worried and it had been 'a tough two years' but he was adamant that he wasn't depressed. More expansive than he had been when I'd seen him before, he explained his attitude: he felt talking about difficulty made it worse – it multiplied it. Watching sport on TV soothed him when he was worried and helped distract him from the discomfort he felt post-surgery and -chemo. He became quite feisty when she suggested he had no hobbies or social life, and reminded her of his golf and fishing, how Anne had arranged meetings with good friends, which he'd enjoyed. He argued that, as soon as he was fit enough, he'd renew all those activities. He acknowledged, in a way that seemed to surprise Emma, that the clash with his last CEO had partly been his inability to adapt to the new business environment. She challenged him, telling him she'd heard from Anne that he hadn't admitted his part in the ending, but evidently he had understood more than they all realized. He smiled and nodded. Not one for many words, as ever.

Emma had recently gone through a painful separation from her husband. She looked her father in the eye and told him, 'You were the only person who didn't ask why. You just asked whether there was something you could do – could you fix something, move any furniture, did I need money?' As they talked together about how difficult that time had been for everyone, Geoffrey was able to take on board, it seemed to me for the first time, that his presence, his lack of judgement and his love had been instrumental in Emma's recovery. I felt moved by the gift her honesty offered him. She'd said only a few sentences, but I knew he'd go back and rekindle them.

When I met them for the last time Emma said, with tears in her eyes, how helpful our previous conversation had been. Having the opportunity to talk in a way that felt safe had enabled them to voice the things they had known about the other; having their words reflected back to them had been simple but surprisingly powerful. As she looked towards her father, she told him how fortunate it was that since her divorce she'd really come to know him as a person, not just as her father, which wasn't true of many of her friends. She told him how happy their closeness made her. Geoffrey's face pinked with emotion, which intensified when I said he'd obviously been a fantastic father, and how touched I was to witness their relationship. He muttered that it was nice to hear that from someone outside the family, and I could see his confidence expand a little internally.

Clearly feeling uncomfortable, Geoffrey shifted the conversation to his new resolution: he wanted to help Anne more with the cooking and be more involved. Emma smiled and questioned whether it was because when she'd lived with him she'd 'refused to wait on him hand and foot', so he'd had to think for both of them, and wondered whether it had given him a taste of what

Anne had to deal with. In his usual manner, which I now knew covered a big heart, he said he hadn't thought of it like that, but couldn't disagree. They both laughed.

When I left, getting a polite goodbye from Geoffrey with a big smile, and a hug from Emma, I had learned that being stoic can be a successful way of adapting to change. But my old adage that we need love when we hurt was affirmed. I felt privileged to have witnessed such a loving father–daughter relationship. It felt rare and special. Her words stayed with me: 'He always has been a great father, and it is a role that is still vital to my sister and me. While other roles have fallen away from him in his later decades – breadwinner, manager, leader, keen outdoor sportsman – this role remains, and it will always remain, and he steps up to it and revels in it.'

Ayesha

Menopause, Redundancy and Family Relationships

Ayesha was a wordsmith. She was super-smart. I sensed her carefully edit her sentences before they came out of her mouth to fit the narrative she wanted me to hear. Or the version of herself she felt she should present. It led me to feel she had had to work herself out, on her own, her whole life. As if she knew deep down no one could help her. I looked across the room at this woman who was in her fifties, dark and stout, partner to Paul for twenty-five years and mother of seventeen-year-old son Ravi. Her folds of flesh fitted who she was: she seemed comfortable in her body. She exuded the confidence of a woman who knew she was beautiful, and a fear that perhaps she wasn't. Her exquisite earrings, a nod to her Pakistani mother, jingled when she brushed her short dark hair behind her ears. I was struck that she had enough honesty for me to be engaged with her, but I felt her guard her inner life. How I reflected back her words to her would matter. I'd need to balance enough emotion to connect, but not too much, which would scare her away.

Why had she come to see me, and why now? Ayesha felt she'd been in the centre of a vortex, her life spinning out of control, and at the time, she wouldn't have been able to use therapy usefully. But now she felt she was more psychologically able to look at what was going on and wanted to take the necessary steps to adjust more happily to this next phase of her life. I asked her to let me know what had been happening.

Ayesha had had an affair three years ago when she was peri-menopausal. Not really an affair, as in a love affair, more of a sexual obsession. I could see the pain of remembering it shoot across her eyes as she spoke. She told me it was with someone she hadn't even liked – she swallowed hard, trying to push the feeling down. At the time she had been on a desperate hunt for a man, a voracious hunger she couldn't sate, 'like the sun is brightest before it goes behind the cloud . . . the last chance saloon'. It had felt like adolescent madness, but for a woman who was fifty years old, and it had lasted three or four months. A hedonistic reset. Her last hurrah, sexually. Then her sexual hunger switched off as forcefully as it had turned her on. Now she felt no sexual attraction for anyone.

When she was talking, I was aware that she was a woman of extremes, all or nothing. I imagined her ferocious hunger for intensity was because, without it, she felt dead, and wondered out loud if our work would enable her to live somewhere in the middle.

In her most clipped voice she said, 'The very words "good enough" or "happy medium" strike fear in me.' Now aged fifty-three, for the previous two years Ayesha had been fully menopausal and described how it had turned her life upside down. 'I didn't want to acknowledge it. I wanted to dampen it down enough to believe it wasn't happening to me. I was to be the anomaly.' But it was happening to her. She had ignored the clear signs and the lack of periods. She remembered coming downstairs one morning, her anxiety spiking, her body shaking uncontrollably. It was as if some deranging virus had taken over her body. It seemed to come completely out of the blue, and her whole system crashed. Normally she was someone who juggled a thousand tasks, but at times like that she couldn't even put on a wash. No one had told her the menopause was this bad.

She went to her GP, who confirmed menopause. He prescribed a low dose of HRT (there was a history of breast cancer in her family), which reduced the symptoms but didn't eliminate them. Ayesha had white nights of no sleep, or deep sleep when she was woken by surges of heat. She experienced regular burning flushes and high levels of anxiety that only fast walks on the Heath, and yoga, could reduce. She was still getting hot flushes, and hated that they were unpredictable, and particularly hated them when she was with other people. She was permanently stripping off and spritzing herself with the cold spray she kept in the fridge. She looked down at her tummy, as if it were an alien appendage that shouldn't belong to her, and commented, with contempt, 'I can see my tyre growing. Weight I used to lose quickly sticks to me.'

She'd started wearing baggier clothes, and Paul had commented that she lived in black. Occasionally, she felt thirty-five years old inside, but when she looked in the mirror, she wondered who that old woman was. Other days she woke depressed, telling herself she was dried up, old and unattractive. Surrounded by family, it was the loneliness that hurt, the loneliness from shutting down on herself – unable to give or receive love. She couldn't get out of bed. She'd lie there ticking off all the things that had failed in her life, like a dog vomiting and going back to eat the result. Her well-honed weapons of self-attack upped her self-loathing to levels that were hard to witness. As an aside – she whispered this as if they were in the room – her husband and son said she was very grumpy, much more impatient and moodier. Answering them back, she agreed that her capacity for everything had diminished, and she gave me a sad smile.

At times it was hard to keep up with her volley of words, which could obscure rather than clarify what was going on. I didn't need to understand every detail, just hold on to the central themes. I could feel the weight of her sadness at the loss of her young self, but weightier sadness at being unable to picture a future she could invest in. I had such a different picture of her than she had of herself. I could see she was clever and curious, an original. Those were tremendous qualities to take her through into the next phase of her life. I even had marvellous pictures of her being wild and glorious, dancing in the rain. But she wasn't in a state to hear me. I could hold on to them for her, until she was ready to befriend herself. What was my best way into her? I tried asking a challenging question: she was drawn to intensity. Was she prepared to face the discomfort of change? Change is an active process that requires commitment and endurance to look at uncomfortable truths. It doesn't happen by recycling misery.

Ayesha wasn't sure. She crossed and uncrossed her legs, her anxiety spiked by my question. She looked down, and spoke haltingly: 'Obviously I want to change, but what if I can't? I'm frightened of having hope and being disappointed.' She shook her head. Her earrings jingled. I acknowledged that hope is a risky business, and daring to try takes courage, and feels dangerous. Only she could decide. There was a long silence, unusual for Ayesha. She sat up, took a deep breath, pressed her palms across each other, not quite a prayer, more a gesture for a wish: she didn't have a choice – yes – she wanted to change. She didn't want to be like her father, who had died broke and alone, shouting, 'I don't need you,' when he meant the opposite. She wanted to adjust to her new circumstances and in the process regain her zest for life. I felt that lovely spring of life in witnessing a shift. Ayesha had made the step to actively support herself and with it the decision to change.

Before she went forward, she needed to put together the jigsaw of her past. Ayesha spoke fast and described vividly her father's misery. I asked her to slow down as I needed to know what her parents had been like. She gave me powerful images of why she felt insecure, which played out in her life, every single day, as an adult. I was touched by Ayesha's vivid description of herself as an unsettled baby who didn't feed well. I felt a lump in my throat when she described the voiceless cry of that hungry child. She had images of sleeping outside her mother's bedroom, longing to be in the warmth of her bed, and her overriding memory was of her mother 'peeling me off her like onion skin'. She remembered her mother leaving her with a friend, and Ayesha being in abject fear that she wouldn't come back. She didn't feel safe: there was no stable base to rest on, only shifting sands, which left her feeling fragmented. It helped me to understand her need for routine, the necessary structure of a habit that helped her weather life's unpredictability. But in Ayesha's case she used it as the carapace that kept the world out. It intensified her emptiness. As for her father, the story was equally difficult.

Ayesha's parents' relationship had broken down irretrievably by the time she was four years old. When her father, who was British-born white, turned against her mother, he also turned against her Pakistani ethnicity. Ayesha was her father's favourite child for a while because she didn't look Pakistani, unlike her brother. But when she was a teenager he'd started criticizing her for being fat. His love was conditional and no more reliable than her mother's. When he had left her mother, Ayesha had a memory of her four-year-old self standing in the window and 'crying for the longest time'.

It was this picture of Ayesha aged four, distressed and alone, that stayed with me and became the pivotal image of our work together. I told Ayesha, and surprised myself by the force with which I spoke, that I felt a stab of outrage for that poor child, and a sense that that four-year-old was still screaming, locked in a cupboard. Not only was no one listening, but they'd all thrown away the key. I wanted to access that child and comfort her. She looked at me with warmth and didn't say a word. Although I hadn't as yet reached that four-year-old, the knowledge that I had her in my mind was a good first step.

With the rationale that Ayesha would have more hope for her future if she could parent that poor desolate four-year-old, I suggested we do a visualization. I was surprised by how open she was to it. She saw herself with her mother and brother on the Heath, with a pink lozenge in a box that said 'Eat Me'. She could feel being thirsty, longing for a drink. She looked up and saw the leaves on the trees, which were shimmering as if they were crying. Crying with relief. Crying good tears (tears were running down Ayesha's face) that were a release. I guided her to see that this was a place where she wasn't hungry, where she wasn't frightened. I invited her to breathe in the peace and calm in nature, to feel it through her body. She smiled quietly and said, 'Nice.' I suggested she pick up her four-year-old self. She breathed in. I could see it was hard to trust herself. Eventually she picked herself up. Silence as she held herself. She felt calmer. I was moved. Relieved. After quite some time, we agreed a safe place to put her young self, knowing she could come back to her whenever she chose.

As she came out of the visualization she felt she could build on that image, her own nirvana. Perhaps with animals. 'I want to step into this safe place.' I gently told her that I was touched by what she had said. Ayesha put her head to one side, gave me a warm but brief glance as she recognized that her tears were healing ones: 'Not crying is when I'm rigid with terror, like when it's so cold it can't snow.'

I was feeling emotionally open, moved by our visualization, and noting we were coming to the end of the session, when she threw me a googly. Ayesha neatly tucked her hair behind her ear, looked me bang in the eye and said, 'My queasy relationship with addiction became a full-blown addiction to cocaine.'

Bam. Perhaps unconsciously she had chosen to tell me at the end of the session to block any opportunity for me to look at it with her. Or was it to sabotage our lovely piece of work? Therapists call it the door-handle drop, when a client says something crucial just as they are leaving the room. I realized it was because addiction is soaked in shame. The defence most commonly used when feeling shame is to disconnect, to move away from it, and hide. Which, of course, means the person receives no empathy or understanding. Shame is a virulent feeling that overrides all it comes into contact with. It can be interrupted by speaking it out, and receiving empathy, for shame grows in silence. It was likely that, as a child, Ayesha couldn't voice what she was feeling – she didn't feel it was allowed, or that she would be heard – and that would have created a perfect recipe for shame inside her.

Interestingly, I found I wasn't that surprised. Her tendency to seek intensity was a horrible but familiar bedfellow with addiction. The need to anaesthetize pain had inevitably blocked all feelings, joy and happiness too, and triggered the cycle of needing more to overcome her emptiness. The false feeling of control that drugs gave her, cleaving to routine, eating the same things every day, was a key part of it. With as much warmth as I could show, I acknowledged how difficult that must have been, and suggested we start with it the next session.

The following week, Ayesha came into my room with a kind of dark impatience. I realized she wanted to be the first to put herself down so that I didn't beat her to it and humiliate her. She described her painful descent into full-blown addiction. She examined where it had come from. Her voice hardened as she remembered herself as a child, as if it was a well-worn script – she was particularly cutting when she described the emptiness she'd felt as a child, it felt intolerable, and how she had constantly tried to fill it: 'When I was little I filled it with sugar from the larder.' For a moment she became more thoughtful, connecting her hunger to her relationship with her mother, who had been post-natally depressed, and had had difficulty breastfeeding. She knew her relationship with food was linked to those first months of her life. As I was picturing this baby, longing for consistent affection, she cut herself short, telling me, 'It's my shit to sort out now.'

I spoke gently: 'You are not alone right now. I can feel bubbling up in me your pain. I can't heal those early wounds, but I want to get across to you that I am here, I am on your side, and let's work on this together.' It is unusual for me to be that overt, but my instinct told me I had to stand up and fight for her. Fight to let her know she was no longer alone, that that child could be heard and could be looked after now. She softened for a moment, gave me a half-smile, which I returned. I felt she let me inch closer to her.

Ayesha mentioned, as if it wasn't out of the ordinary, that her mother had put her on prescription drugs when she was seven years old. It had come about when she'd been asking questions about death, which her mother couldn't answer, and Ayesha had had a full-blown panic attack. Her mum took her to the doctor, who had prescribed Valium. Her voice tightened as she continued that it had haunted her ever since: 'Death is my real block. It really is coming closer, and it frightens me. It has informed my life every day since then. If I could accept it, everything else would fall into place.'

That brought up for me the inevitable link between menopause, and its association with decline and decay. Menopause shouts 'ageing', 'getting old' and 'closer to death'. I could see Ayesha physically retreat into herself as I spoke. I'd gone too far. I said it was something that we could work on together, but she refused for fear of another panic attack. We agreed we could come back to it when she was ready.

From her story, it seemed to me that Ayesha's cocaine habit, which had started in her early forties as recreational fun, had been lying in wait to hit her. Its escalation was a script that was already written. The amazing thing was that she was in recovery, and I asked what had got her into a rehabilitation programme. It had been over New Year: her addiction was always bad at Christmas, when there was more food and more alcohol. She was ill with a chest infection, her hair was falling out, and the last straw was that her teeth were rickety. On New Year's Eve she drank a whole bottle of vodka and a bottle of wine. 'I was so desolate, and I hit my personal rock bottom. I've had mini rock bottoms before, limping along. How was I going to exist without drink and drugs?' Paul had recognized how desperate she was, could see she wasn't coping, and that she had to get help. He would pay for her to go to rehab. He wanted her to take responsibility and find the place.

'I walked into the rehabilitation clinic and it felt like going home. It was enjoyable for me. I had focus and I didn't have to deal with anyone. It was such a relief not to do drink and drugs any more. As an addict you feel this obligation to drink. The community of people who are my age are still all in the programme. I love that community of sober people not medicating.' The simplicity of her experience, the lack of coercion imposed on her, and the release she felt in surrendering her addiction illustrated that 'Recovery is not for people who need it. It's for people who want it.'

Addiction and menopause were not the only difficulties Ayesha had to contend with. She quoted Shakespeare: 'When sorrows come, they come not single spies, /But in battalions!' Six months prior to seeing me Ayesha had been made redundant from the literary agency she had worked at for the last eleven years. Her boss, whom she greatly admired, had sold half of the company to a younger partner, who wanted 'new blood'. It meant axing the old guard, which included Ayesha. But the numbing of drugs, and then the recovery programme, meant she was only now feeling the full impact of the loss. She realized anew how work gave her much more than money. As she was talking, it seemed to dawn on her how desolate she felt without a job to go to. She missed the tribe, the being together, the chatter, the joint purpose and structure. I could feel the space in her where there had been this whole hub of connection. Now it was empty. She could go for days sitting at her computer in her pyjamas. She had limitless time to brood, which engendered 'stinking thinking.' The looping agony of purposelessness', and she had images of herself as that mean old lady in the supermarket, who hates noise and shouts at everyone.

As the weeks passed, inch by inch Ayesha began to trust our process and herself. She was surprised, saying, 'I've had something of a breakthrough.' She began to watch as she punished herself when she was doing anything pleasurable, whether it was eating or buying her son clothes. She saw, with more forgiving eyes, that everything she did was laden with judgement – there was a build-up of it in her chest, like a physical block, cutting off her pleasure. As she talked about her shame, the heat of it was in her body. I saw her get slightly clammy.

Understanding the cycle of cutting herself off clarified her 'relentless emptiness'. She would stop herself taking in and feeling the pleasure of what she wanted at the very point she got it, like refusing to enjoy the taste and pleasure of a delicious orange at the very moment she put it into her mouth. Ayesha linked it to her work, where she would complete the piece of work she was set but not allow herself the acknowledgement she deserved. Or with people she would get to a point when she felt happy and would need to withdraw. 'But the visualizations are good for me. Loving Ravi helps me see myself as a lovable child. When I soothe my child, I soothe my hunger.'

Ayesha became quite animated as the clouds seemed to clear in her mind, as she recognized that her 'habit', as she called it 'of bingeing and purging' was to do with control. She had an on–off switch but no gears. She liked the thought of introducing gears in different situations. She laughed with excitement. 'I'm either hyper or asleep. I can quieten the crowd of people on my shoulder who are criticizing me . . . That's why the image of the four-year-old me is so good, because my emotion then is pure. I wasn't a ball of artifice when I came out of the womb. I had a delight in the world. I have that kernel of realness. I need to access it, to peel the layers of artifice off.'

The big shift emerged when Ayesha had an image in her mind of the 'loving moderator lady', a higher power, who told her she was okay, she was 'enough'. She gently nudged Ayesha in the right direction to help her make better decisions, which meant she didn't hate herself and had more satisfying days. The changes in her happened so quickly that we both understood the work she'd done in therapy before: the wisdom she'd learned in rehab was now playing a part.

I wondered aloud whether Ayesha would spit me out at the point where she was getting something. She wasn't sure. Yet she showed up every week. She was feeling a lot calmer. She did yoga and had acupuncture as well, and used her visualization regularly: it had the power to soothe her in the way no drug or food ever had. She'd stopped using social media: 'Comparing my insides with everyone else's outsides is pure poison.'

While Ayesha was on holiday she felt at peace. She almost

couldn't believe what she was saying. She argued that the blue sky and sunshine of a holiday were a false dawn. But I countered that in reality holidays are often when family difficulties intensify: people have the time to face each other and themselves. She slept well and wasn't battling with food; she had a potent memory of swimming, feeling, Wow, this is complete. The image remained alive in her as she spoke and could nourish her after the experience.

Her yoga practice, which she'd begun at home, became a meditative pleasure rather than something she 'should' do. She and Paul had good conversations with Ravi, and felt he was calmer too. I could see her pride in him shining in her face. She'd moved towards her husband for a hug, and it had felt like going to a source of life as she breathed in his familiar smell and felt the warmth of his body. She read my eyes and, without missing a beat, Ayesha firmly told me she didn't want sex again: it was too dangerous. Then she was surprised to realize that that was a message from her mother, who'd transmitted the power of infatuation, and that it was too risky to fall in love. Never fall in love. Sex and death were issues I would have liked to work on with Ayesha, although I knew she wasn't ready as yet. In the end she stopped our therapy before we could attempt it. Therapy rarely fits tidily with our wishes.

On her return from holiday, there were green shoots of hope for work: a publisher had contacted her about editing a book, another about ghost-writing a biography. Ayesha was holding herself differently, her arm above her head, lying back in the chair, open and relaxed – using her newly discovered mechanisms to move between different emotional states: being all on or all off was no longer her only option. She had come back with a tan, and she seemed sensuous. I felt moved seeing her embrace her body and her life. I was interested that, in the next breath, as she acknowledged she felt at peace, she looked to seek nirvana through yoga. I challenged her, chuckling, wanting her to take in what she had before she went on a quest for a higher plane. She laughed in acknowledgement of the truth.

Ayesha had come a long way. She said she had to remember her moderator: 'I've always felt that aloneness, and it's about having that higher power, that voice, whatever you want to call it, who's on my side, that wants the best for me. It's been illuminating. I'm thankful. And, fuck, I love the idea that, instead of winding down, this is a really important part of my life. It is kind of exciting, this next part of my life. Not seeing myself constantly through the prism of others. I have value innately . . .'

Ayesha was no longer stuck. She gave herself permission to be who she was. She was facing the uncomfortable truth of change and adjusting to it. Death scared her, but it also gave her a nudge: life was short, she'd better *carpe diem*. She wanted to remind herself to be happy, to be grateful for what she had. 'Maybe I'm allowed to reap the benefits now. Maybe the best years of my life are ahead of me.'

Ben

Cancer as a Single Father

Ben walked into my room, head slightly stooped. He was tall and constantly on alert for low ceilings and door frames that he would knock into. Ben had come to see me because he had feared his prostate cancer had come back, needing to have multiple further tests after his three-month check-up, having been treated eighteen months earlier. With no preamble he told me, 'I've reached breaking point. People are saying, "You look so much better." Yet there's barely a day I haven't been in the Cancer Centre – although the results this time have turned out okay, I've lost all belief in my future. I feel I've gone from being young to old almost overnight.'

Ben was in his mid-forties, wore a khaki jacket and T-shirt. With his small beard, his looks shouted cool. He was a freelance camera operator, but he was also a bereaved husband, whose wife, Lisa, had died four years previously in a car crash, leaving him as a single parent of a thirteen-year-old daughter, Tia, and an eleven-year-old son, Jax. In my notes I wrote, rather randomly, that he was probably someone who would write in brief, to the point, no extraneous words or Xs or 'darling' – telling me that he had no spare words or affection to give.

Ben spoke fast and articulately, giving me lists of the aspects of his life that were impossible: he knew his children needed him more than ever, but he was working harder than ever to keep the show on the road, not giving them what they needed – he was 'ruining' his children's lives. 'I don't want to be a fucking patient. I want to be a normal healthy father, like the rest of the kids' parents.' They were a 'broken family': he didn't have a good relationship with his father and brother, or his wife's family. Ben's mother had died of cancer when he was sixteen years old, which was a haunting parallel to his own children's grief. When he spoke, it was as if he was digging stakes in the ground to mark how untenable his life was – and he'd certainly had more untimely death to deal with than seemed bearable. He had acute insight into himself, and I was moved by his courage in facing these immense difficulties.

I could see the dark stains of exhaustion on his face, set against his ice-white skin. In response, I found myself wanting to give him confidence that I could help him. I felt the push inside me to imbue him with hope while I knew it could come only from him.

Ben's recent health scare had wiped out the small steps of strength he felt he'd built since his last brutal operation and treatment. But it was the initial cancer diagnosis that had been the killer for him. He'd just begun to dare to trust he could have a new future, even think about having a new relationship after the death of his much-loved wife, when he'd gone for an annual check-up and his GP had told him that his blood test showed his PSA (prostate-specific antigen) levels were raised. The MRI scan confirmed cancer, an aggressive form, which required an operation, radiotherapy and chemo, for it had spread into the lymph nodes. It had taken a year out of his life, the recovery from the operation, and he had tried to work between bouts of treatment. A hellish year with the terrible side effects of chemo, the fevers and vomiting, exhaustion, sore skin and hair loss. He had lived in that vortex of pain, on occasion feeling better only to be thrown back into it. Telling his children had been one of the hardest things he'd ever done in his life, and then seeing them worry and being at the brunt of their anger, while he was unable to protect them, was horrendous. It had left him afraid of absolutely everything.

He bent back his hands as if by stretching his palm he could stretch his internal world to fit the chaos that was circulating in him. I had an image in my mind that I wanted to create the space that would allow him to scream out his distress, then breathe, and slowly examine his different thoughts one by one.

I tried to explain his feelings to him: of course he was at 'breaking point' – he was only just beginning to step out of the grief for his wife's death when his own life was seriously under threat; and he knew all too well from his mother's death that cancer could kill. I told him that grief starts at the point of diagnosis, and a new loss will always bring back previous losses. For him the losses were overwhelming – his mother's death, his wife's sudden death and now his prostate cancer. There was an understandable lag between his capacity to adjust internally to the many external events. I could see him nodding, even agreeing with me, but felt my words fall away, into the effluence that ran through him.

Ben described in clinical detail how he'd been emotionally broken by his first diagnosis: 'Fairly sure I was going to die, I sobbed uncontrollably' (something he never ever did) as he gave the news to his father and brother. To my shock, I heard they had been repulsed by his tears. They had looked at him with contempt, as if his distress was a personal failure. They even voiced their disgust, telling him to pull himself together and stop being pathetic. Ben's hurt and inevitable fury meant the end of any contact at all with his father, and only perfunctory contact with his brother. As he spoke, his acute insight recognized that his internal voice mirrored that of his father: he had a punishing internal voice that 'told me I don't need this indulgent pampering . . . get a grip. It makes me physically rigid.' He described a ceaseless background commentary in his head, brutally critical, that was like a pain in his chest but felt as 'normal as breathing'. He looked at strangers on the tube with envy. They had health. They had it with such confidence they didn't even think about it.

It didn't end there. With tears in his eyes, he acknowledged, 'I could feel myself withdraw from my children. I was aware if I was terminally ill I had to shut down.' It reminded him of the death of his mother: everyone had told him how much she'd loved him, but it didn't ring true, and he could see now that she, too, had had to withdraw when she was dying. He hadn't been able to say her name for decades and had rewritten the story in his head that it was good she'd died. Ben's acid accuracy noted, 'I killed her before she died and killed her again after she'd died.' Yet as he talked more about his mother, a softening opened in him. Again there were tears in his eyes as he questioned, 'What have I lost? When I became a father, oh, my God, my mother felt this about me, I know she must have loved me. The way I felt about my kids felt like it was a muscle memory of my mum's love . . . I want to be like my mum, but I'm terrified I'll be like my dad.'

As moved as I was by the enormity of what Ben told me, I was left feeling I couldn't access him. It was as if the heart of him lay beneath years and years of autumn leaves and cold winters, which no spring or summer warmth could get through. This had been wired in him young, learned from observing his father: it was his best and safest option, protecting him from future hurt. It gave him an ongoing hurt of a different kind: utter loneliness.

But from the outside Ben's life was a constant round of busyness – getting jobs done, meetings, juggling filming TV shows with the endless problem-solving, travelling for work, working long hours, not being in charge of his schedule, having more to do than it was possible to fit in.

I'd asked him what he did to support himself. Nothing. He had good friends, some of whom had been incredible. I wondered, while recognizing the reality of all he had to do, how we could create space: we wouldn't get anywhere until he allowed even a little space for him to breathe, to open a tiny inch. Although I acknowledged his sense of responsibility for his children, and saw that he didn't have the luxury to stop, there was another aspect to it. He saw everyone else go home to their partner and he used work to fill the void of not having one. I voiced to him the contradiction he had to wrestle with: on the one hand, busyness gave him no time to really feel how miserable he was; on the other, he'd told me, 'I don't know if this fundamental deadness inside me is permanent or not. I wake up every day and say, "Fuck me, I've got to do it all over again."'

Ben moved around in the chair when we touched on a topic that was uncomfortable. His mantra was that he didn't know how to feel, yet he had just let us both know vulnerable aspects of himself that he hadn't known before – tears in his eyes, which he swallowed, but as he spoke, they came through. He quickly wiped them away and talked about his valiant self. I took him back to his tears: they hadn't had enough space. I felt closer to him for the first time, and that I could help him. Before, I felt he'd built a wall of words that kept me out, rather than allowed me in.

The next few sessions we talked more openly. He was genuinely engaged with me as to how he might show more vulnerability. He knew that if he showed his vulnerability, it created intimacy and closeness, but in his experience it created more debt to the people who'd been kind to him. We explored what looked like a barricade of defences built by his head and his heart: his head, which said, 'I don't need anyone or anything'; and his heart, which was shielded and kept everyone away from his real feelings. He sighed as he said, 'And it's lonely.' We were both almost taken aback in recognizing how incredibly powerful his father's teaching was, how alive it was in him, even though he had no contact with him. We agreed he'd spent forty-five years being defensive: change was going to take a long time.

An important moment happened minutes before the end of our session. Ben asked me how other people opened up: could he copy them? I took time to reply. I told him I didn't think it was something he had within him just yet. He'd developed, vitally, this very strong mechanism to defend himself: when he had shown vulnerability, he had received only his father's icy contempt. I felt nauseous, even in voicing what to me was the reverse of any parent's response. Ben's interest was piqued. He had thought his reflex to switch off was his fault, self-blame mixed with shame. As he talked, he recognized he could open his heart to other people's difficulties, but he never felt sorry for himself. He could see sadness in my eyes. We didn't have to speak. I quietly added that the work is not about having the same universal response to everyone but to try small experiments, even momentarily of being open with one or two people. He left wondering who they would be.

We had a gap for a number of weeks, which meant we lost some of the connection we were tentatively building. When we met, Ben's anger was back in force: he felt overloaded with all he had to do, and as he reeled off his list of tasks, my head spun. I could see why he found it hard to get up in the morning: the weight of it all sucked the joy out of life. His was a familiar description of the burden of being a single parent, the tasks combined with the absolute responsibility for his children – all alone. His total love for his children meant they engendered a kind of fury when he couldn't give them what they needed – not against them, but a rage in his heart, fuelled by love and fear for how he might fail in his responsibility to care for them properly. He looked with unmasked envy at other families who had more support. It's true, it takes a village to bring up a child. In an ideal world every child should have at least nine adults who are invested in their life. Ben's children had their dad.

As we talked, the intensity of what he felt became clear. Ben didn't think anything would fall into place any more. His assumption now was that nothing would turn out well – not only that but he had a permanent feeling that something terrible was going to happen. He felt 'superstitious. The most dangerous thing I can do is think everything is just great – just before Lisa died, I remember thinking, I've got everything I want in my life, and then, so soon, it all went, and on the anniversary of her funeral, I remember thinking there are nice things coming up, and five days later I'm

told I've got cancer. It's as if I'm being punished if I believe everything is okay.'

It was his cancer diagnosis that brought the worst pressure: the
fear that he had no viable future. He was in a double bind, for right
now he was well, but if this was as good as it got . . . It was shit,
yet there could be worse to come if his cancer returned. He
summed it up: 'Even if God gave me a guarantee that all would be
well, I can never go back to being who I was. After Lisa died, I
thought, I'm young enough, this is early enough into the book of
family life for me to be able to create a whole new chapter. Cancer
has meant I'm too near the end of the book.'

His life was balanced on rocky foundations: he was constantly
aware of the scarcity of time, both in the twenty-four hours of a
day and in his own life. He questioned the point of trying to make
good stuff happen, since nothing good stuck. He wondered about
the purpose of our counselling, whose benefit he'd slowly seen
before our break.

I jumped to my optimistic self, assuring him we could work to
change this, that I had ideas of how he could find space within him
to come alive a little – suggesting regular exercise, creating positive healing rituals with Tia and Jax. I reminded him that he
hadn't had a say in getting cancer or being bereaved, but he could
choose how he responded to it. If he held on to the limiting belief
that he was doomed he would succeed in detonating the good
things he did have. Pragmatically that was true, but in my supervision later, I realized I was working hard because his doom
scenario had transferred to me. It took quite some discussion to
get back to my own view, which was counter to Ben's fear-laden
magical thinking. He believed if he let himself have hope the
gods, who were watching and laughing, would smite him down in
punishment.

Over time my concern reduced as Ben began to talk more
openly. He cried out loud. He told me he didn't feel judged by me,
and it surprised him that he felt better. The barriers between us
lowered, and I felt we were making progress. More importantly,

his life seemed to be getting back on track. His work was intense, but his children were happy at school and doing well; he had moments of real joy with them. There were difficulties, such as his car being stolen, but as he told me, many times, he was a problem-solver: those things were stressful but didn't blow him off course as he could sort them out. Ben's confidence grew, and he decided with some energy that his new project was to find a girlfriend.

A flicker of worry must have crossed my face. Ben was sharp: quick as a flash he retorted, 'The mechanics down there are fine.' We laughed, lovely connecting laughter. He continued that finding someone to share his life with would reawaken his heart and give him hope. Furthermore, it would solve a lot of his problems – of loneliness, money worries, his burden of work and parenting, and could potentially make him happier. We both felt optimistic.

I didn't see Ben for a number of weeks. He didn't show up for appointments or respond to texts. I was surprised, but assumed it was because he was happier. I texted him on the day of the last session we had in the diary. He agreed to come in.

He was more stooped than ever and wearing dark glasses. He fell into the chair. He covered his face with his hands. He didn't want me to see him. I learned there were unconfirmed worries from his last cancer-test results. 'I can never escape the cancer . . . it's all so futile . . . I want to give up the struggle. I'd like to go away and die – sooner the better. This is unbearable . . . There's the scorching humiliation of keeping on having hope and being beaten again and again. Cancer has destroyed my life and destroyed me . . .'

I felt his plummeting despair in my stomach, with a kind of growling fury that he should be suffering again. I, too, had desperately wanted Ben to have a fair wind, to have some relief from dealing with bereavement and life-threatening illness. I needed to check whether he was suicidal, and he reassured me that he would never abandon his children. But he had let us both know how unbearable his pain was. He went on, 'I don't recognize myself. I didn't think I'd be a broken person . . . but Lisa's death is not fix-able, and now I may be ill again, I may not earn . . . Money would solve a lot of my problems . . . It wouldn't cure me, but it would stop me worrying so much . . .'

I couldn't argue with Ben. He had more to deal with than one person could manage. Hardship came on too many fronts. His family of origin didn't support him, he was bereaved of his mother as a child, his wife had died, he'd got cancer and he didn't earn very much. If he could have grieved his loss, perhaps he would have developed the resilience to overcome his difficulties. But the combination of all of them was literally overwhelming. Ben didn't believe talking to me could help, because what I offered was connection for him to express his pain, and then incrementally gave him the desire to rebuild his life. In Ben's case hope was now too dangerous. It had let him down too often. It had shattered even the wish for it. He told me, 'There's a deadness in my soul. I'm not alive.'

At the point we stopped speaking he wanted to stop fighting. Sometimes we don't want to have hope because it can't protect us from the hurt of disappointment. But nothing can shield us from that pain, and hope is the single force that can offer light when life is darkest. Hope is the alchemy that can turn a life around. Rightly we hold on valiantly to expressions like 'It is darkest before dawn.' But for Ben, just as he was on the tipping point of finding light in his life, he was hit again. Eventually hope needs to deliver. Ben had suffered, for now, too many disappointments to dare to have it again.

I worried about Ben. I kept trying to look for answers in my head. I heard his voice, everyone tried to give him solutions, but he was the best problem-solver on the planet: if there was a solution to this he would find it. I knew he was right. In discussion with my supervisor, I came to the conclusion, I hope correctly, that fundamentally Ben was a fighter. At heart, he was a survivor. It was in every cell of his body. Completely understandably, he no longer wanted to come to see me. But if his doctors could get his cancer in remission, he would, with time, rebuild his life. For that, he needed medicine to work, to be physically well. He needed a more reliable income. I prayed to whoever might listen that he had good fortune.

Reflections on Health

Health is invisible until we are ill. Health is the absence of suffering: we regard ourselves as healthy when we wake up every day and can reliably function mentally and physically, and our focus is tuned to those around us, to what we need to do to get on with our day, however difficult or easy that is. Ideally, each healthy day builds a healthy life. For most of us, it isn't until we age that ill-health emerges. For an older person, often with multiple health problems, having an accident, perhaps a fall, can have serious consequences: it is harder for them to recover than it is for a younger person.

Ayesha, Geoffrey and Ben's stories show how changing health and ill-health impacted them. We see what supported and hindered them as they learned to live with their conditions. What became increasingly clear to me was that when we are suffering it is totally preoccupying: the greater the pain, the more pervasive it is, and it limits our capacity to engage with the aspects of life that give us joy and make life worth living. It is a particularly cruel cycle. Inevitably it has a massive knock-on effect on those around us, who by proximity suffer too.

What also became apparent was how Ayesha, Geoffrey and Ben's attitudes, understanding and consequent behaviours influenced their capacity to manage their health. Their minds and bodies had equally important parts in their recovery. They couldn't choose how to react: that pattern was set in them already, and was instantly triggered by their illness. But when they found a way to accommodate their ill-health, they were better able to support themselves. Evidence shows that doctors and medical protocols cure us, but multiple research studies show that developing positive coping strategies, which may include alternative medicine, mean people feel less pain, recover more quickly and have more joy in life.

For Ben, having a life-threatening illness at a relatively young age, being a single parent and having no family support (although good friends) meant that his suffering was greatly intensified. By the time I stopped seeing him, even daring to hope felt too much. There is no doubt that we all have limits as to what we can endure, and Ben had reached his. What he needed was good news, some good luck: good things needed to happen to him, not good counselling. Geoffrey and Ayesha's ill-health injured them, stalling their progression in life, and knocked their trust in themselves and their future. But we saw that through reflection, and allowing themselves time to process, they could shift from their first response to be more hopeful.

Health and Wellbeing

I was interested that statistically we are healthier and happier than I'd expected. In 2011 in England and Wales 81 per cent of people reported their general health as either 'Very good' or 'Good'; in England it was 81 per cent and in Wales it was 78 per cent. The measure for personal wellbeing was similar – life satisfaction, feeling what you do is worthwhile and happiness were all above 70 per cent and the figure for anxiety was lower than 30 per cent.

According to the 2012 King's Fund report, there is a direct link between socio-economic background and health and wellbeing. Those with chronic conditions are more likely to be from a particular social class and type of employment. Those living in the poorest environment have a 60 per cent higher chance of developing long-term conditions than those in wealthier areas.

More than two-thirds of NHS spending in the UK goes on the over–65s. The data shows that an eighty-five-year-old man costs the NHS about seven times more on average than a man in his late thirties. This means that for those who are living longer, their final years are increasingly spent in ill-health, often with numerous chronic conditions.

Loss of Health and Recovery Post-diagnosis

The moment a person is given a life-limiting or life-threatening diagnosis their perception of themselves as healthy is irrevocably changed. It turns their life, as they knew it, upside down. The shock and the fear feel like grief. It is change that they did not want or choose. The psychological adjustment that has to be made from 'I am healthy' to 'I am ill', whether through accident or diagnosis, requires a shift in identity that is extremely unwelcome and hard to negotiate. They grieve for that innocent version of themselves that could count on their health. Those who are able to feel their loss and maintain their regular routines (by carrying on with existing activities and nurturing current relationships) are more robust when navigating their ongoing illness.

Research shows that how we come to terms with the diagnosis has significant consequences. Recovery is not the same for all, even when the health issue the person is recovering from is the same. Those who have strong relationships with family and friends, a comfortable living environment and purpose before the onset of illness are more likely to be able to recover and want to recover. When they understand their illness and what they need to do to manage it, they fare better. Those who choose active coping strategies, like talking about how they feel, fare better. For instance, if they are in a relationship maintaining physical intimacy (which can be sexual but not necessarily) they are more likely to feel alive and attractive than when beaten down by illness; that also enhances the capacity to be patient and kind when the going is tough. Doing what they enjoy, even if limited, exercising and meditating will lower their risk of depression.

Older people with multiple health complaints, who have experienced loss and have less secure relationships, will find it harder to recover. Many factors come into play, starting with how they now see themselves, as they face this new daunting reality of what options are open to them. They could frame their illness as a personal failure, and believe that it has robbed them of more than just their health. Research shows the consequences of such a negative perspective may mean they deny the importance of their treatment, may stop taking their medication and not attend hospital appointments. They may also stop taking care of themselves, which creates a downward cycle. Their outcomes are worse medically and psychologically, not because the treatment doesn't work if they aren't positive, but because their negative attitudes and behaviours can lead to further ill-health.

The complexity of a patient's emotional response, particularly those with treatments like chemotherapy and radiotherapy, stems from their improvement and deterioration through the course of the treatment, with no certainty as to the outcome. The rollercoaster of feelings, happier when feeling well and low when feeling ill, is hard to endure. There are often additional changes that illness enforces, to lifestyle and work, which may add to their stress. A study showed that 20 per cent of those with chronic conditions, such as rheumatoid arthritis, are at risk of being depressed, and with cancer it can be 30 per cent. After the imposed structure of treatments, patients can find the open-ended time that follows unexpectedly hard, the months and years of not knowing if the cancer will recur if nothing active is done to stop it.

For those with chronic conditions it is helpful to reframe the term 'recovery', as it implies a fixed destination and a return to their former self. The recovery is more taking each step at a time, with many stages and possibilities rather than an end point. It helps to keep their outlook for the future short, in the day, this week, not escalating fear levels by looking into the abyss of the unknown. Each person can define their own recovery with small steps, succeeding in activities that were not possible before, like going for a walk. It is rarely linear, with many ups and downs, but it helps to celebrate the small victories. It is key to know that you have both learned to accept the limits the illness imposes and done all you can to support your recovery, and live as full and happy a life as possible.

For many survivors of a life-threatening illness, there is often a major shift. Their perception of the world is enhanced, which brings a more satisfying engagement with and love of life. They may have learned for the first time how loved they are, when they have been explicitly shown love by close family and friends. Their confidence in their robustness to live and survive difficulty also grows.

Family Systems and Health

As we have seen in the case studies, it is by no means only the patient who suffers when someone is ill: it has a ripple effect, which is widespread and profound on all those close to them. Their family is affected in multiple ways when the illness is long term: it impacts every aspect of their life – their relationships, their emotional and financial health, their use of time on every level, socially. It is complex too, because the person who is ill has to move up the hierarchy of priorities, yet often those who love them are worried and stressed but feel they cannot turn to their sick family member for support.

Research shows that those who are fully open with each other, express their feelings directly and solve problems collaboratively feel less anxiety and experience lower levels of depression. They see it through the lens of the family system: the chronically ill person, as well as everyone else in their family, influences and impacts the others. A family needs to work together to meet the changing demands of the sick person and share the workload. Each member may be affected in a different way, and if that is accepted and everyone is free to express how they feel, the unit can cope. This works best when families balance the illness with doing enjoyable activities together.

Within each family there are beliefs and attitudes towards health and ill-health that are unique to them. It may be that they are a family that underplays sickness, whose members are expected to be stoic and not complain. At the other end of the spectrum, sickness creates a drama that attracts attention: every minor ailment is talked about and attended to. And there are myriad different versions in between. Understanding the beliefs of one's own family helps clarify what is going on when someone's behaviour is causing upset, which may be because it isn't aligned with the family's belief system.

A NCBI (National Center Biotechnology Information) study in 2013 showed that in a family of someone with a chronic illness '92% of the family members interviewed were affected emotionally by the patient's illness, mentioning worry (35%), frustration (27%), anger (15%), and guilt (14%). Worry was reported when the family members were thinking about the future or the patient's death. Further psychological effects included feeling upset, annoyed, helpless, stressed, and lonely.' Being worried is normal as they begin to take on board the implications of the illness, which information and a clear plan help to alleviate. Frustration and anger are linked to being unable to make better the person they love; it also means they have to do more chores and are likely to be fighting more, as everyone is on a short fuse. Financial problems can occur, which certainly adds to the anger. The guilt is usually because they feel they should have only love and compassion for the person who is ill and feel bad that they are furious and want it over with as soon as possible. It is exhausting.

Friends who support the family can make a huge difference. Acknowledging the illness and then listening is key. The language a friend uses when they speak, being warm and compassionate without that doomsday poor-you head-on-one-side tone, helps. Often, offers of practical help, like bringing food or caring for children, freeing the parents to spend quality time together, are significant. Or perhaps organizing a surprise treat to bring joy and distraction. It is possible to buy little windows of pleasure for the friend, maybe a massage, or flowers, and sit down to chat together. Small gestures can be immensely comforting even when the illness of the friend is very serious. When friends want to fix the situation, by imparting magic diets, magic pills, stories of success, it tends to be less helpful, as well intentioned as it is. Maintaining gestures of help in the long term, not just in the crisis, really matters. Each family is unique and needs to find its own solutions. But offering loving friendship, listening, being available and emotionally present, that is where the magic lies.

Menopause

In the UK the average age for women to experience the menopause is fifty-one, but having it at any time between forty-five and fifty-eight is normal. In rare cases a woman can get early-onset menopause, before the age of forty.

Menopause can last from four to eight years, and the symptoms are well known, but the most common are hot flushes, poor concentration, fatigue, sleeplessness, anxiety and mood disturbances; some women are lucky enough to have few or no symptoms. Ayesha demonstrates how seismic it can be, and without the right understanding and support, menopause can bring with it a swathe of destruction. The shame and taboo that are wrapped around it increase the disruption. I have seen many long marriages and careers crash on the rocks of menopause. All of us need greater depth of understanding of its impact and consequences. Of the 4.4 million women over the age of fifty in employment, a recent study showed half of them found it difficult to work, and more of them difficult to talk about their menopause.

As with all things physical and psychological, there are unique responses and ways of being that help or hinder menopause. Women who had multiple roles in their life were less prone to depression and were less concerned about the loss of their fertility. Conversely, but not surprisingly, those who had more symptoms were significantly more worried about the effects of menopause on their attractiveness: pouring with sweat, feeling exhausted and anxious are not exactly conducive to feeling sexy and vital. This is accompanied by a Western society that reveres youth and beauty. It is very common for middle-aged women to say how invisible they feel, or how their skills and talents are undervalued because of how they look.

The menopause represents a step into another phase of life. It is the physical embodiment of no longer being fertile. Sexuality, fertility and motherhood are often a key part of a woman's identity, and perceived societal purpose. Therefore, finding a way to carve a new identity and purpose can give renewed meaning to her life. But this does not happen overnight: there will be upset and disquiet in shedding one identity to move into another.

Work has an important role to play. Women who gave up work to parent, often a difficult transition in itself because they lost status and structure, may find it particularly hard. Menopause often coincides with children getting older and no longer needing their parent as much. The consequent loss of meaning and purpose can be debilitating, and the obvious step would be to go back to work. But often they have little confidence in finding a new job if they have been out of the market for two decades.

We need to talk more openly and honestly about menopause and andropause (the male menopause) with men and our children. Miseducation on this has damaging outcomes for women and their families. It needs a multi-generational, multi-gender approach; older family members who have experienced menopause must talk to younger ones. It is important to talk about women's hormonal cycles and periods generally, creating a culture and role-modelling an attitude that this is not a shameful subject to be whispered about in corners but a normal healthy part of being a woman. Fortunately voices are opening up important discussions and campaigning for improved work practices through organizations like Plan International UK and Menopause Support UK and movements like #HotWomenOnly.

I have been interested to see in my practice that some women from a higher socio-economic background struggle with menopause in a different way: they do not see it as a normative life phase, having the money to feel they can 'fight' it. Their modus operandi can be to set their will and their experience as successful women to beat menopause. And perhaps they can, because HRT puts off menopausal symptoms. Thousands of women, from all socio-economic backgrounds stopped taking life-changing HRT because of research that linked it to higher rates of breast cancer. This has been toned down now. For some, bio-identical hormones are the new, increasingly popular answer to menopausal symptoms. However, even without menopausal symptoms, it is essential to face up to this life transition. A middle-aged woman needs to reflect on and address what matters to her in life; she needs to ask what this next chapter looks like and how she can fulfil her potential.

Employment

Illness for Ben and Geoffrey curtailed their ability to work for a significant time. Being employed improves our health, and being healthy is a predictor for employment – people think of healthspan interchangeably with lifespan. As the statistics show, ill-health has a massive impact on work life: 11 million people in the UK have a long-term health condition; 50 per cent of them say it affects how much and what work they can do, with many more negative consequences than just the financial – one in five employees with a physical-health condition also reported having a mental-health condition.

When an employer takes the care to adapt their employee's job to fit their capacity they are often repaid ten-fold in commitment and loyalty. This requires both parties to communicate honestly with each other on many levels: they need to weigh up the employee's realistic ability, and what can be accommodated within the job to meet it. The employee needs to learn what his or her options and rights are and find ways of being assertive in stating them as well as what will give him or her personal satisfaction.

Ageing

Ageing is better than its alternative! If we are lucky we grow old. As human beings we are genetically programmed to procreate, support our children's growth to maturity, and be alive for the birth of the next generation. Our bodies are not built to grow very old. In 2011 life expectancy at birth was almost double what it was in 1841. A man born in 2011 has a life expectancy of seventy-eight years, a woman of eighty-three years. The number of centenarians has increased by 85 per cent over the last fifteen years. Increased life expectancy has brought with it the problems of a population that is more likely to have ill-health, and the opportunity to have another whole phase of life our parents' generation couldn't have dreamed of.

It is clear through the case studies that our attitude to ageing is changing. Geoffrey has a stoic attitude, with low demands and expectations compared to Ayesha, born in the early 1960s. She found it hard to transition into the next phase of her life, for many reasons, but one was the pressure to maintain a young-looking body.

According to research that focused on longevity hot spots around the world, known as Blue Zones, ageing is in fact only 10 per cent genetic and 90 per cent lifestyle. This is helpful if it means we make better health choices, but unhelpful if we think we have absolute control over our health.

The reality is that as we age we deteriorate physically. Researchers identified that a realistic picture of what being older means to a particular individual helps them. For each person to engage in a vision of their life in old age, to be curious, look at what excites and interests them. It may bring sharper focus and a better use of their limited time. Plan new positive activities and ways of being that maintain mental, physical and psychological vibrancy.

Loneliness in Old Age

Loneliness and isolation are killers in old age. The majority of the 7.7 million people in 2016 who lived alone were women. It is therefore women who are at the highest risk of getting long-term chronic illnesses, like diabetes and heart failure, as a consequence of that social isolation. In England more than a million older people can go for over a month without speaking to their family, friend or neighbour. Often they are the sole survivor following the death of their spouse and friends, or they may have a disability, or are physically weaker and no longer have social connections through work.

Being frail as an elderly person leads to less activity, which can affect memory and cognition. If you don't use it, you lose it: the adage is true of old age. We need to accept that ill-health is likely, but it helps to stay interested and as active as possible by building a set of achievable goals. Most important of all is staying connected to family, friends and neighbours, even if it is only by telephone.

Hope

For patients and their families, hope is key. Research shows it is one of the predictors for long-term survivors of HIV infection and breast cancer. Healthy coping is different from the more simplistic approach of 'positive thinking'. It implies the ability to tolerate and express worries, fears and sadness while still hoping for a good outcome.

No one who is ill is able to shut out their anxieties, although there is often pressure from family and friends to look at the sunny side, but this is usually more to do with their own difficulty in sitting with the distress of chronic illness. While the health professional may be drawn to optimism, they play a significant part in conveying realistic hope. It is important, although difficult, for them to negotiate the path between giving hope and being honest, holding both with equal weight, which protects against false hope and builds trust.

Identity

'Know, first, who you are, and then adorn yourself accordingly.'

Epictetus

Sara

Escape from Raqqa to Berlin

Sara, a Kurdish Syrian, now living in Berlin, spoke to me through Skype. She was twenty-four years old, but looked sixteen, her innocent brown eyes piercing me with engaging warmth. I was astonished by the resilience with which she presented herself, given that she had endured years of living in a war-torn country and, most recently, a terrifying journey. I could feel myself stepping towards her, wanting to connect on a deeper level, drawn in by her bubbly sense of humour and bouncy optimism.

Over time, as our conversation developed, I saw that this was by no means the whole picture, but it was a necessary and useful survival response that helped her manage her place in a frightening and unpredictable world.

Sara had been living in Raqqa, a normal middle-class life, with her two younger brothers and her father, a dentist. Her mother had died of cancer when Sara was ten years old. She had just finished high school and was studying for university when the rebels seized the city and the bombing by the regime started. It didn't stop: there was a constant downpour of bombs twenty-four hours a day. She was rigid with horror, couldn't eat, and was terrified, knowing they could die at any moment: walking along the street, sleeping in bed, eating a meal. One of her brothers would look up to the sky and shout, 'Why are you doing this to us?' but Sara would tell them both not to move, stay still, be silent and pray, in the hope that if none of them moved the bombs would miss them.

I could see the startled look of unprocessed shock on her face, and feel the fear that pulsated through her body, which she seemed not to know how to express. I needed to be careful with my response, not wanting to crash through her necessary coping mechanism by prodding. I wanted to let her know I was alongside her, although I could never truly know what she had experienced. Ninety per cent of Raqqa was destroyed, and she told me shocking stories of the many dead bodies she'd seen and, horrifyingly, of her cousin's head being blown off.

Being Kurdish, they were forced to leave Raqqa, Isis having declared that Kurds were the devil. Each new atrocity shook me. I acknowledged it was beyond comprehension. This seemed to resonate with her: she agreed and told me people use the word 'terror', which didn't do justice to what had happened. 'I lose words. No words describe it.' I checked with her as to whether we'd talked enough for that day. She told me it was good to go back to those moments, that avoiding them was not good: 'It is simple words or moments that take me to an exact memory. I'm not crying now, but I can't control my tears when they do come . . . It is in me all the time.' Although she had been in Berlin for a year, she had never told anyone her story.

Her family moved to Tal Abyad, a northern border town in Syria, but that was attacked too, and was soon reduced to rubble. They escaped to Turkey where they stayed with cousins, but after eighteen months life there was too expensive: they had no work, no official papers, and they moved back to Tal Abyad. Her family had remained neutral throughout the fighting, not wanting to be a target for any side. But six years after the first uprising Sara felt her powerlessness draining the life out of her. As a survival reflex, she became an activist, posting messages on Facebook.

Almost immediately she was telephoned anonymously, commanded to stop posting or be killed. The image that she could die from a slit throat, drowning in her own blood, overcame her terror of the risks involved in leaving Syria. Beneath this lay her determination, which I could see in her eyes as she spoke, to do something with her life. School friends of her age were getting married, but she didn't want to be submissive to a husband: she wanted to be in charge of her own destiny. She was desperate to get a proper education – she wanted to be a doctor.

Sara made the decision to leave, knowing hundreds of people who tried were shot or beaten up. It took her four attempts to cross the border. On the first three she was shot at and had to turn back. Each time she tried, she cried when saying goodbye to her family, and she was afraid, but there was a stronger drive in her to go forward. On the fourth attempt she succeeded: the actual crossing took two minutes, and a waiting van drove her and some others to a bus station. From there, the same night, she paid a smuggler for a boat. A dinghy that was designed to hold fifteen people had fifty-two in it. She was frozen, water was pouring in, and people were screaming for help. She couldn't swim and was certain she would drown, though she felt 'It's not my time to die. I haven't spoken to my father and I don't want to see these children die.'

Thankfully, they were rescued by a Greek Navy ship, whose crew yelled at them angrily, and she was afraid she would be sent back. But she was taken to the big camp in Lesbos, from where, thanks to money from her cousin, a smuggler flew her to Berlin.

Sara's story was familiar in that I'd read it many times, yet hearing her tell it, while I looked at her young face, stirred a response in me of an entirely different order. I felt shock for what she had been through, admiration for her capacity to fight for her life, and a pull to rescue and mother her. I wondered if I, or my children, could have been as courageous. Her humour and positive personality were strengths that shone through. They must have influenced the judge in Berlin who interviewed her: he laughed at her jokes, immediately accepted her refugee status and gave her the required papers. Usually it takes at least two years to receive the certificate that allows a refugee to stay, if it is granted.

I wondered what her life was like now. I heard more of what was beneath the surface as she described the opposing forces in her. There was the ever-present fear for her family, assuming they were dead if she didn't receive a response to her texts. She dreamed of her father being murdered, and being unable to protect her brothers. She felt selfish and a bad person that she was worrying about her university place when they didn't even go to school, couldn't read or write, and could be blown up at any moment. 'I feel survivor's guilt all the time. If I see a young child who has died, I ask, why her, not me? My family are still there. How come I am safe, and they are not?' She told me other refugees sometimes felt so powerless at not being able to defend their family that they wanted to return to Syria.

She heard two voices. One was her primitive instinct to survive, and the other questioned her right to be safe when those she loved most were not. I acknowledged that both voices had an important place in her and needed to be heard. It would drive her crazy if she tried to block one in preference to the other.

I could see Sara's shoulders drop a little in response, then felt her tighten immediately when I said she had a right to live the life she had now. She explained that in Syria, as a Kurd, she hadn't known who she was. She was treated as a second-class citizen and was consistently on the end of racist attacks. She remembered being bullied at school by a classmate jeering, 'What are you?' and her response, 'We are aliens.' It was a typical experience of someone who is not being seen as a person but as an object of distaste.

At work she felt cross when she was introduced as a Syrian refugee – she wanted to be introduced as a colleague – and then if she was asked where she came from. When she was asked, she usually paused before she responded. She worried the person could be anti-refugee or, almost worse, she would get the 'pity look'. She wanted respect and to be valued for who she was.

I suggested to her, perhaps being too hopeful, that she might

belong in Berlin. Sara was clear in her response. She was grateful
to Berlin for giving her a place to live, and some money, and for
their police force who were trustworthy, unlike those in Syria,
and for her rights as a woman. Being respected as a woman (a
courtesy not accorded to her in Syria) meant a great deal to her.
But she was not a citizen in Berlin, she was 'a stranger'. She felt
scared all the time. She felt no one wanted to listen to her or cared
what happened to her or her family; she was a long way from
belonging. Sara was suspended above ground, untethered and
alone.

Although Sara started each session by telling me, with a cheer-
ful smile, she was 'fine', she began to be more open. Turkey was
attacking the Kurds, and her nightmares increased. She dreamed
of her brothers being buried under rubble, her father tortured.
The fear leaked into her days, and at times she couldn't stop herself
crying, feeling she was going mad. For the first time I heard the
anger, beneath her foreboding: 'We are all victims of bigger plans
that destroy our lives. My brother was a baby when it started – all
he has known is war. It is unfair. Just as I was about to go to university it was taken away from me, and now all I think about is
how I am going to survive – and will my family die?' She was
trembling as she spoke, apologizing for crying and for speaking
too much, distraught as she told me she could see no end to it. She
could suppress it some of the time, but felt it was always there.
She wanted a doctor to cut it out of her brain.

I spoke gently, telling her I could see that the terror of her experiences was alive in her body, and that it was constantly being
triggered, by images on Facebook, even cars backfiring. Everything she had believed in and known had been blown up – her
basic safety, her home and neighbourhood, going to school, the
simple necessities of life, like having food on the table. The threat
was present every day. How could she feel any differently without
being a machine?

My words seemed to calm her as she spoke with renewed
energy, the fighter in her coming to the fore, telling me she wanted

the rights and life of any other young woman, not to be a victim refugee. She felt, 'They are stripping you away from a normal human being and they turn you into someone who doesn't have anything else. I want more than safety. I have a right to think about other things. I want my bachelor's degree. I'm angry at being told to forget it, or postpone it. I want to study.' And as I looked at her, in the moment of her valiant outcry, I could see her being hit by the underlying fear that she wouldn't succeed. She cried more deep tears. She was a fighter and a victim of events over which she had no control. The weight of both was greater than her confidence.

Identity has not challenged me personally. I'm lucky in that my identity is that of the majority in the UK. Through Sara's eyes, I saw how dehumanizing being labelled could be, her identity as a refugee, a Syrian, a Kurd. She is always seen initially as an outsider who threatens the host country's way of life. I wanted my genuine warmth for her to reach through the Skype screen and help protect her against the cold she often had to endure. I would also need to connect to her core sense of identity, informed by her upbringing, and see whether that would work for or against her.

Following discussions with my supervisor, I felt I needed extra knowledge to be able to support Sara as effectively as I could. I read papers about trauma from war; I went on a four-day residential course with the leading expert on trauma, Bessel van der Kolk; and I read widely about identity. Even when we don't expect it, clients teach therapists, and Sara taught me to look deeply at my assumptions from my own life, where I had blind spots, and to examine my own prejudices. It left me with a feeling of discomfort at our inequalities, and I hoped a heightened sensitivity to her experience. I questioned how I could best respond to her, given that trauma work is ideally done with two people in a room together or using EMDR (Eye Movement Desensitization Reprocessing), which I didn't do and she'd never be able to access in Berlin . . . In some ways, reflecting on it in this way supported me with my own sense of helplessness, for there was nothing I could actually do to give her what she wanted. But if I could build a true connection with her, attuning to her effectively, from a position that was well informed and compassionate, but not patronizing, maybe I could make a difference. My intention was that through our relationship she could find a way to face the consequences of the devastating events she'd experienced and live her life fully.

As much as Sara wanted a doctor to cut out her memories, we agreed that our work was to process the traumatic experiences she'd had, for they were in her, poisoning her mind, and to find ways of soothing her when she was hit by waves of distress. I did a relaxation exercise with her, and she sighed with relief. We'd done some good work – put words to the scrambled story in her mind, helped her find a narrative she could understand; she had expressed some of her fury and cried necessary tears – all of which enabled her to be calm. She was beginning to take on board that her instinct not to touch her distraught memories kept them heightened in her: she needed to let them run through her if she was to heal. I saw that at the heart of Sara there was a young woman whose identity had been shaped by others in ways that did not fit with whom she believed herself to be. I wanted to be an advocate for this ambitious, clever and creative young woman, who had a right to an education and a voice that needed to be heard.

In the next few sessions Sara felt bleak, with increasingly bad news from her threatened family: 'I'm scared. There's a stone in my heart, and my hands start shaking, my fingers hurt, and I start sweating. There's something so heavy on it, I cannot breathe.' She saw the faces of dead people, and wanted to remember her mother, but couldn't draw on an image of her. Her eyes darted past me, looking for somewhere safe to land. I felt protective of this young girl all alone, shaking in that whitewashed bare room, with a single bed and a table and chair – a room she felt safe in but looked grim to me. I thought perhaps doing a visualization exercise might help her find a safe place within her, but when I asked her to close her eyes, breathe in, and tell me what images emerged, she could see only black, which disturbed her: she was worried it meant she was empty, and that equated to weakness. She feared if she allowed herself to 'give in to sadness, I will be worth nothing and I will fail . . . If I work hard enough, I will achieve.'

She wrestled with her reflex to shut down but slowly, over time, she came around. Doing the relaxation and talking to me helped her: 'I feel relieved when I speak. I feel more relaxed. When I keep it inside, it piles up like a jumble of words.' I felt we were on track: I could see her rummaging around inside herself for the right word, and looking relieved as she voiced it. She agreed, telling me, 'When I find the word then finally the person I'm talking to knows what I mean.' What she needed was not complicated: she needed to be seen and heard as the person she felt herself to be. No more, no less.

Over the months Sara did good work which enabled her to ground herself in the present. She had developed various strategies, sometimes breathing, at others doing yoga or dancing (which have been shown to be powerful antidotes to trauma), and talking to me to counter her fight, flight and freeze response when it was triggered in her body by a sight, sound, scent or touch. That was by no means all. Sara had been enterprising in integrating herself in German life: she'd learned German, and found a job. Her trauma was not stalling her progress, but circumstances were. She had processed the adjustment in her sense of identity and felt herself to be someone worthy of respect and value, but she badly needed to be living that next step. We both felt she could even manage the disturbances of fear for her family, which would continue, if she had enough positive experiences in her life.

The springboard for Sara's future was a source of great frustration and at times rage. More than anything in the world Sara wanted to go to university: it was why she had borne being shot at and nearly drowned. It was her stepping stone. 'I had hoped I would live normally. I want a BA and then a PhD. I think I'm getting away from the things I want – they are walking away from me. I keep following them, and they are faster.' Her head slumped as she cried despairing tears. She had applied to many universities and had no replies; there had been fragments of hope for scholarships, but they had seemed to disappear. For a place in Berlin she needed to pass the equivalent of her high-school exams all over again to be eligible to apply. This outraged her: she had done exceptionally well and having to repeat them seemed pointless.

As she spoke I understood that going to university meant more than an education: it was a central part of her identity to be seen as someone of worth. 'If you don't have a degree people don't take you seriously. They won't look at you.' It represented her winning her fight over her powerlessness in all she had been robbed of. There was also a time pressure: her visa was for three years, and she had to secure her place before that time was up.

I thought about the serenity prayer and its central message to accept what you cannot change, and have the courage to change the things you can. I wondered with Sara, given there was a great deal she had no control over, what she could change. She was lonely. There were a few older people where she worked part time in a craft and design studio, and young people where she was learning to code, but no Syrians. She missed her brothers, who had often driven her mad, but she could talk to them at night when they couldn't sleep; one brother made her laugh, and she missed her father's hug, the familiarity of being at home.

We had a pivotal session in which Sara cried in a way she hadn't before, rocking backwards and forwards, her hands over her eyes, lifting her head up to the ceiling as she drew other painful memories from what felt like the depths of her being, taking in big breaths as she remembered each one. She had never spoken of them to anyone before. She'd believed she would never talk to anyone about them but would have to carry them for the rest of her life. They were as much about missing her mother, and the impact her death had had on her whole family, as the war.

I had felt brutal leaving her at the end of the session, having agreed what she could do to look after herself, and I started the next with some trepidation, wondering how she'd coped. I heard it had been immensely cathartic. 'I haven't cried like that for years, and there is a huge burden lifted off my heart and my shoulders – it gave me courage to do things I haven't been doing for months, even years. After I spoke to you, I decided I needed to deal with it. It felt like a spell had come over me – I felt so strong.' She felt much happier, she had greater clarity, and was more confident that she would get what she wanted in her life, to trust in herself, even if it took longer. And she made the decision not to listen to the negative voices in her head, when 'I overthink and catastrophize', but to keep her thinking in the present and focus on the good things she had. I could feel her immense optimism lift her into a different place and felt a surge of warmth and affection for her, with the hope that that optimism would be met by a positive future.

Over time, with occasional dips, when I saw Sara it was as if the sun had gradually come out inside her. This wasn't a brittle version of her putting on a show: I saw her smiling face beaming at me, which ignited a responding smile in me. She had been busy, which had stopped her ruminating about the past, and she'd accepted having to do her exams again. Life had more possibilities and she felt stronger: 'I've seen I've grown. I'm more independent. I'm not the same person. There are things I've been through I never imagined I would get through – the sea, being shot at. I was running, and my brain focused: "Get to the other side." If I'd asked myself before, I'd have said I was a coward, but I think I've become braver. I was shy, but I don't have that now. I've always been a kind person but I'm more compassionate now.'

I felt proud that she was on her own side, standing looking at herself, and had seen she was stronger than she'd known. It helped build her resilience in an environment over which she had very little influence. I took on the baton of hope for her and told her I wanted her to have fun. I encouraged her to get out of her room and meet people her own age. She told me she'd been thinking of going back to basketball, which she used to play, and learning to swim, which had always terrified her, and hopefully make friends.

She wanted to find friends who were like-minded: she had strong views that often people from her country disagreed with, particularly about being a feminist. She had been mocked by Syrian friends, which infuriated her. Part of her developing self began to recognize that her beliefs were fundamental to who she was, and she wouldn't compromise on them to have friends. I was reminded of Viktor Frankl, holocaust survivor, psychiatrist and author: 'Everything can be taken from a man but one thing: the last of the human freedoms – to choose one's attitude in any given set of circumstances, to choose one's own way.'

In the sessions that followed it became clearer to us both that Sara's sense of identity had multiple facets that would operate in different situations. There was the version that had immense confidence, could speak to anyone and was full of bubbling energy. The sunny Sara, the Sara who liked being seen, and liked to feel she was making a difference. Doing good helped her feel she belonged, that she wasn't an outsider who was regarded suspiciously. This Sara trusted she would go to university and then change the world. I'd seen much of her recently.

But there was also the sad little girl, who badly missed her mother, particularly when she had to deal with bad news. Or when she was ill. She felt no one cared about her because she didn't belong. There was the young woman, too, who could have fun when she went out with her friends, but who was vulnerable to any criticism and could easily be upset.

Sometimes she felt most alone when she was with other people because she didn't believe they understood her, perhaps didn't value her beliefs. Then there was the young Sara, shaped by the criticism of her father, who had said, 'Whatever you do you aren't good enough. You will never have what you want.' This voice scared her most. It could come out of the blue or was triggered by an event. I reminded her not to conflate her feeling of fear with fact: fearing she wouldn't go to university didn't mean she wouldn't. Feelings are not facts. Sara was fundamentally resilient, and once she had spoken, cried, been heard, it freed her to breathe. She said, 'Thank you. It's like I'm burning all the time when I'm scared. When I'm breathing it's like turning on a fan. It's cooling air.'

We agreed that Sara would inevitably be shaken by news from her family or events in Berlin. She couldn't fight it or block that out. Her passion to go to university and her family's safety were at the centre of her fear. Yet she had no control over them. But she did have control over her response. Sara said, 'Better say, "Come in, do your mess, and leave,"' each time she was hit by a storm of fear. She could support herself to withstand it.

When she reclaimed her sense of calm, it freed her to hold on to the value of herself, a young woman full of potential, for whom labels gave false information. She was able to be more assertive in her university applications, and eventually she received good news: she had passed her exams and her place at university was confirmed. I was thrilled, and happy to hear the excitement in her voice as she told me, 'I feel finally something is moving forward. It's not just talk and emails and promises – something is actually going to happen which is good . . . I've waited years but my experience is not wasted. Now I will be in a better situation for my work . . . Everything is good. Today I'm a complex person. I do feel broken at times but I don't let it affect how my life is going. I cry but then I continue. I want to make a difference . . .'

I have no doubt she will.

Owen

Coming Out

Owen had just left university. Despite his beard, he looked even younger than his twenty-two years. He had chestnut-brown hair, which he flicked behind his ears with tanned, elegant hands that matched his slim frame. Clothed in well-fitting jeans, a shirt with a pop of colour at the collar and cuffs, and Birkenstock sandals, he looked as if he was about to go on holiday. He wore heavy-framed glasses, which didn't hide the deep brown eyes that looked at me with hope and uncertainty. Owen spoke quietly, with an accent that showed both his early Welsh and then American roots, following his father, an engineer, who had worked all over the world and lived in London now. He'd heard about me through a friend of his. I had no idea why he'd come.

Owen started hesitantly. He wasn't sure I could help him or whether talking would make any difference. I could feel myself gently moving towards him and him incrementally stepping away from me as I tried to connect with him. I had to sit on my instinct, which was to say what I felt he was doing. That might have shut him down or shamed him, I needed to step back and wait for him to move when he was ready. He took a breath, smiled and said, 'I had a pretty dreamy school life, in hindsight.'

I questioned whether life was a bit too real now. I could see him working out in his mind how much to say, and he told me he'd had a difficult time since he'd come out at university. Following this, he had begun to question everything, and started to feel uneasy and awkward around people who had previously been his bedrock. When he told me, 'This was the first time in my life I felt an outsider,' I experienced an involuntary shiver, the chill of his new loneliness.

Over the next few sessions a picture emerged of the schism in Owen's internal world. He'd been born into a loving family with two sisters. It was a heterosexual environment: there were no role models or important relationships with gay people with whom he could identify. He told me, 'I knew from a very small age that something was up, something was different. I remember being eight years old. We had moved back to London from the States and, most basically, I knew I found men attractive and not women.' What he saw on the outside and who he knew himself to be on the inside didn't match. 'My whole life was so great, apart from that, I immaturely thought, I can't be bothered, I'm not going to deal with that, and throughout school I didn't focus on it.'

We recognized together that, by not putting words to it, he

could suppress it. His reflex as a young boy, and all the way through school, was to be the same as his peers, and he added poignantly, 'When you are the same as everyone else you don't necessarily recognize it. It's only when you're not, you notice it.' He smiled as he looked back at his blissfully contented childhood and confident self, which had changed when he got to university.

But I wondered what the long-term cost to his sense of self and confidence would be in having denied such an integral part of himself during his key developmental years.

One of the many reasons for his build-up of anxiety was the nightmare of going out at night, realizing that the only thing his male friends went on about was 'how to get with a girl', and that the girls seemed to dress up for the single purpose of pulling. He dreaded the idea of having to get with a girl because he knew it wouldn't do anything for him. He'd got drunk or high to cover it up. 'I always knew it was there, but it wasn't until I was absolutely forced, kicking and screaming, that I came out. It built up like a pressure cooker. I remember being in my room at university, quite clinically realizing this unbelievable pressure was now worse than if I released it and am open.'

Owen went home to tell his parents he was gay, saying he had something really big to tell them. They looked frightened, as if he was going to tell them he had a life-threatening illness. They were surprised: they hadn't known it all along. They were, despite their shakiness, very supportive, wanting to understand how he felt, and reassuring him of their pride in and love for him. He was never teased or bullied for being gay by any friend or family member. Ironically, he had been teased for being gay before he came out because he didn't pull girls, but only because his friends were sure he wasn't. He softened as he remembered hearing his parents fight, whispering in shouty tones, over whose fault it was that he was gay, and had a tear of pride in his eyes at acknowledging they had to go through their own process of coming out as parents of a gay son and having to face their unconscious homophobia.

I could see him looking at me. I wondered what he was looking for. I sensed that our openness in talking about sex and sexuality was unsettling. 'When I did come out that pretty much changed my entire life. Not necessarily for the better. Of course for the better in the round, but my comfort blanket, my confidence, my sense of belonging were flicked away – because when you're being uneasy in your own skin it becomes self-perpetuating. I got very paranoid and anxious that people were seeing me differently.'

His worst critic was inside himself. His gay part felt uncomfortable to him, which meant he behaved awkwardly around it. He lived his discomfort before me: he didn't move around in his chair, it was in his eyes – they looked scared. There was an undercurrent of guilt, which seemed to pervade every corner of his life: guilt that he'd had a comfortable childhood, loving parents and a good education. Interestingly, the thing that soothed him was being gay: 'At least I've suffered with that,' he said, with relief, as he stroked his lower lip.

I could feel myself getting angry and combative, wanting to fight his guilt, wanting him to enjoy and take pleasure in the good things of his life. I reflected afterwards that perhaps the guilt was anger turned inward. Perhaps in hiding his sexuality for all those years, his inability to be completely honest with those he loved most blocked intimacy with them. Wasn't that more likely to be the source of his anger and guilt?

Owen had experimented with different ways of expressing himself as a gay man, both sexually and romantically, but hadn't yet found what he called his 'natural self'. He described what a hurdle it was to tell people that he was gay: quite often they didn't believe him and said, 'You're joking.' There was a girl at a party who'd really liked him and was gutted when he told her. I could feel Owen was pissed off too – it would have been so much easier if he'd been attracted to her.

It became clear that two parts of him clashed: the conventional part, which wanted to belong to the majority, and the gay part, which in some ways liked being different but didn't know how to live fully in its gay self. The two parts didn't converse. We shared a moment of meeting when I reflected back what I thought he felt: that being gay was really bloody complicated and not what he would have chosen, had he had a say. I had an image of a steel block dividing him in two: our work was to find a way to soften that block and allow both parts to integrate. It seemed the conventional aspect of him had matured, but the gay part hadn't been out and about, literally, so didn't yet know how to be gay socially or sexually.

We talked about the need for him to experiment and discover this new and emerging part of himself. He sighed as he said, 'When I fully accept who I am, and I've come to terms with my sexuality, I will be very glad for it. It will probably take being in a long and fruitful relationship.' This was thwarted by how difficult he found it to meet gay men he really liked: he'd tried Grindr and gay clubs but found them slightly sleazy. Part of him debated with me whether he needed to go abroad to discover the gay version of himself, but eventually came to the conclusion that he'd take his resistance with him. He needed to assimilate it before he lived abroad.

I asked Owen how the therapy was helping him. I didn't have a magic answer, and I acknowledged that at times I was a little intimidated by the power of his capacity to articulate himself, yet I couldn't really picture what was going on underneath. I could see that finding words for what had been unvoiced his whole life was therapeutic, but I wondered whether the steel block I'd envisaged was this articulation, and maybe his work was to allow himself to be messy, almost blobby. The words were useful but not if they armoured him against his feelings.

Owen didn't move, his brown eyes looking steadily into mine as he silently breathed in my words. He had enough internal strength to take them in. There was no need to speak. I guessed it would be something he would reflect on when by himself.

Owen's sexuality was not the only alien landscape he was confronting. He found the world of work, and living in London as an

adult, bewildering. He felt completely unprepared to face and deal
with adult working life. He had done some internships while at
university, but that didn't help to guide him through the maze of
employment agencies and application forms. Talking about this, I
saw his anger for the first time, how absurd it was that throughout
his school career he had had one rather inadequate day of careers
advice. Similarly, at university, the quality of the careers fair had
been abysmal. With friends, he'd had a debate about ambition,
what was meant by vocation. Generally, they felt they'd been
offered a false promise: 'Not only that once you get through all
the barriers of exams and university the world is your oyster, but
you have to find what makes you tick, your passion.' Owen was
furious at how unlikely that was. He understood why half of his
friends had gone back into education or travelled abroad to delay
the decision.

Having looked at all his options Owen decided accountancy
would give him the most flexibility in the future. Over the weeks,
I saw him struggle to find a position, how it shook his confidence
and raised his anxiety, not knowing whether he should come out
as gay in his interview, and when he didn't, he felt ashamed. It was
complex. While looking, he had part-time low-paid jobs in bars
and restaurants, which was better than doing nothing: unemployment raised his anxiety to intolerable levels. Finally, his persistence
paid off: following a gruelling interview process he was accepted
at a medium-sized accountancy firm. He loathed it. The people he
worked with were okay, but the daily grind of auditing, matching
numbers with invoices, pages and pages of figures was utterly
deadening. The loss of freedom was what got to him most, having
no choices, being told what to do every day, and the lack of holiday: that first year he was told he had only four days from January
to November, a brutal contrast to university life.

At university he'd felt he and his life were expanding. Now he
felt as if he was packed into a very tight train in a dark tunnel,
which was bleak and meaningless. He felt frustrated: as a perfectionist he wanted to do his best but he could never do the job

properly because of the short deadlines and lack of auditors. It meant his work was never rewarding, and he was working ten hours a day doing something 'I don't give a shit about'. He woke every morning with a sense of dread. He felt when dressing in his suit that he was putting on a costume and found himself screaming out loud, while on a run, 'What the fuck?' many times over. He'd kick the fridge a lot. But then he'd feel ashamed of himself: he should grow up, he'd signed up to do this, and he had to complete it. He lived at home, he couldn't afford to move yet, which was claustrophobic after the freedom of university. Owen knew it was coming from him, but everyone irritated him, and his mother clucking around, trying to feed him and cheer him up, drove him nuts.

Owen was a deep thinker, and I was moved by his capacity to reflect on himself. The one thing he liked about doing accountancy was that it gave him an answer to the repeated question 'What are you doing?' It gave him security, and a goal to work towards; he had hated not knowing. What he couldn't fully clarify in himself was whether he had given up on the dream of finding work he was passionate about, or whether this would enable him eventually to do so. He didn't know whether he'd sloughed off the skin of being a child, and now had to step into being a working adult. It was a difficult transition, as to whether he had just cut off an important part of himself. Through talking, he realized part of his hatred for the job was having the responsibilities and life of an adult: it felt like a prison sentence. Even acknowledging that freed him to breathe a little easier.

We managed to work out that eventually he wanted his job to have a creative element, and maybe he could combine that with his accountancy in the future. If, as we discussed, this was the first step into a long and multi-stage life, it could give the others secure foundations. He knew he was hungry for experiences, for variety: when he was fifty he wanted to look back on having lived a full life. Strangely, that gave him hope that he could manage this bleak phase.

Unusually for me, I pushed Owen to talk to me more about dating. He didn't like it. He changed the subject and would go back to talking about how much he hated work. But I felt the chicken-and-egg bind he'd got himself into: he wouldn't be happy with his identity until he was having a sexual relationship with someone he liked, this being blocked by his wall of resistance to it. He got quite cross with me, wanting me to understand how difficult it was: only 3 per cent of the population was openly gay (2 per cent outside London), and he met very few gay men in his friendship group. He was tired: the idea of going out on some clunky date with someone he didn't know, rather than meeting his mates, didn't inspire him. I acknowledged that, but pushed back a little, not too much. I didn't want to shut him down – but suggested that unless he made a decision, and got active in meeting someone, it was less likely to happen. He nodded rather glumly. Finally he agreed there would be a tipping point in him, similar to when he'd come out, that his longing to have a relationship, someone to share his life with, would outweigh his resistance, and then he would put in the time and effort. This felt an important shift to me.

We explored both the stereotype and the reality of the gay community in London: bi and gay men having random sex with random others, the binge-and-purge aspect of it, when men would totally lose control, then wrench it back. Owen had had some experience of that: there was an element of self-loathing in the lack of intimacy, which we both found painful and fed into homophobia, which was equally painful. But there was also a freedom, fun and richness to it, which was exciting. It was full of possibility and free of outdated views. Owen felt that wasn't what he wanted. He spoke quietly, his head down. He told me he'd sat on a bus with Grindr on, and the whole journey home he was fired with hot messages. He could have got off the bus at any point and met someone. But he knew that instant gratification would swiftly be followed by a sense of emptiness.

Owen wanted a loving intimate relationship. He fundamentally believed that love was what life was all about – and he knew there were gay men who had loving family relationships. The only role model we could both think of was Elton John, which probably reflected our lack of openness. He acknowledged that if you were gay, London was the best place to be – I suggested he join gay communities, not go to clubs or on dating apps, but communities that shared his interests – design, art, photography. He nodded blithely.

Owen had a friend, who'd become very spiritual and was now a yoga and meditation teacher. He inspired Owen in the way that he lived in the moment, was grateful for his day, and seemed at peace. It was a little like the diner scene in *When Harry Met Sally*: he knew he wanted some of that for himself, and he started meditating. It was tough, and he hated it at times, couldn't do it, felt frustrated, but there were moments when he felt at peace. He could feel that at times it flushed out his internalized shame, the poison, and he was calmer.

I felt a deep fondness for Owen. I knew we had built a good working relationship. But on reflection, I wondered if I, at this point in his development, was the right therapist for him. Being a heterosexual woman, I was a mirror image of his experience with his family and played into all his prejudices. I suggested to Owen that he see a gay male therapist. He wanted time to think about it. He sent me a few text messages, wanting to know whom I'd recommend, and needing further explanation as to why I'd suggested it.

In our session I told him I had no intention of rejecting him. He'd learned the value of talking and being heard: now he had an opportunity to get that with someone who could offer a gay male perspective. I told him about my colleague, whom I rated very highly. I guessed it would be both illuminating and liberating. Owen agreed to have a few sessions with him. Due to our code of confidentiality I have no idea how it went, and I long to know. Often he pops into my mind. I hope he is more at peace with who he finds himself to be. I hope he has found love.

KT

Beyond the Binary

My ongoing commitment to myself is to keep learning. If I don't step beyond my familiar environment, and out of my comfort zone, I would be the living embodiment of the very thing I encourage my clients not to be: stuck. Or, even worse, come to think I'm always right. The age of digital technology has opened up the world for me in a way that is transformative: not only can I learn from the best psychotherapy experts in the world while I'm sitting at home, but by using Skype and FaceTime I have extended my reach to people I could never have worked with before. Now that I am no longer constrained to be physically in the same room as a client, I can work with people from Australia to China and everywhere in between. London, as multicultural as it is, is a bubble. When working with people based outside it, hearing new perspectives and ways of being, I can actually feel the richness bubbling inside me. I'm aware of the snap of new neural pathways firing up, energizing me to want to know more, building creativity and a depth of flexibility in how I view the world. For me it has extended not only my geographical reach but my understanding of who we are as humans.

With this in mind, my awareness that I was excluding a whole section of society, the Lesbian Gay Bisexual Transgender Queer (LGBTQ+) community, felt increasingly uncomfortable: I had been working principally with people who identified as heterosexual. Since the LGBTQ community weren't coming to me for therapy, I needed to be active in reaching them. I put a notice on an LGBTQ+ website offering counselling.

KT responded straight away and told me they lived in the north of England. Our sessions would therefore be online.

As I write about KT, who identifies as gender nonconforming, I will be using they/them pronouns instead of the binary pronouns he/him/his and she/her/hers. It feels clunky and awkward initially, which perhaps represents how unfamiliar KT's world is to me. In Sweden there is a specific word for a gender-neutral pronoun, which is more elegant: *hen* is the alternative to the gender-specific *hon* and *han*. Or is that my leaning towards making gender identity neat and tidy, when it is infinitely complex and particularly seeks not to be tidied behind fixed boundaries and boxes?

For our first few sessions I didn't see KT's face: we communicated via Skype audio. The reason for this was internet-related, not because either of us wished it. As it turned out, it influenced the quality of our relationship. When I first spoke with KT I immediately felt at home in their world, although I could only know them from their words and their tone of voice. It gave KT the necessary protection they needed to build trust with me, without the exposure of me looking at them and making the inevitable assumptions one makes when looking at someone's face as we seek visual cues. I could hear in KT's voice a tentativeness, in how they chose their words, the space between words, a deep layer of trepidation, although it would take some time for me to find its source.

KT contacted me telling me it was perfect timing for them, because they wanted to explore gender identity, and their sexual orientation. 'I've known I wasn't straight from a young age, and I've been getting through life, maybe too lazy, thinking this gender thing doesn't matter, but I probably should be thinking about it more . . . when it comes to dating. I want to know who I am, be myself and not hide anything.' I reflected that KT was wise, in knowing they needed to understand themselves before they could form an attachment with someone else, and it also felt like a quest to know where KT fitted in.

Before we went further I told KT this area of gender identity was new to me, to the extent that when I trained it wasn't even on the curriculum. I had recently done some further learning but still asked that they tell me directly if I said anything that upset them through my ignorance. I wanted to be sure that there was a straightforward honesty from our first encounter. It was of key importance for me to protect KT from experiencing with me the prejudice and ignorance they had to deal with on a daily basis. What I was confident about was that I could offer KT a non-judgemental empathic relationship. I knew how to build trust.

I learned more about their history. KT's family comprised their younger brother and their parents. Due to their father's job, throughout their childhood they had moved every few years around the world, from West Africa and South-East Asia to Europe. By the time KT was twenty-one they had lived in twenty-two different homes. KT told me it meant they could 'settle anywhere but struggled to put down roots'. Consequently, KT had only one friendship that had lasted since their childhood, and that was intermittent, speaking twice a year by Skype. 'I have a lot of friends but no very close friends – I know a lot of people but not many people really know me.' When KT was eleven years old, they had formed some close friendships, but then had to move, telling me, 'I felt I lost my life.'

It was a pivotal experience. As a way of coping, in their next school KT reinvented themselves from the quiet one to standing on the stage and making speeches. They soon became head of the school council. KT felt released from the pain into a stronger person, sloughing off their previous identity. But from then on KT found it difficult to trust people, as KT assumed, correctly, their family would be moving on and, once they'd left, the friendship would be over. It meant KT had cut off and consequently didn't form close attachments.

As KT spoke I felt the slicing of that cut inside me, remembering how friendship had been a cornerstone of my childhood, the years of time and memories that had built a solid base I could rely on. I reflected that what had formed in KT as a necessary coping mechanism had developed into an embedded attitude towards the world, of being high-functioning on the outside but not feeling much. And others encouraged this disposition, since working hard and keeping it together were useful for everyone else.

KT thought for a long time, sighed deeply and spoke quietly:

'It brings a sense of loneliness . . . *big sigh* . . . but also security knowing I'm not cutting off from much . . . preparing myself to move on.' KT voiced in that sentence their dilemma: loving is risky, but a life without love is lonely. There was also a dissonance between the KT who was successful at work, and the wound they were carrying internally, which was blocking KT from forming close relationships. Part of our therapy would be to get the two parts to integrate.

KT's job was as an ecological field worker, which meant long hours, often in bad weather conditions, all night, while studying the habitat of animals in their environment. A couple of evenings a week they volunteered with a group of troubled youths. KT, as many of their generation, felt the pain of the world's inequalities, poverty and suffering, and wanted to fight against it. Images, stories and live streams of global cruelty and trauma were pouring into their phone, which saturated their life and filled their mind. It brought with it anxiety about the lack of safety in the world, and how uncertain their future was. They told me, 'I measure myself by the work I do, and its impact on others.' I felt a real respect for their high-mindedness, and empathy that their future seemed very challenging. I also felt a pang of loss for their lack of innocent joy as a young person. The blissful ignorance of youth that feels immortal, full of hope and has fun seemed to have passed them by.

As KT began to open up more, I heard about the two immensely damaging sexual relationships they'd had. The first one was the most abusive. I could feel the raw pain in KT as they told me about it: there were big gaps between words. They struggled to find the language for what they didn't want to remember, yet knew they had to come to terms with it if they were to have another relationship. It had lasted two years when KT was aged between seventeen and nineteen. It had been abusive emotionally and physically: he had lied, sexually assaulted them and manipulated them into staying in the relationship by threatening suicide. KT had reported the assault to the police; it was not followed up.

I went numb as I heard KT's words, though I guessed that beneath the numbness was rage. There was too much to feel. Perhaps because of that, or intuitively, I felt it wasn't the right time to go deeper into it – though I knew that we would need to revisit it many times, and at depth. It had taken immense courage for KT to tell me what had happened. They hadn't fully voiced the fact that he'd assaulted them ever before – not even to their mum, to whom they were close. That first relationship with someone is formative, and shapes our sense of self as an adult, as a sexual being and, as far as I had known, our sense of identity as a man or a woman. The implications for KT would need to be fully explored if they were to heal.

KT then spoke with more force, as if their story had been waiting to be told with a momentum of its own, fighting to be voiced. KT's second relationship, which had started a few months later, had been going well, KT had thought, until nine months in he 'ghosted' them. He completely disappeared. KT had been frantic trying to find him. As they searched they were panicked, and then, as they realized he'd deliberately disappeared from their life, they were furiously angry. Then KT cut off, tried not to think about it: it was too painful, all the not-knowing gave them multiple scenarios of what might have led to it – the imagination is limitless and often tends to be worse than the reality.

I recognized that a version of ghosting had always happened, but it seemed more frequent now. It seemed more brutal too, when there were countless ways to make contact without seeing someone – it was incomprehensible to me that someone wouldn't say goodbye. How relationships end, as with how people die, has a huge impact on the partners' capacity to recover. There are definitely good and bad endings. For KT the impact was that they hadn't had a relationship with anyone for four years.

I felt angry, the quiet anger that sits and stews. I didn't even recognize it as anger – but knew the signal: if I want to retreat and not speak it's usually because I've got that low-level anger. Most likely it was transferred into me from KT but intensified by connecting to my own experience. I didn't speak for what seemed a long time. Then I swore: 'What a complete fucker.' Sometimes a short, sharp profanity does the business, more empathic than long-winded responses. Then I found myself leaning towards KT and saying simply, 'I'm profoundly sorry this happened to you. It shouldn't have. You need to let yourself know this is not about you, this is his stuff.' KT cried, quiet tears. Cleansing tears. Their story was out, no more holding it inside with shame. I'd heard it, and I moved towards KT, wanting them to know they were no longer alone with this.

As I understood KT from their brief history, it seemed to me KT's default position was not to trust, the world felt unsafe, and as a result many of their issues centred around power. Since the power dynamic between us was unequal – I held more power as the one who listened and didn't reveal myself – I wanted to be sure that we had equal power. There were the further external markers of power: I was considerably older than KT's twenty-four years. My experience in life was as part of the majority: white, heterosexual, married. I had never known what it was like to live in a minority, to feel the sting of prejudice or be excluded. It meant I wanted to be vigilant in not making assumptions. Neither did I want to be the one to push KT's process: I wanted KT to go at their own pace. I wanted to understand them. I didn't have an agenda, or a place I wanted to get to. I felt that the more KT could own their power in our relationship, the more they could learn to hold it internally, and then externally, while engaging with those around them.

I was speaking at length, too much, and KT cut through it all: 'But I trust you.' The fragility of KT's voice when they had spoken before, versus the confidence in KT's words in that moment, went straight into my heart. KT's raw vulnerability elicited a pull in me: I wanted to match that rawness with my own authenticity.

I wanted to get a broader picture of where KT could access support. I was glad to learn that their family was '100 per cent on board'. Their mother was positively active about KT being bi. She had also researched gender identity, and even asked for clarity around terms like 'gender neutral'. I could hear the pride in KT's voice that their parents were unusual in this, much more open-minded than many of their peers, which was warming. KT hadn't come out as non-binary or asexual as yet, although they knew in theory their mum would be okay with it. KT felt it was a bit of a jump at present. Their mum used sensitive language, like 'my child', not 'my daughter/son' and 'lovely person', rather than 'lovely girl/boy'. KT's dad didn't engage with anything very much, although he asked a few soulful questions. He wasn't critical, 'it just wasn't his thing,' which didn't seem to upset KT, more an acceptance of their father's personality.

KT felt their mum had learned a lot from seeing many different cultures, which had opened her mind to be less rigid. When their mum was younger she'd devotedly followed the Christian doctrine: they had driven miles to go to church every Sunday, wherever they lived. Now KT's mum challenged the Church on many issues, including gender identity and sexual orientation.

Finally, our broadband was restored, and I could see KT. It didn't bring the extra depth of connection I had expected. By this point I felt our alliance was deep and I had made pictures in my mind from KT's narrative. It meant I attuned mind to mind rather than face to face. It had succeeded in slowing me down, being more careful in my choice of words, listening with greater intensity. It meant I felt I was more accurate in seeing KT from the inside.

Reading my client's face is my go-to way of being, as it is with all of us: our brain uses assumptions about looks as a shortcut to see if there is love, hate, danger or safety. When I saw KT, they matched my internal picture: slicked-back black hair, elegantly cut, a contrast to their pale flawless skin and hazel eyes. KT dressed in dark trousers and checked shirt, which didn't manage to conceal their tiny waist and full chest. KT's figure was a classic 1950s hour-glass. It was their nails that demanded attention: they were bright green. KT told me, 'The colour was a bit weird, so I liked it.' But seeing KT's body language was helpful: when they spoke they pulled at the edge of the chair, systematically and rhythmically at the corner, leaning slightly forward. KT shifted their attention and examined a mark on their trousers and rubbed it, as if looking and rubbing would magically make it vanish. I couldn't know what it meant as yet, but I clocked KT's need to self-soothe: it was most likely anxiety . . . I wondered if there was something about KT knowing all of their internal world which at present didn't match their outside image.

KT had applied for various ecology jobs, in different cities. Over a number of sessions, we examined what their need for a new job was about. It gave us insight into KT's opposing internal forces. KT had lived in York for the last six years, which was twice as long as they had ever lived anywhere. There was an itch to move for 'new life, new friends, new energy . . . When people have known you for a while they have expectations of what you're like. When I move I play around with who I am, and what I'm like . . . I've been the same person for years and I want to break out of that a little bit.' I wondered what KT was breaking out from now. KT felt that 'moving away lifts a weight', which I understood to mean that when there was a part KT didn't like, KT could reinvent themselves elsewhere and feel lighter. 'Part of it is gender identity. I want to get more into the LGBTQ+ community, build more meaningful relationships with people. Here I'm limited, it's a small community . . . and when I broke up with my first boyfriend, Joe, I cut off from a lot of friends.'

Interestingly, at the point KT was thinking of moving, a close friendship, the very thing KT said they longed for, was developing with an ex-colleague. This person had been their boss and mentor but had left. Prior to KT's interview for a new job she had taken the time to give KT a pep talk, telling them how much they were valued. KT had cried with her. This wasn't something KT did: it was an entirely new experience. But it also shook them: 'I've never really felt vulnerable like that before.' I could see tears in KT's eyes. Recalling the memory had reignited the depth of the feeling. We both felt it showed KT was longing for connection, to be known, and be liked for what was seen – their friend believed in KT and knew KT had potential. It meant KT didn't have to put on their armour. Nor had KT sought this new connection: 'It happened without me realizing.' What had particularly touched KT was that their boss had left but 'she hadn't forgotten me, the realization that she had moved away, but it wasn't the end, she remembered me, I was still in her mind . . .' Which was the reverse of what KT did in their own life: 'That's it, the friendship is over.' KT knew how to travel, how to keep moving, and certainly knew how to arrive, but didn't know how to fully connect with someone: that was a major theme.

I was silent for a while, not because I didn't have words, more because I felt the depth of KT's sadness, the quantity of losses that were heaped together in their life, throughout their life. I felt in my breastbone, going all the way up to my chin, piles of stacked-up grief: KT's loss of places, homes, friends, schools, all blocking their openness. KT, of course, had researched this, the 'third-culture kid' phenomenon: someone who spent their formative years in a culture they weren't born into, didn't identify with the local culture, and then sourced identity through their family. Lost friendships created suspended grief; the multiple losses meant the person couldn't grieve for them properly. They're what I call 'living losses'.

I asked KT what they were feeling in their body. 'I don't know, I guess it feels heavy. I haven't spoken about everything before, and I've said so much, we've spoken about so much, but you are the only one I've told. It feels good to talk about it . . . actually a bit scary, a bit exposing and a bit phew . . .'

KT didn't succeed in getting the job. They felt it had been a useful experience and they'd been given good feedback. It brought back the debate for us as to whether KT's need to move geographically was a reflex: was the itchiness of never staying anywhere too long a habit, or was it what was best for them? KT reiterated,

'I feel a bit trapped here – doing the same job, same town. It gets a bit boring . . . I want to learn a bit more about myself. Moving is an opportunity to change.' I reflected that people who are distressed yearn for the relief of boredom, and when people were bored it was often a defence to block the true feelings beneath.

KT looked startled, realizing that being an outsider was the position they wanted to change. 'I don't ever think to initiate contact. As a child I complained to Mum, "They won't play with me." I didn't initiate the play, then if they did, I'd insist on playing my game . . .' The habit of needing control had early roots. As KT recognized this, they wondered whether they were more a prisoner of their own painful thoughts than actually of being trapped in York. I questioned whether staying in the same place would give them the opportunity to expand internally, when they didn't have to grapple with finding their way round a new city, new job, new friends. KT responded, 'Can I stay here, get growth and broaden my world? If I did that, it would be something very different to what I've always done . . . I don't need to grow the number of people in my life, but I struggle with depth of relationships. I have none to stay for.' I felt the icy wind of KT's loneliness.

It led KT to acknowledge that they had started looking for a new romantic relationship. They'd tried all the dating apps, met a few people, but once they got past a certain point, KT withdrew. 'I go on a date then I don't answer messages. I get the feeling they're being overbearing, too clingy. Then I disengage – cut them off.' Internally I clocked it was an echo of what had been done to KT and was wondering whether it was appropriate to voice it as yet. KT voiced it for me and acknowledged how frustrating it was: they wanted a new relationship but, when faced with the prospect, couldn't quite put the effort in: 'The risk of the relationship not working out . . .' KT leaned forward, rubbed their nails, spoke slowly, discovering the meaning of their words as they came out of their mouth: 'I don't want to open up to someone and rely on them . . . in case it comes back and bites me . . . and they leave.'

I asked KT what happened in their body: it felt heavy, tight in their chest and shoulders. KT shivered. I asked KT to breathe and go into their body. On closing their eyes, they focused and saw a black space, then the image of Joe. He was the worst. He was the only person KT had ever been really open with. When KT was vulnerable Joe would say he couldn't deal with it, invalidate their emotions and shut KT down, then make it about him. It stopped KT ever saying what they felt. The second boyfriend KT hadn't really trusted, but his disappearance reinforced KT's belief that people generally couldn't be trusted and left.

I was aware that a bad experience sticks like Velcro in the brain for good evolutionary reasons, to protect us from that kind of bad happening again, but it was by no means always helpful. It needed to be processed and released in order to allow the new good feelings to grow. We both saw how those two boyfriends had deeply injured KT. I asked KT what they wanted to be different. 'I would like to be able to let people in, find the right people to trust in. Often for people coming out is their big step. For me it pales in comparison to being emotionally open and vulnerable.'

We explored how openly showing what you feel, however untidy, is how we can connect truthfully. We laughed as KT talked about 'radical vulnerability'. I'd never heard of it, but that 'radical' intensity of sharing and being open was on brand. When KT saw people on Facebook being open, they admired it and wished they could do it, but 'I don't want to burden people, don't want to open up to people. If I do, they leave.' As KT spoke, their voice slowed again. Their hands pressed on to their eyes. I checked if they were crying. They were. I quietly said they were being vulnerable with me. KT agreed while wiping away their tears.

As our work continued I realized I wanted clarification about KT's gender identity, wondering how KT would describe themselves on the inside. They told me, 'I'm bisexual and my gender identity is non-binary. In the broadest sense, I'm not a man or a woman. And I lean more towards asexual. I don't have sexual attraction. Desiring sex is absent or infrequent. It's more to do with the emotional connection.' Which led me to be curious as to how their sexual orientation operated, knowing that their previous sexual relationships had been with men. 'I'm looking for either gender, who I get on with – sex isn't at the forefront when I'm thinking about a relationship. Sex would be an added bonus. It comes after everything else . . . For friends of mine, sex is one of the first things they go to.' I reflected my understanding in life, up to this point, was that sex was often the catalyst for the initial attraction between two people: liking the look of someone, being drawn towards them, talking, spending longer time together, then the first physical contact, often a kiss, either led eventually to sex, or not.

KT clarified it wasn't that they didn't want sex, but it came later, which was often frustrating because people wanted sex immediately. This was a sensitive area, one I was new to. In order to respond to KT while bringing in my thinking, I wanted my response to be accurate. 'I want to say it back to you, and check my understanding – your relationship with yourself is important. Your gender identity is non-binary, neither male nor female, and that is how you want to be treated when you are dating. Being asexual, you are looking for ways of connecting with the qualities of that person and that is your route to forming a relationship. The most common one, the fast-track one, is through sexual attraction. What I'm thinking, and maybe this is wrong, so put me right, in some ways being able to choose a man or woman gives you lots of options, but finding someone who has the same perceptions as you, who wants the same kind of relationship as you, narrows down the field. In a practical way, is it harder to find someone? Does it limit your choices?'

KT agreed that dating was generally a nightmare. Not only did people want to have sex but their views 'are inherently sexist, misogynistic, and navigating a world where men are used to dating a certain way. They see me as a woman and expect me to behave a certain way when dating.' I could hear KT's frustration and wondered whether their style of dress, which was mainly from the men's section, didn't fit with their body shape and meant they were seen as a woman which they particularly didn't want. I could hear KT's anger: the mismatch of how they saw themselves yet were seen as a woman in the street; how patronized they felt at being called 'lovey', 'darling', 'miss', 'lovely lady'. 'Men holding the door for me. I don't identify with that.' Even when volunteering, when KT asked for the plural pronoun to be used, it wasn't always taken seriously.

I had a moment of clarity through the twists and turns of dating and pronouns, which I wanted to try out with KT. They were navigating new and uncharted territory to manage the daily challenges of how they saw themselves versus how they were seen, which required a certain robustness. Romantic relationships felt new territory as well. KT had traversed many continents, spent their whole life travelling: wasn't KT now doing what they'd always done, but doing it psychologically? KT's response was, 'I might want to move because it's hard work looking in. A new place might be a relief from myself. While I'm itching to travel, I want to stay here, spend time on myself, stick with it for a while.' It seemed a real shift. An important revelation.

We had a wobble. I had forgotten to tell KT I was going on holiday. When I told them, I heard their voice recede, and in that moment make a dash for the exit. I had done what they feared. The one thing I had intended not to do. I acknowledged my mistake and did my best to reassure them I would be back, and that we would work together for as long as it took. KT seemed placated but cancelled the next two sessions: one for work reasons and the other a migraine. It was my responsibility to repair the rupture openly and honestly, and vital to us going forward. KT would have to be able to tell me how angry they were with me, how let down they felt. I had to allow those feelings and then be present, not reject them. As bad as I felt for the rupture, I knew it was inevitable in all relationships, and it is the capacity to repair that builds trust, not perfection.

After the summer I emailed to recommence our therapy and

heard no response. I felt as if they'd disappeared on me with no explanation and no goodbye. I thought perhaps I had lost KT and I felt ghosted. I felt the anxiety of it, the obsessive seeking and wondering and not finding. A few weeks later, which felt longer, I was immensely relieved when KT did text me. I explained my process and KT apologized profusely for being rude: there had been multiple issues at work and KT had forgotten me. I was curious to discover if anything else was going on but KT was not interested in looking at any unconscious processes, and our work continued with no further ruptures.

I had discussed KT with my supervisor and out of the blue she had asked me what KT's relationship to their body was like. I took the question to KT who answered: 'I don't have a relationship with my body. I try to disengage from it. I'm not happy or particularly unhappy with any part of it . . . I have a resigned acceptance of it.' They crossed their arms firmly as they spoke. I felt 'ouch': that was a tough response to their body.

The reason was many-layered. KT had grown tall young, and got their period at nine, much younger than their peers. Being different meant KT drew apart from their peers. It hadn't totally freaked KT out, but it had felt complicated. 'It felt as if my body was working against me.' KT had loved running around with no clothes on, and that had stopped immediately. When buying clothes, they'd never liked the girls' section and always gone for tomboyish clothes. Putting their head to one side as they recalled, KT had never thought they weren't a girl, as it hadn't crossed their mind as a possibility. But KT felt from then on they were never able to wear the clothes they wanted to wear, because their body shape of tiny waist, full hips and large breasts didn't fit easily in men's clothes. From that day their body image felt off kilter. They would have liked to be more straight up and down, less curvy. Sometimes KT wore sports bras to flatten their chest, and knew people who bound their chest, but didn't go that far. But when KT looked in the mirror they didn't like what they saw.

I questioned whether that linked to KT's asexuality: was there a disconnect? Were they stopping themselves having a sexual relationship? KT didn't move, looked up. 'You've hit the nail on the head.' KT's first boyfriend had punished KT when they'd initiated sex: 'He made me feel terrible for wanting sex – he would instigate things and if I reciprocated he'd accuse me of rape.'

By this point in the drama triangle of persecutor-victim-rescuer, KT moved between rescuer and victim and never found their voice to speak up for themselves. KT had never had an orgasm with another person, or even felt pleasure with another person, only alone. The damage had sat in their body in the subsequent years, too painful to go near. KT had given up on it. I challenged KT that perhaps they weren't asexual but simply had had damaging sex.

KT was silent, nodded, and then laughed. And cried. Then KT was deep in thought, pulling at the chair. 'I lean towards being asexual, but I am not 100 per cent sure if it's to do with my disconnect with my body.' I asked KT what was happening in their body. They said it was 'tense', then told me they had to go. They'd had enough for now. The revelation was scary for KT, as well as offering possible new directions. We had done an important piece of work, uncovered the terrible legacy of that destructive man.

KT had made the decision to stay in York: 'I can put down roots. I can focus on doing things long term, without fear of thinking every few months it will change, and life won't exist any more . . . Staying feels like change, spending time on myself, and my friendships and not being in survival mode. I'm committed to working on not being an outsider.' It seemed to release new energy in KT. They were given a new and exciting project at work, which built their confidence as a professional who was competent in their field. They were having conversations they'd never had before. 'I've pushed myself to be more open with people – after last week I had a friend help me with the presentation to get that project – the first time I've ever done that. Normally it's me being there for other people, not this way round. It felt really good.' I felt a beam of pride in KT for daring to take the risk.

KT began talking more about their gender identity and how it was evolving. KT had been interested in non-binary four years ago with their boyfriend. Being him, he'd invalidated KT's experience and consequently KT had repressed it. KT could remember the exact moment when their gender identity emerged more clearly. KT was on the phone to a good friend and he'd called them 'woman'. 'Something in that moment made me feel really strange, nothing I'd experienced before. I wasn't expecting to feel that way, but I knew he wasn't right – I felt, who is he talking about? He's not talking about me. It threw me.' In fact, it kicked off a process that awakened KT to dare to discover their gender identity.

We spent a lot of time testing KT's inner voice and how that related to the outside world. 'Being non-binary is confusing. The world tells you you are A or B, and the world is geared that way. From the toilets, to forms, to birthday cards, I am constantly fighting what society is telling me . . . It is difficult having confidence in my identity, and I know my doubts come from wanting to fit in.' We went back and forth with this dilemma, and through an incremental process of owning and allowing their internal promptings to align with how they described themselves, it was clear KT was non-binary. They did not see themselves as either a man or a woman. 'I look at both sexes and fit in a little bit in both of them – I don't want stereotyped perceptions, assumptions made of me. I hate that. I hate the distinct different male/female responses. That is not me.' KT became clearer that they absolutely did not fit in a neat gender box: they wanted to find their own path and way of being as non-binary.

Although KT had wondered if the questions were undermining, it emerged that 'questioning' the Q from LGBTQ+, alongside 'queer', was a key part of discovering who they were. Each time KT checked, they found their own answer, 'This is me', 'Oh, and this is me', until it became consistent and clear. 'I'm listening to my doubts less. I'm more able to ignore them. The more I come out to people and they accept me and correct themselves using pronouns, and listen to me, the more confident I get in myself, the more I listen to myself.' I was witnessing change, that messy, tricky thing, as it happened before me.

On hearing how dating through apps was 'a nightmare', I felt for KT. When KT would say they wanted to get to know someone with the intention of a long-term relationship, they were met with silence. Men were looking for sex: 'It's demoralizing. I've lost interest in it. It's humiliating too – there is an entire cohort of men who ignore my gender identity and call me "baby", "love", and just want sex. The internet allows people to be sexually explicit in a way they never would be face to face – and it allows them to let you down without feeling they're letting you down. I send a message and people don't reply, or they lie.' We agreed that KT should change tack and meet people in real time.

Within weeks, despite being full of fear, KT took a deep breath, overcame the fear, joined a walking club and signed up with a friend for a speed-dating night. And told me proudly, 'I'm getting out there.' I felt excited for the possibilities their future now held.

As the weeks passed, we were both aware that KT was growing in confidence, increasingly connected to their internal world and, importantly, an integrated sense of themselves as a whole: their vulnerability, strengths, weaknesses, talents and, of course, their gender identity. KT was giving themselves time and attention. Having spoken about their body awakened KT to choose to do things they enjoyed, to befriend their body and get fitter. The damage caused by Joe was no longer a raw wound: 'I'm okay with what happened with him. I barely think about him now. I've reconciled what happened, looked at it objectively. There are some things I will take responsibility for, but a lot of it was not my fault. For the most part, a lot of the things that happened he manipulated, he created the situation. It was all on him and whatever he was going through. I know it was unacceptable.'

Music to my ears. KT had reframed the whole experience to fit more accurately with its truth, and in the process allowed it to heal. It freed KT to dare to build closer and more open friendships, which felt meaningful and satisfying, though still bumpy at times – it is always risky. 'I'm really investing in relationships. I knew it on paper, but now I'm putting it into practice and I'm not being held back – I'm living what I instinctively knew. Having a clear sense of myself is a big part of that. I'm clear I'm non-binary. There's work to be done as to whether I'm asexual or not. Having stability and staying put for a while will help. I have given myself that time to find out.'

Our work together was, for now, complete. I have been fortunate to receive an update from KT: they are happy, their work is going well, and they are dating.

Reflections on Identity

A personal point

I agree with Reni Eddo-Lodge, a Nigerian-British journalist and author: 'Britain is still profoundly uncomfortable with race and difference.' For that reason, although I have not needed to own my personal circumstances in any other section of this book, I found I could not write about identity without acknowledging where I come from. As someone who was born into the dominant culture, and whose way of living aligns with the majority, I have an innate sense of belonging – how I feel, who I am, how I live is to me 'normal'. It has meant in the area of my identity I have navigated through the world easily. I've had the privilege of not having had to wrestle with identity. When I became a therapist, identity was not on my radar, ignorance that would not have been possible if I had been born into different circumstances. Even as a therapist my training included race, class (minimally) and sexual identity, but there was nothing about gender or religion. Despite my best efforts, it may mean I miss the sensitivities, nuances and life experience of those who've come from a minority.

When we ask ourselves, 'Who am I?' it is often through identity that we find our answers. I believe identity is the foundation on which we build a life. I define identity as being made up of a series of building blocks. Ideally those foundations support self-esteem and confidence. Some of the building blocks are fixed, like our race. Others can remain fixed or develop over time, like our sexuality, and yet others change over the lifespan through the roles we have at work, in love and life. Part of our identity is formed from our parents, peers and other role models, and our developmental task as we grow through life is to align them with who we find ourselves to be. Through the choices we make, our identity expresses our values and beliefs. The crucial understanding is that within each building block is the basic need to be loved and to belong. If that need is not met, it leads to fear of rejection by family or society, which causes profound distress.

Identity is complex and hard to pin down. We can all hold multiple identities and multiple selves at the same time: for instance, we can be British, a Catholic, a scientist, a mother, a single parent, and feel and even behave slightly differently when we are in those different roles. As we progress through life and change happens to us, there is always an adjustment to be made in our identity. The changes can be simple or complex: examples include becoming a husband or wife, changing political persuasion, changing gender, moving social class or migrating to another country. Identity is at the heart of change, and it is where some of the difficulties around change reside. We may fear that being who we are now will mean we won't be loved any more. We may resist change for it may put under threat our sense of power and status.

Coming out as gay, like Owen, for example, may expose a sense of vulnerability as a man, and the isolation of being in a minority. We may even be in denial for a long time, when what feels true to embrace in ourselves is not socially accepted. We resist it for it means going from the known to the unknown, from safety to danger. Eventually we may no longer stay in denial when the pain it induces is greater than the fear of the danger.

In our innate need as human beings to belong, we tend to see difference as a threat, usually through ignorance about the other. This can create internal conflict within the self, or external conflict between people with different identities. It is only through compassionate dialogue, when difference is examined and greater understanding is opened up, that we see there is more that binds us than separates us. Part of the challenge for those who are born with an identity that is at odds with society as a whole, like Owen, Sara and KT, is how to be fully themselves, given they cannot always change the judgement of others. They may also have internalized shame, when the culture they've grown up in is a shaming culture.

My focus through their stories is to illustrate this complexity. How their sense of gender, race, sexual and cultural identities impacted their lives through the process of change – how they saw themselves was at odds with how they were seen by others. Their context played a central part in their empowerment to transition successfully into their new identity. Owen and KT were broadly in an empathic environment, which supported their change. Sara, who did not have a supportive family on hand, had to fight for her empowerment: she had to learn a new language, access education, learn skills to earn money and be extremely adaptable to fulfil her dreams. Through them we see that being confident in their sense of identity was fundamental to how they operated in their world. While they were at odds with it, it undermined their wellbeing and capacity to engage in their life.

As children, as well as adults across the lifespan, we learn the rules of embracing our identities, which aspects are approved and those that are forbidden or hidden from our family, community and cultural context. Never underestimate the power of those messages, which are transmitted before the child has language or the opportunity to question or make sense of them. These rules are learned implicitly and explicitly. Key issues often arise for those who choose to act against their traditional family, community and cultural identity, when they fear they will no longer be loved or have a sense of belonging.

Identity is an issue of increasing importance within our society: it can cause conflict for those whose lived experience is imbued with prejudice. Some of those who have not been given a voice fight for it, and through them our understanding grows – or we refuse to listen. Through research, my aim is to illuminate the issues that arise psychologically through identity, and in doing so expand our understanding.

Identity and Evolution

Reza Ziai, an American psychology professor, explains through evolutionary science that the reason for our drive to be seen as a unique individual is to stand out and attract a potential mate. We do it by displaying our particular characteristics, whether looks, skills or personality, to outshine the competition.

We have an innate desire to be unique, yet a need to belong to a group. From an evolutionary perspective, it is logical: being cast out in the times of our ancestors could mean death through loss of resources, mates, status and threat from predators. The physiological legacy of our ancestors is alive in us today: being expelled from a group (whatever the group is) triggers a stress response that feels like physical pain.

Further research from Professor Ziai shows that hearing dissonant messages also triggers the stress response because it confuses our sense of group connectedness. Again, from an evolutionary perspective assimilating a dissonant message, contrary to the narrative of one's group, could lead to ostracism and potential death. This is understood to be why groups and individuals react violently when they perceive their ideas are being attacked.

Historically, more dissonant groups of people have come together in the last decades than at any other point in man's evolution. Today we live in a highly connected world through travel, technology and globalization. In contrast, our internal systems have not adapted as fast as these changes. Primitively we are wired to see difference as a potential threat to our existence: 'stranger danger'.

It seems we often lack awareness of this evolutionary response, and don't use our cognitive skills to wind down our system in order to countermand our reflex, and allow for a more reflective, thoughtful one.

Historical Influence on Identity Today

An aspect of identity that is often ignored is how large a part the past has to play in how we view identities today. Our history is often told by the dominant culture, lacking the voices of multiple perspectives, and thereby shaping the narratives with which we view identity now. They have created a dynamic image of the 'good guy' and the 'bad guy' to tell their story. The consequences are manifold: if we are told we are the 'bad guy', do we subconsciously start to manifest 'bad guy' qualities? If we hear only stories describing images of ourselves then our identity is strengthened, but is it at the cost of not building empathy and insight into the identity of others? If we are not represented and heard, this makes specific aspects of our identities feel less important and less understood. Since stories are how we understand ourselves, we cannot truly learn about ourselves if our history is deleted or distorted.

The combination of history intersecting with our current identity often creates challenges to our personal and social meaning. It would be in our best interest to learn and not repeat the behaviour of the past, to understand and create new social norms and rules evolving with the modern world.

Power and Identity

There is a personal and individual element to our identity. We have to recognize that some people have fewer challenges when it comes to identity than others. If we have a 'popular' identity or one that is recognized as 'better', it is likely we will navigate the world more easily. On the whole it means judgements and barriers are not imposed, which makes the progression of life more successful. This is particularly true in the hierarchy of the white race, which, in the West, has greater power and privilege. It can be viewed as a structural pervasive cultural force, viewing the white man as good, and necessarily marginalizing others to bolster the chances of the majority. There is a vital political dimension to identity that is not explored here, the focus here being psychological.

There is a particular tension around power and identity at the intersections of marginalized and mainstream identities. Challenges of intersecting identities could be, for example, being gay but practising a religion in which that religious community interprets it as immoral to be gay. Research indicates that 'Black women are socially ignored given that they are neither the prototypical Black person nor the prototypical woman.' Kimberlé Crenshaw, who coined the term 'intersectionality', argues that if you are (like a duo of women calling themselves 'the Triple Cripples') black, female and disabled, you face societal oppression at three different levels. You have common ground with other women of colour as well as white women, common ground with other disabled people of all ethnicities, and common ground with all black people. All the oppressions faced by those three groups will apply to you. You don't only face 'black' or 'female' or 'disabled' oppression but all three at once. All three of these are your identity – plus if you happen not to be straight, maybe there's more.

Gender and Sexual Identity Research

Generally, straight men and women are thought of as the norm, from which others deviate. Yet we now know the differences between men and women, their sexuality and relationships, are on a continual variable line, and where your place is on that line can be affected by external elements. Those who are seen as nonconformist in gender, sexuality and relationship preference have often suffered psychologically: they experience higher rates of mental illness than straight people due to being marginalized, discriminated against or viewed as abnormal.

It is important to view how the landscape of sexual orientation is changing fast, and this can be seen clearly through the statistics taken from the UK Office for National Statistics.

- In 2017, just over a million (2 per cent) of the UK population aged 16 and over identified themselves as lesbian, gay or bisexual (LGB). [This was 1.7 in 2015.]
- The population aged 16–24 were the age group most likely to identify as LGB in 2017 (4.2 per cent).
- More males (2.3 per cent) than females (1.8 per cent) identified themselves as LGB in 2017.
- The population who identified as LGB in 2017 were most likely to be single, never married or civil-partnered, at 69.4 per cent.
- From March 2014 to October 2015, approximately 15,000 same-sex marriages were performed in England and Wales; 55 per cent of these marriages were between female couples and 45 per cent between male couples.

Currently there is a lack of data from the ONS on trans identity: since 2009 they have recognized a need to collect and record information as part of the 2021 census. This reflects how recent changes in our views on gender identity have evolved and hopefully come into the forefront of the 'mainstream'.

Research shows that young people, like KT, find it easier to come out to their peers than their parents, guardians or anyone of an older generation. If young people find it hard to come out to older generations, it may be that older individuals may struggle to be honest about their sexual orientation with their (comparatively older) peers, often hiding it or living with dual identities.

Young people, eighteen and under, are identifying more frequently as LGBTQ+ and living in an environment that is perceived to be more accepting. Also, young people are having more discussions on sexuality and gender and seeing more representation on social media. It is also important to recognize that young people like KT are generally developing psychologically at a slower rate than the generation before them, having more time to explore who they are. It is predicted that their gender fluidity will continue as they grow older.

'Binary' is a relatively new term, although not a new concept. According to Jack Drescher, a psychologist, it was in 1970s Western culture that gender variations emerged to challenge the binary norm of male and female. In numerous cultures varying identities had been documented but only represented poorly as the 'mentally ill or sexual deviants'. His view is challenged by others who see it as ahistorical and untrue. Research shows that social media has enabled this minority group, and others, to be represented with a louder voice.

The research for those who identify as non-binary, meaning that a person does not identify their gender as either male or female, is emerging at a greater rate. Mairéad Losty, the Irish psychologist, states in her article 'Falling Outside of the "Nice Little Binary Box"' that 'their discovery of the non-binary gender category allowed them to put their unique experiences of identification with and/or dis-identification from their biological sex into context.' Unsurprisingly, the experience of rejection and invalidation when the category of non-binary was not acknowledged has been shown to damage self-confidence.

Using correct terminology is important: it is not simply using the right words, but a sensitive use of language generally that allows a person to feel they have a better sense of their own self. These terms are not just for others to know what box to put someone in, but for the person whose experience it is better to understand their identity. When speaking about gender, the language we use to those who are gender nonconforming is essential: they want us to use correct terminology, for example using the pronoun 'they' instead of 'he' or 'she'. It is important to give a sense of ownership to those who often feel as if they are being marginalized.

Research on Gender Development from Birth

A study asked new parents following the birth of their babies for the most frequently asked question from friends and family. It showed that 80 per cent of the initial questions were about the baby's sex: 'Is it a boy or a girl?' I know it's the first question I ask, and somehow it seems important, but I cannot put my finger on why. I wonder if it is because we want to have a handle on this newborn baby. Since they can't speak and we don't know what they look like, we seek connection through gender. Once we have a gender in mind it gives us an image of how that little girl or boy will be in their family.

From our very first days the most important definition of our identity is our gender: that of boy or girl, blue or pink, with no grey area coming into question. Certainly, it is in our early years that our sense of our own gender develops: research shows that important developments in gender formation occur in the first two or three years of life. Children understand their gender and that of those around them and, from the age of three, make decisions based on gender, such as haircut and voice. This is not completely surprising when gender has been such a big part of how they have been perceived in their formative years.

There remains a debate as to whether masculine and feminine behaviour is conditioned. But increasingly gender is broadly recognized as a social construct.

Migration, Refugees and Identity

In 2017 258 million people were migrants, roughly 3 per cent of the world's population. As of 2017, 64 per cent of all international migrants worldwide – equal to 165 million international migrants – lived in high-income countries. The migrant population has grown 200 per cent in the last fifty years.

Although it is obvious, it is still worth stating that it is only those from minority groups who are viewed as having ethnic identities, while the majority have the nation's identity. Not forgetting that, on a global scale, white ethnicity is the minority (11.5 per cent globally). Sara encapsulated the experience of this when she said, 'I don't want to be ashamed of being Syrian, but I don't want racism or pity. I want respect and value for who I am . . . I'm treated as a stranger.'

As I have shown, belonging is a central drive of identity and for those who migrate to new countries, whether it is forced or anticipated, they no longer belong. It may be that someone in their country of origin was seen as successful, educated and upper class, but when they migrate, that no longer holds value. Whatever their previous background, there is loss of status, social regard and a shattered identity. They arrive, disconnected from all they have known, and face the formidable barriers of their new country, not least that they don't speak the same language. They are given this new unwelcome identity of 'refugee'. Societies categorize people, labelling them 'refugee' or 'migrant', which reduces their perceived human qualities, then limits our openness to them, as one human being to another.

Part of the hugely complex difficulty in assimilating themselves in their new culture is that a person may have come from somewhere that has one type of established rules, such as those for women, and then move somewhere with another set of rules or social expectations. Those rules may compromise the person's identity and may promote segregation and an inability to adapt socially to certain activities. This is particularly true when the person comes from a non-Western to a Western country: the difficulty of perhaps coming from a rural environment to an urban one, feeling overwhelmed and lost with none of the skills that are needed for working in a city. The stigma of being seen as a refugee, combined with the lack of power, whatever their personal plans or wishes, means they are at the mercy of their new country. In addition, their status is often uncertain, and there is the fear of being sent back to the country they fled from in terror or poverty. In recognition of the difficulty, a specific type of stress has been defined: 'acculturative stress' is 'the level of psychosocial strain experienced by immigrants and their descendants in response to the immigration-related stressors that they encounter as they adapt to life in a new country'.

Unsurprisingly, the ultimate success or failure of the migrant or refugee to integrate into their new country is dependent on both the personality type of the person migrating and how the receiving country responds to them. The process of assimilation is extremely difficult. Those who succeed in their new society have to shed the identity of refugee, and as they struggle for a sense of belonging, they need to negotiate their new identity and rebuild their life in their new environment – this takes time. But they also need a welcoming environment and systems that support them. If we do not value diversity or continue to increase our awareness, we do not allow for cultural bonds, thus making it harder to take on or adapt an individual's identity to a new setting.

Social Media and Identity

Social media will play a fundamental part in the representation and, most importantly, the correct representation of all ways of identifying. As Ann Morning, the American sociologist and demographer, cogently stated: 'What is new about public contestation today is the way in which social media provides a vast arena – well beyond the town gossip circle, the courtroom, or the municipal registry – in which multitudes of everyday people can follow and weigh in on debates about selected individuals' racial identity.'

The Process of Change in Identity

The first step in the process of change is awareness. We may say to ourselves, 'This is who I am,' because who we are has been laid down in us from birth and it is all we know. Most of us do not choose to examine those messages and beliefs, or question if they fit us, or if they limit us, because it is frightening to break the bond of connection from our birth family. Being different from all we know can feel alienating.

Discomfort is usually the siren call to change, telling us that how we are living or being seen does not fit any longer. Change may be forced on us by circumstances beyond our control, which intensifies the level of distress. We may seek control and a longing to cling to our past self, but we have no choice other than to surrender to this new situation. It will force us to differentiate how we were shaped in the past, in order to receive love and acceptance, and how we see ourselves now. This covers all domains of our personhood, from our sexuality, gender, religion, work and life roles, to our inner sense of self, conditioned by our parents and environment.

It takes courage, self-compassion and determination to dare to step outside what has been projected on to us. To find clarity in this evolving dimension of the self involves a great deal of back and forth in the mind and through talking. The pull between the two poles of the birth identity and the real me or new me, in whatever shape that takes, is hard. We may be thwarted by our internal critical voices, what I term the 'shitty committee'. It is helpful to hear clearly what those voices are telling us and challenge them: they can mutter quietly and create toxic self-loathing. We can develop a kinder inner dialogue that is curious, compassionate and patient, a positive voice to support us towards opening up this new dimension of our self.

The process of change is supported by experimentation with new actions, connection with new groups, knowledge building to create better understanding and familiarity with this new landscape. To find a new sense of belonging is a kind of grief: the pain of losing the past self in order to be able to step into the new self: the greater the change, the greater the loss. As with grief, the paradoxical nature of the process is true. To quote the American psychologist Carl Rogers, 'The more we can accept the aspects of our self that we find unacceptable, the more likely it is that change will occur.'

Continuing the relationships with those connected to our past self, if possible, is important. It is achieved through building bridges of understanding with those pivotal people in our life, not about alienating and cutting the past. There may be very painful situations in which that is not possible. The key in coming to terms with all loss is support. It is not possible to undertake this process in isolation. In addition, it is important to remember that this takes time, longer than most people want. Patience is the required abiding attitude.

As we change our identity the meaning we make of life, or wish to make, will inevitably change too. This will involve finding answers to questions of what makes our life meaningful now. When we feel fulfilled and at peace with who we are, we have greater depths of satisfaction. Making meaning of our life, as opposed to seeking happiness, leads to long-term wellbeing.

If, over time, a person can change into who they want to be, or adapt to the new circumstances in which they find themselves, it is painful but empowering. It is necessary. Living an inauthentic life is too high a price to pay for the fear of change. Given the complexity of the identity structure for any individual, this is unlikely to be a one-stop shop. As we step into new phases of our life, or new circumstances are imposed on us through its different aspects, our identity will require ongoing negotiation.

Conclusion

I have loved writing this book about how we change, what we feel as we change, how we develop from it and what stalls us. It has felt a very personal project, pulling together what I have learned from my clients, my research and my personal life. I wanted it to be the book that I wished I had been given in my twenties to help me understand myself then, and again in every phase of my life as a guide and source of insight for life through time. I want it to be a book, once read, that sits on a shelf as a reminder to be not self-destructive but self-compassionate in times of change.

If I had only one wish for this book, and in truth I have many, it would be that those of you whose relationships have become conflicted through the process of change, either between others or with yourselves, will find a route through these pages to understand better the self and those you love. I hope the stories and reflections help clarify what has blocked you, open up new ways of being and help you recognize that, as abnormal as you may feel, you are normal. That this new wisdom enables you to forge closer bonds with those you love and need most, including themselves.

When change hit my clients, particularly unwanted change, they, as we all do, tended to revert to their natural defences: lashing out, shutting down, being difficult, which brought further distress. It is a cruel truth that when we are hurting we often behave in a way that leads to negative responses and consequences. As I wrote the stories of my clients' lives, I was ceaselessly in awe of their courage in resolving their difficulties. They instinctively knew, which research repeatedly shows, that the sooner their difficulty was faced, the better their outcomes. In many of the stories we saw the contradictory nature of human beings, the friction between the desire for predictability versus freedom – safety versus excitement. Human nature operates best with regularity, and we prefer habit, but we can find that stultifyingly dull. Then we put our heads above the parapet to look for something new, which sets in motion the battle between order and chaos.

These stories show how this process was played out personally. They illustrate how we can manage change in small steps, but sudden or big change hits us as if a tiger has jumped out at us and sends fear cascading through our whole being. Through these stories we learn that pain doesn't kill us: there isn't an actual tiger threatening us. We understand that, for the majority of us, when we trust the ebb and flow of our feelings, and have the endurance to stay with the discomfort, ultimately we will grow.

My clients questioned, as most of us question at some point, what is it fair to expect of our life and what do we have to accept? We are told to jump to the moon, and then we will reach the stars. For some, luck, life and dreams come together. For others, the reality is a world away from their vision, maybe through bad decisions or most frequently bad luck. Or perhaps the dream was unrealistic. I have emphasized throughout this book the importance of hope, but when is it false hope? People often say they dreamed through a whole decade of their life or didn't know what led them down a particular path of work or relationship, their vision of their unlived life being far more alluring than the life they were actually living.

These stories affirm for me the value of spending time examining our life and our dreams. By exploration we recognize how we've been shaped by our experience, that embracing change expands us while blocking it diminishes us. We cannot do that alone. For that we need a good listener: a friend or therapist to discover who we really are, what matters most to us and what it means. It can protect us from a lifetime of regret.

This book may have brought up very strong feelings: you may vehemently agree or disagree with its contents. Whatever the response, it is useful. It is information that can help clarify what we do believe, what matters to us and what we don't want. I also imagine many readers will have looked for a particular story that would illuminate their own experiences or fears and may not have found it. If I'd had different clients, someone experiencing a more destructive divorce than Isobel's or a more difficult transition in retiring than Heinrich, it would have been a different book. But my message would remain the same. It is a simple one. Life is change; we cannot avoid it; our capacity to adapt to change usually takes longer than we imagine; and it rarely happens without bringing up many feelings – disquiet at the least difficult end of the spectrum, pain at the other. The more we are able to adapt, the richer our life is likely to be; unresolved issues from the past lead to more difficult transitions in later life. Crucially we need the love and connection of others to hold us together when we fear we might fall apart.

Finally, we also need to find ways to support ourselves through it. For that reason, I have developed the 8 Pillars of Strength, outlined below: it is a concrete guide of the actual things we can do to help us when we are overwhelmed and immobilized by present feelings, or focused on an imagined future we dread or long for. If we do these things, we can help ourselves build our robustness.

My wish is that whoever reads this book, for whatever reason, while living their life of baffling, fascinating complexity, will find some wisdom, or solace, or a light-bulb moment within it. That it will help them take their next step forward in the natural momentum of life, with a little more joy, clarity, confidence and, of course, hope. In the knowledge that 'This too shall pass.'

The 8 Pillars of Strength, for Times of Change

| Relationship with oneself | Relationship with others | Ways to manage emotions | Time |

| Mindbody | Limits | Structure | Focusing |

The 8 Pillars of Strength

I have developed this model from my work with clients and research. It is clear that talking and reflecting while we are in a phase of change is key if we are to fulfil our potential and thrive. It is important that we take a holistic approach and become aware of how everything we choose to do, or not do, has an impact. The 8 Pillars of Strength is a framework to find the attitudes, the ways of being and the good habits that will help build our strength to manage the highs and lows throughout our lives.

I cannot state strongly enough how important it is for each of us to develop our own toolbox of support, to find our own particular way of doing this. It requires work to build the pillars, and commitment to keep going. They work best as an integrated whole. You choose which ones are key for you.

1. Relationship with Oneself

The relationship with oneself is the pillar that influences every other relationship in our life and is central to our wellbeing. We need to be aware of what is going on inside us and accept who we find ourselves to be. A good guide is to be as kind and respectful to ourselves as we would be to a good friend.

What helps:

- There may be many different conflicting and confusing messages going on in our mind. A useful way to find out what we are thinking is to write a journal. Writing down the competing messages, and what we are feeling, enables us to begin to clarify what is going on inside us and gives us the information to ensure we find the right support. Journalling is a well-researched source of self-support that has been shown to be as effective as therapy. Perhaps do this before or after the relaxation exercise in the mindbody pillar.
- We all need defence mechanisms: learn what yours are, and work out, for this situation, whether they are still helpful or not. For example, if you tend to shut down and withdraw from other people when you are upset, it may mean you don't get the support you actually need. It is useful to be aware of that and tell those close to you that you need them to listen to you or comfort you or help you work out what is troubling you.
- As we change over time, our confidence and sense of self change. We may have relied on our physical strength or looks, our job, memory or talent, which may have diminished or changed. We need self-compassion to support ourselves to mourn the loss of those attributes and be active in finding new sources of confidence and meaning.

- Having an attitude of gratitude for what we do have, rather than seeking more externally, is increasingly seen as a key component of a healthy relationship with oneself. An exercise that is quick and easy is to keep a note on your phone or keep a book by your bed and jot down every night three things you are grateful for that day – even tiny things can help. When you look back at it weeks later it is often a lovely tapestry of memories, which gives a rich and rewarding underpinning to your life.

2. Relationship with Others

Having good strong relationships with others is the central tenet to a good and happy life. Relationships require self-knowledge, commitment and time, as well as love. If we are to thrive we need to do the work, and it is hard work, to ensure we give and receive the love that makes life worth living.

What helps:

- Recognize that as we change in life so our relationships will change, with our partner, family and friends. That means we need to find ways of communicating our love, what we need, as well as having difficult but important conversations, and ways of repairing the rupture after a fight. The secret power in communication is the capacity to be able to listen – yes, we need to be able to communicate honestly, but unless we are fully heard the purpose is lost. It is the capacity to be reflective through listening. By 'listen', I mean actively listen: listen with your heart, listen with your eyes so you pick up visual cues, and listen so you actively pay attention to what is being said, not busy rehearsing what you want to say. The honesty from those conversations builds trust, one of the foundation stones of good relationships. A useful exercise is to take it in turns to speak, five minutes

each, and the listener has to reflect on what they've heard
before taking their turn to speak.

- It means making our key relationships a priority,
  which involves really making time: time to have
  fun together, play together and time to just be
  together. Perhaps regularly have a date night, or
  commit to do a hobby together or simply go for
  walks together.

3. Ways to Manage Emotions

If we could force our feelings to obey our thoughts, life would be
infinitely less difficult, but also flatter and duller. Although we
cannot control what we feel, the more we are aware of what we
are feeling, and the self-chatter that is whirling around in our
head, the more likely it is we can protect ourselves from letting
those feelings taking control.

There is a part of our brain that is constantly on alert to look for
danger – it is there to protect us – but it means we have a negative
bias to look for bad things rather than good. If that part of the
brain is triggered, by, for example, hearing bad news, it can turn
on the fight-flight-freeze system, which, again, is there to protect
us, so we can flee or fight, but it stops us being able to think clearly.
We need to develop ways of mediating that with a 'yes brain' so
that if we hear bad news we don't go with our first reaction, which
is likely to be negative. Take time to calm down, think more
deeply, discuss it with others and then respond.

Eighty per cent of decision-making is influenced by emotion,
and our previous experience. The more we have a handle on what
is going on inside us, the better informed our decisions are.

A key contributor to a successful life is impulse control, the
ability to delay gratification or choose what to say and when. This
means we need to find ways of calibrating our extreme feelings so
we don't use bad habits, like drugs and alcohol, to anaesthetize
them, or vent them on those closest to us.

What helps:

- Take responsibility for ourselves and the impact we have on others.
- Awareness is the first step, knowing what your triggers are. HALT: hungry, angry, lonely, tired are vulnerable times when we could for instance fire off an angry text. Don't. HALT.
- Take a breath when you can see a likely trigger heading in your direction. The big step is to slow down, take time out.
- To stop a persistent urge or recurrent bad image, it can help to close your eyes and visualize that image on a television screen. Take a breath and switch the channel. Visualize a positive image, or your safe place, look around it and breathe it in. Take another breath, open your eyes and move your attention to doing a task. This can be repeated a number of times. Using it regularly increases its speed and efficacy.
- Feelings are not facts. We may feel omnipotent or, at the other end of the spectrum, guilty and powerless – but feeling it does not make it so. Being able to identify all our different emotions gives us more clarity in knowing how to respond to a particular situation. It ensures we are guided in the right direction to fit with who we are and what we believe.

4. *Time*

Our relationship with time is radically altered as we age. When we're young we feel life is for ever, we feel immortal, but as we age we have a scary sense of our mortality. Time has different hues, depending on our mood: when we are unhappy, time slows down. The more we can be mindful of the day and the moment we are living in, the richer our life can be. As Annie Dillard wrote, 'How we spend our days is, of course, how we spend our lives.' It is worth remembering.

What helps:

- Being mindful means focusing one's attention on the present moment, being aware of the sensations in our body, of the sights and sounds around us, while calmly accepting our feelings. Apps like Headspace are useful guides. (See also Pillar 8 on page 281.)
- Adapting to change takes longer than anyone wants or expects. We cannot fight it or wilfully hasten it. We can only find ways to support ourselves in it. Accepting the change, being patient and kind to ourselves means we are more likely to adjust faster. In the long term we will thrive.
- Allowing more time than is often expected to make decisions, both immediate but also life decisions. We can feel a pressure to take action because the sense of powerlessness is so strong, but only time allows proper reflection to ensure against regret.
- Our relationship with time feels changed. The future can look daunting and we may long to be in the past. The best we can do is keep our outlook short, keep our attention focused on today and this week. When you find yourself making a film in your mind of your negative unknown future, bring your attention back to the present, the task you are doing, your feet firmly standing on the ground, breathe, and plan what you need to do today. 'Keep it in the day' is a very helpful AA mantra to hold on to.

5. Mindbody

The mindbody is now thought of as a single unit, not two separate systems, mind and body. We know our thinking/feeling mind affects our physical body, and vice versa: at all times what we are thinking will send a signal to our body, and a sensation in our body will send a signal to our mind. The mindbody is a set of interweaving connections, and profoundly influences our mood, choices and behaviours. It is often our most powerful source of information. The famous neuroscientist Antonio Damasio said, 'The body remembers, the body holds the score,' meaning every experience we have leaves a mark in us, which can be ignited by our next experience.

It is important to recognize that what we allow into our mind will have a fundamental influence on our emotions. We need to be as aware, for instance, that what we are watching or listening to has a powerful influence on our mood. Its impact on us is similar to how what we put into our mouth, or how we are moving or not moving, affects our body.

Regular exercise is a keystone of a healthy life, it is more effective than any pill yet developed for both physical and mental health. For the best possible outcome, a pattern should be established from adolescence and continued into old age, although it is never too late to start. Not only does exercise help prevent the onset of many diseases, it can also help to cure or alleviate others.

NICE (National Institute for Health and Care Excellence) guidelines state that *regular* exercise is the equivalent of a low dose of antidepressants – it lifts our mood.

What helps:

- Cardiovascular exercise is the fast-track route to de-stress your body. Our stress levels ratchet up with the daily juggle of life, while running, walking or any sport instantly decreases our cortisol levels; having exercised, our body is told not to be on alert, we are safe, and releases the feel-good neurotransmitter dopamine. Never ask yourself, Shall I exercise today? Have a clear decision: JFDI (Just Fucking Do It).
- Follow exercise with a relaxation/meditation pratice that helps manage your anxiety. This could be through an app, a YouTube clip or just breathing in and out.

The simplest breathing exercise is to breathe in for the count of five, hold for the count of five, breathe out for the count of five, hold for the count of five, and repeat.

- This should be combined with eating healthily. What we eat and drink affects our mood as well as our health. When we are stressed we can be drawn to sugar, coffee and alcohol – thinking of them as treats we need to feel better but in fact make us feel worse: they send the body peaking and crashing. This does not mean never eating sugar or drinking coffee or alcohol: a fun night and treats are important too.
- Give yourself a treat when you have completed this series of tasks, which helps embed it as a regular habit. For example, if you do this in the morning, make a delicious breakfast as your reward.

6. Limits

As we age many different limits may emerge, those of our success, our capacity and our life. If we actively address each one, such as our reduced capacity, recognizing that we get tired more easily, we can be creative in adjusting our schedule to match our energy levels, rather than battling to do what we've always done but ending up exhausted.

It helps to:

- Learn how to say NO with conviction. Being assertive and having a confident 'no' rather than saying 'yes' to something you don't want to do in order to please others means you have more enjoyment in what you have said 'yes' to as you are more invested in it.
- Introduce boundaries, which are crucial to our sense of order in a world that can seem overwhelming. For example, the 24/7 culture and its limitless capacity to transmit content: turn your telephone off from 8.30 p.m.

to 7 a.m. Personal boundaries protect you from being
intruded on, like putting in place time to be on your
own. With professional boundaries, make a distinction
between work and home, an increasingly important limit
to put in place.
- Recognize the limits of what you can control,
  change and influence – not confusing hope or will
  with reality.

7. Structure

Structure helps to stabilize us and gives us a foundation on which
to stand when our world feels shaky. It helps to build a pillar of
structure, although allowing some flexibility within it – too much
controlling behaviour can be counterproductive. But in times of
change we may need scaffolding to see us through.

Develop good habits, such as:

- exercising first thing
- engaging in work or chores
- making time to reflect on the present and on the past; use
  the learning to think about future plans, get informed
  about possibilities, do some research, have lots of
  conversations with different people to explore ideas
- actively choosing to do soothing, calming things – like
  buying flowers, having a massage, cooking nice food,
  watching box sets, listening to music, reading (although
  for some it takes a long time before they can concentrate
  on reading)
- ensuring regular good sleeping habits

Developing a structure of good routines has the multiplier effect:
the more we do them, the better we feel. It takes about six weeks
to develop a good habit for it to become so automatic we do it
without thinking.

8. Focusing

Our minds often ruminate on what we cannot change, or an experience leaves us feeling frustrated or numb. Those feelings usually sit in the body unvoiced but we know we feel tense and unsettled. Focusing is a way of connecting to the sensations in your body and finding words for those feelings: it is the technique that helps you open and release your bodily intelligence. It can be done in a matter of minutes or much longer.

Doing it regularly helps you feel calmer and able to meet each new day afresh.

The focusing technique I ask clients to do, which you can do for yourself, is:

Close your eyes.
Breathe deeply and slowly. In through your nose, and out
    through your mouth. Three times.
Move your attention internally.
Move your attention around your body until you find the
    place where there is most sensation.
Breathe into the place.
Find a word to describe that place: does it have a shape, a
    colour? Is it hard, soft?
If the image could speak, what would it say?
Then follow where the image takes you.

Last Word

There is a great deal of information in the 8 Pillars, but don't let that put you off. Start by choosing one or two and work out how you can integrate them as part of your daily life. When you've got your head around doing those, choose another. Once you feel the benefits it will be easy to keep going.

Appendix: Lifespan Development

We like order: we want to be able to make sense of our life, and although logically we would agree there isn't a fixed way to mark the narrative of it, we do like a story with a beginning, a middle and an end. Here I have shown that story from a psychological perspective. Lifespan psychologists have devised a number of helpful frameworks to look at the lifespan and I think this is the most useful.

Developmental Tasks

Developmental tasks are a loose list of what we might face, and when. Organizing a lifespan into chapters like this lets us consider all the types of tasks that someone might be facing at any given stage and provides a kind of cross-section of an individual. Whether we are looking back at our past or envisaging our future, viewing life in stages helps us to construct a narrative, which is crucial to building and maintaining a sense of identity – as I have argued already, a cornerstone of psychological stability. It also gives us the direction of travel that we are aiming for, purpose and goals. The overarching vision of the tasks is for them to create a life of successful achievement – with its individual definition of that success – which brings happiness. For every individual, success and happiness will look very different. I am more interested in the moments when people struggle to achieve their developmental tasks rather than identifying them; following this new phase of our life is more about understanding, facing, making the adjustment inside ourselves and then achieving it.

These adult developmental tasks cover the range of social,

physical and spiritual challenges that people typically face. Some tasks arise from individual desires (falling in love); some are physical imperatives (going through the menopause); some are social constructs (retirement). Many are a mixture of all three, so they depend to a certain extent on the culture and time in which we live and the things that society expects. Of course, not everyone will choose to take on every task and the list is always open to change. A summary of developmental tasks amounts to a description of what people tend to do at a particular time in life. Most of us have a 'social alarm clock', which measures in our minds whether we are ahead, on time or behind our peers in these tasks – for example, our friends getting married and having babies when we remain single. It goes against our survival instinct to see ourselves as behind: it gives us the feeling that we are at the bottom of the ladder and everyone else is ahead of us, which is both annoying and frightening.

What is the definition of an adult if it isn't judged by the legal age of eighteen or twenty-one? I would define an adult as someone, whatever their age, who knows themselves well, whose choices are informed, who is aware of and takes responsibility for their duties and obligations. An adult is a person who is accountable for their actions, how they affect others, as well as themselves, has higher impulse control than when they were young, and has the discipline to follow through on commitments.

The case studies in this book chart those uniquely individual processes, the meaning, the sense and lack of sense each person has made of them, and how they have come to accept them or not. For although there is much to be gained from a framework that tells us what tasks our life might hold and when they might arise, it can't paint the full picture. It doesn't shed light on how those tasks might feel to an individual, or how well equipped they are to weather them. In other words, it may tell us about *what* we face, but it doesn't tell us much about *how* we face it. To learn more about this, we need to focus on the person, not the event – more specifically, how that person handles the process of transition.

This will depend on their unique balance of psychological and social resources. What are their coping strategies and character strengths? How strong is their support network? What is their health and socio-economic status? How stable are other areas of their life? And, crucially, how do they interpret the event? Is it welcome, unexpected, controllable, temporary, familiar, challenging? Answers to these questions will help to place an event in the unique context of an individual life and give some idea as to how someone will approach the transition.

For those, like me, who find a map useful, here are the developmental tasks loosely grouped into different life stages. They have been devised by leading American lifespan psychologists Philip Newman and Barbara Newman, who identified five stages from early adulthood to old age.

Life Tasks

EARLY ADULTHOOD (18–22 YEARS)

- Autonomy from parents
- Gender identity
- Internalized morality
- Career choice

YOUNG ADULTHOOD (22–40 YEARS)

- Exploring intimate relationships
- Childbearing
- Work
- Lifestyle

MIDDLE ADULTHOOD (40–60 YEARS)

- Management of career
- Nurturing the couple relationship
- Expanding caring relationships
- Management of the household

EARLY-LATE ADULTHOOD (60–75 YEARS)
- Promotion of intellectual vigour
- Redirection of energy towards new roles and activities
- Acceptance of one's life
- Development of a point of view about death

LATE-LATE ADULTHOOD (75+)
- Coping with physical changes of ageing
- Development of a psychological historical perspective
- Travel through uncharted terrain
- Facing death *(my addition)*

Context and Definition for the Different Generations

The Traditionalists – Born 1928–45

The Traditionalists have been called the children of crisis. Their parents fought in the Second World War and brought them up during the lean years that followed. They grew up conscious of the sacrifices made on their behalf and were unwilling to rock the boat. They came of age in a time of relative prosperity during which their socially conservative attitudes worked to their advantage. Those who played by the rules were able, with relative ease, to find jobs, buy homes and see their savings increase. They enjoyed better health than previous generations and retired early.

Unlike their parents, who were forced to grow up fast by war and economic necessity, the Traditionalist generation was among the first to enjoy a 'youth culture', facilitated by the rise of television and consumerism. While parents were pleased to see their children enjoying the opportunities of peacetime, it also became harder for the two generations to relate to each other, fuelling intergenerational anxieties. When the Traditionalists became parents themselves, the generation gap left them struggling for role models. This was the first generation to make widespread use of parenting manuals, the prevailing wisdom of which was to encourage parents to follow their instincts and let the natural progression of childhood to adulthood ensue, marking a major shift in parenting styles. The Traditionalists married young, and while divorce rates started to rise among this generation, to be single or divorced was still the exception.

Traditionalists are characterized as being loyal, dutiful and respectful of authority. They have a strong work ethic, are unlikely to change career, are fiscally prudent and abhor waste. They may struggle with change and ambiguity and can be seen as inflexible. Some Traditionalists find it hard to understand why younger generations battle with their careers and finances, and may harbour a belief that the young are simply not trying as hard as they did in their own day. They believe in making the best of a situation with minimal fuss – a stoicism which can mean they are less likely to share their problems or seek mental-health support.

'Baby Boomers' – Born 1946–64

Nowadays the Traditionalists are perhaps known for one thing above all others: the number of babies they had. Peace and prosperity led to a spike in birth rates, creating the famous 'Baby Boomer' generation. They were born into peacetime conditions and enjoyed a growing youth culture. Baby Boomers rebelled: where their parents were silent, they made noise. Encouraged by their parents and by marketers of consumer products to see themselves as special, the Baby Boomers grew up believing they could effect change, then putting that belief into practice. These were the radicals of the sixties and seventies, and the yuppies of the eighties. Indeed, some have seen the real 'boom' of this generation as being not the birth rate but the seismic impact of their countercultural attitudes and activities.

Defining events for this generation included the moon landings and civil-rights movements, the Cold War, the Vietnam War and anti-war protests, Watergate, the Swinging Sixties, drug experimentation and increased sexual liberation, thanks to the Pill. This heady mix fostered both free-spirited idealism and a mistrust of authority and government. Above all, it encouraged individualism: many wanted to define their own values.

They were also more likely to say they wanted to give their children 'good values' than material inheritance and were keen to spend time with them. And yet they raised the first 'latchkey generation'. The Baby Boomers' pursuit of individual fulfilment, combined with a strong work ethic and increased maternal participation in the workforce, meant that they had a more detached parenting style than previous generations. This generation also saw the first leap in divorce rates, inevitably leading to a higher incidence of absent parents.

Boomers eschewed reliance on institutions and on each other; and while this independence delivered rewards, it also weakened traditional societal and family bonds, leaving them more vulnerable to isolation and loneliness. As it grows old, the generation that revelled in youth culture is having to face the challenges of ageing. For many, the prospect of losing their much-valued independence is deeply unsettling, while in pragmatic terms, the sheer number of Boomers is placing pressure on services.

Generation X – Born 1965–80

Sandwiched between the Boomers and the Millennials, both of whom generate more column inches and interest from marketers, Gen-X is sometimes seen as the 'neglected middle child' of the generations. In demographic terms they are relatively small, as a combination of contraception and economic downturn led to a 'baby bust'.

Significant events for Generation X include the end of the Cold War, the AIDS epidemic, MTV, video games, rave culture, Thatcherism/Reaganomics and the emergence of the internet. But in many ways the defining influence for this generation was the long shadow cast by the values of the Baby Boomers. Gen-X children experienced the full range of parenting styles, from the attentive to the permissive to the utterly hands-off. Divorce rates soared, and school systems fragmented. This is not to say that Gen-X did not experience nurture and love, but they learned not to *rely* on their elders or institutions and became self-sufficient realists.

This independence had a distinctly more pragmatic streak than that of their parents, and Gen-Xers are more likely to focus on the bottom line than on their personal journey. This has led some to characterize this generation as ironic, detached, cynical, while others see it as a necessary restoration of sanity after the failed utopianism of the Boomers.

Once again, there was a generational correction in terms of parenting styles, with Gen-X becoming attentive and even anxious parents, keenly aware of safeguarding issues and hopeful of spending more time with their children than their parents did. Much has been made of Gen-X's determination to strike a fulfilling work–life balance and the high value they place on employment flexibility. While it is true that some – particularly men – are actively choosing to be more involved in family than their parents were, others have had little say in the matter.

Gen-X has been hit hard by successive booms and busts, culminating in the prolonged downturn from 2008, and their part-time involvement in the workforce is not always voluntary. In material terms, Gen-Xers are lagging a long way behind their Boomer parents, particularly in terms of home ownership, and this discrepancy can foster deep-seated anxieties and intergenerational resentment. Gen-X mothers also find themselves caught in a bind, encouraged on the one hand to capitalize on hard-won feminist rights with high career ambitions, and on the other to be attentive and present parents. Feeling unable or even reluctant to 'have it all' can be harboured as a guilty secret.

The Millennials (Generation Y) – Born 1981–96

Throughout time, older generations have looked to the younger to comment, criticize and voice their hopes and – more often – their fears for society's future. The generation now occupying that spotlight is the Millennials, also termed Generation Y, born between 1981 and 1996 (the end date still being a matter of debate). Perhaps more interesting than what is being said of them is the sheer intensity of the focus, which betrays the presence of a significant generation gap. Older generations are struggling to make sense of Millennial behaviours and mindsets, as well they might. On the most important fronts – parenting styles, political and economic circumstances, and technology – the Millennials' experience is a world away from that of their grandparents.

Millennial children experienced more adult attention than any other generation living today. Parenting styles had become much more hands-on, and safeguarding issues rose up the social agenda. Parents monitored their children's activities more closely, from their safety and whereabouts to their academic and emotional development, and were encouraged to reward their offspring not just for achievement but for effort. This has led to accusations that 'helicopter' parents are raising a trophy generation that expects prizes simply for participation, but it should also be noted that this shift in parenting styles seems to have strengthened family bonds. Today's young adults are remaining close to their parents as they grow, and studies suggest that they are more comfortable discussing emotional life events with their parents than the previous generation were.

The greatest single defining political event for Millennials was 9/11. Whether they are old enough to remember the attacks or not, this generation grew up against a backdrop of international terrorism and prolonged yet loosely defined global conflict. The extent to which this has affected a generation is impossible to quantify, but Millennials can certainly take life seriously and many report struggles with anxiety. The economic downturn has done little to lighten their load, and the Millennials' prospects in terms of salary and home ownership fall far behind those of the Boomers. The stark comparison can be a source of intergenerational tension. The social conservatism of the Traditionalists also seems to be making a reappearance, with the levels of drug and alcohol abuse, violent crime and teenage pregnancy falling.

Millennials' attitude to work has adapted to the economic realities and, rather than job security and high remuneration, some say their life is hard for them in a different way: 'Constantly living in precarity – psycho or economic.' As a counter-attitude to this, they look for inspirational mentors, strong networks and meaningful experiences. Baby Boomer bosses can be quick to interpret Millennials' demands for feedback and involvement as unearned entitlement – another expression of today's generation gap. This gap is perhaps at its widest in terms of the Millennials' relationship to technology. They came of age at a time when technology was reshaping almost every aspect of life – a radical shift that places them in a different age from their elders and brings new opportunities and challenges. The human urge to connect has been greatly facilitated, and Millennials are developing rich ways to strengthen their personal networks and effect political and social change. At the same time, the always-on culture and the pressures of social media are generating anxiety, which parents may note but not fully understand. Those seeking to bridge the generation gap with Millennials need curiosity and empathy to walk with them as they face age-old life transitions in a brand-new age.

Generation Z – Born 1996–2010

As with the other generations, there is some disagreement about when Generation Z starts and ends. Some date it from 1995 to 2009, which would mean that those born between 1996 and 2000 are at university or beginning to work. It is a fledgling generation on which we have only scant insight, but the information we do have is through their digital footprint, although they may be tired of being too networked as they prefer face-to-face meetings and contact to online messages.

It is likely Gen-Z will have a lot in common with Millennials, particularly with regard to how they were parented, although it seems that, characteristically, they are more autonomous and independent than the generation before.

The defining event of their life to date is the economic crisis of 2008 and the subsequent recession. It had huge financial consequences for many of their parents, which they would have witnessed for much of their childhood. It is thought that this means Gen-Z will be less idealistic than Gen-Y and long for both security and money. They will want to make a difference but their underlying motivation is likely to be more pragmatic. They will be a generation who expect to be adaptive, work hard, are competitive but will demand to be paid fairly. In their bid for financial security and given the rising cost of tuition fees, more of them have skipped university and moved straight into the workplace.

They are the generation that was born with the internet: it is as natural to them as television was to the generations before them. Gen-Z are the true digital natives and, as a result, have no problem with switching between platforms and technologies. They are sophisticated and fast in seeking what is relevant to them and will be more inclined to support brands that advocate issues they believe in. They can be entrepreneurial, using their tech-savviness to make money.

Young people, including Gen-Z, are leading the fight to address climate change, campaigning powerfully, collectively, for the future of the planet they believe we have trashed. They are pushing for action across the world, and back politicians whose policies include lower carbon emissions.

They are the generation who hold our future in their hands, despite their youth, already addressing the key issues of the day. We would be wise to listen to and support them, rather than deride their sensitivity and passion.

Myself as a Psychotherapist

I am enormously grateful to all my fascinating and extraordinary clients who allowed me to show the relationship I had with them.

I thought it might be useful to write a few lines about what kind of psychotherapist I am.

While writing, I have intentionally put my focus on the process of change. I have deliberately not used psychological terms or theories. I have kept it 'therapy light'. Even the little I have shown leaves me feeling exposed to other therapists who work differently and may be critical of my approach. But a message has stayed with me since my early psychotherapy training from Carl Rogers: 'The most personal is the most universal.' My work with these clients, although a professional relationship, couldn't be more personal. I am a person-centred therapist, meaning I believe my client is an expert on themselves, and I create a non-judgemental, empathic and authentic relationship, which enables my client to use it for their personal growth. I draw on many other theories to inform my practice. I hold my theories lightly. I don't hold fixed views. My responses are intended to affirm that I can see my clients as they see themselves, and also add something on the edge of our understanding. I can be straight-talking if I think my client is harming themselves, not shaming or critical but honest. Maybe I will get something wrong. At times they may be angry with me and I need to respect that and find out what they are angry about. I will acknowledge it and work with them to repair the rupture. At times we will get stuck, and I will name it. Sometimes we will hit on something new, at others not. There may be questions that emerge. It is all information, and the clarification builds our trust and understanding together.

I am often asked how I can understand another person's difficulty if I haven't had the experience myself. It is a good question and the answer is straightforward: I can never fully understand what it is like to be the other. I do think I can step into their world and see it 'as if' it were mine. At my best, it brings the optimal version of me to the fore. There is a stillness that happens as I move towards the person in front of me. My engaged curiosity is looking to attune to my client, to developing the channel of communication between us. I can hold our separateness while I engage as fully as I can in their perception of themselves. What I see is inevitably influenced by my own experience.

My hope is that this way of relating will connect to anyone reading these stories, who may borrow ideas of the kind of relationship that is helpful, which needn't be with a therapist. Being a loving friend, or family member, who can really listen, without judgement, is curative.

Sources

The place of publication is London, unless stated otherwise.

Title

'The Revolutions in Europe', *Blackwood's Edinburgh Magazine*, May 1848, p. 638

Introduction

Darwin, C. (1859), *On the Origin of Species*, John Murray

Elder, Glen H. (1994), 'Time, Human Agency, and Social Change: Perspectives on the Life Course', *Social Psychology Quarterly*, 57 (1), 4–15

Joyce, L.-J. (2014), *Fertile Void: Gestalt Coaching at Work*, AoEC Press

McOrmand, T. (January 2004), *Changes in Working Trends Over the Past Decade*, Labour Market Division, ONS

Office for National Statistics (November 2014), *Families and Households*, www.ons.gov.uk

— (November 2015), *Families and Households*, www.ons.gov.uk

— (November 2017), *Families and Households*, www.ons.gov.uk

Reitman, F., and Schneer, J. (2008), 'Enabling the New Careers of the 21st Century', *Organization Management Journal*, 5 (1), 17–28

Scott, A., and Gratton, L. (2017), *The 100 Year Life*, Bloomsbury

Waldinger, R. (2017), *75-year Harvard Study of Happiness*, https://news.harvard.edu

The Process of Change in Life

Armstrong, T. (2012), 'The Stages of Life According to Rudolf Steiner', http://www.institute4learning.com/2012/08/07/the-stages-of-life-according-to-rudolf-steiner/

Bridges, W. (2004), *Transitions: Making Sense of Life's Changes*, Boston: Da Capo Press

Dweck, C. S. (2006), *Mindset: The New Psychology of Success*, Random House

Fisher, H. (2015), 'Is There a Biological Basis for the Famous Seven-year Itch?' *SA Mind*, 26, 1, 74 (January 2015); doi:10.1038/scientificamerican mind0115-74

Perls, F. (1969), *Gestalt Therapy Verbatim*, Real People Press

— (1973), *The Gestalt Approach & Eye Witness to Therapy*, Bantam Books

Prochaska, J. O., and Redding, C. A. (2015), The Transtheoretical Model and Stages of Change Health Behavior: Theory, Research, and Practice', in Glanz, K., Rimer, B. K., and Viswanath, K. (eds), *Health Behavior Theory, Research, and Practice*, San Francisco: Jossey-Bass, 125-48.

Rogers, C. R. (1961), *On Becoming a Person: A Therapist's View of Psychotherapy*, Constable

Snyder, C. R. (2003), *Psychology of Hope: You Can Get There from Here*, New York: Free Press

— (2002), 'Hope Theory: Rainbows in the Mind', *Psychological Inquiry*, 13, 4, 249-75

Sugarman, L. (2001), *Lifespan Development: Frameworks, Accounts and Strategies* (2nd edn), Hove: Psychology Press

The Process of Transition, www.bodycoachclub.com/the-process-of-transition/

Whitlock, J., and Purington, M. (2013), *Understanding and Using the Stages of Change Model*, Practical Matters series, Cornell Research Program on Self-Injury and Recovery, Ithaca, Cornell University

Williams, D. (April 1999), 'Transitions: Managing Personal and Organizational Change', Association for Clinical Data Management newsletter

Family

Allen, K. R., Blieszner, R., Roberto, K. A., Farnsworth, E. B., and Wilcox, K. L. (1999), 'Older Adults and Their Children: Family Patterns of Structural Diversity', *Family Relations*, 48 (2), 151-7

Barclay, L., and Lupton, D. (1999), 'The Experiences of New Fatherhood: A Socio-cultural Analysis', *Journal of Advanced Nursing*, 29, 1013-20

Bingham, J. (2013), ''Til Retirement Us Do Part: "Silver Splitter" Divorces up by Three-quarters in Generation', *Daily Telegraph*

Bodnar, J. (2013), 'When the Kids Move Back', *Kiplinger's Personal Finance*, 67 (8), 4

Bostwick, E. N., and Johnson, A. J. (2018), 'Family Secrets: The Roles of Family Communication Patterns and Conflict Styles between Parents and Young Adult Children', *Communication Reports*, 31 (2), 91-102

Brann, D. (2013), *Reluctantly Related*, Ambergris Publishing

Chatzky, J. (2006), 'Just When You Thought It Was Safe to Retire . . .' *Money Magazine*, 35 (10), https://money.cnn.com/magazines/moneymag/moneymag_archive/2006/10/01/8387557/index.htm

Cohen, G. J. (November 2002), 'Helping Children and Families Deal With Divorce and Separation', *American Academy of Paediatrics*, 110, 5, 1019–23

Crespi, I., and Ruspini, E. (2015), 'Transition to Fatherhood: New Perspectives in the Global Context of Changing Men's Identities', *International Review of Sociology*, 25, 1–6

DeFrain, J. (1999), 'Strong Families around the World', *Family Matters*, 53, Winter, 6–13

Dunning, A. (2006), 'Grandparents – An Intergenerational Resource for Families: A UK Perspective', *Journal of Intergenerational Relationships*, 4 (1), 127–35

Fingerman, K., Gilligan, M., VanderDrift, L., and Pitzer, L. (2012), 'In-Law Relationships Before and After Marriage: Husbands, Wives, and Their Mothers-in-Law', *Research in Human Development*, 9 (2), 106–25

Fingerman, K. L., Pillemer, K. A., Silverstein, M., and Suitor, J. J. (2012), 'The Baby Boomers' Intergenerational Relationships', *Gerontologist*, 52 (2), 199–209

Forward, S. (1989), *Toxic Parents*, New York: Bantam Books

Geggie, J., DeFrain, J., Hitchcock, S., and Silberberg, S. (2000), *The Family Strengths Research Report*, University of Newcastle, Newcastle, NSW: Family Action Centre

Grossman, L., Mustafa, N., Van Dyk, D., Kloberdanz, K., and Schultz, M. (2005), 'Grow Up? NOT SO FAST', *Time*, 165 (4), 42

Guinart, M., and Grau, M. (2014), 'Qualitative Analysis of the Short-Term and Long-Term Impact of Family Breakdown on Children: Case Study', *Journal of Divorce and Remarriage*, 55, 408–22

Halpern, H. (1990), *Cutting Loose*, New York: Simon & Schuster

Hermansen, S., Croninger, B., and Croninger, S. (2015), 'Exploring the Role of Modern-day Fatherhood', *Work*, 50(3), 495–500

Hesse, C., Mikkelson, A. C., and Saracco, S. (2017), 'Parent–Child Affection and Helicopter Parenting: Exploring the Concept of Excessive Affection', *Western Journal of Communication*, 82 (4), 457–74

Hideg, N. A., Kristic, A., Trau, R., and Zarina, T. (September 2018), 'Do Longer Maternity Leaves Hurt Women's Careers?' *Harvard Business Review*

Hilpern, K. (13 March 2009), 'Dad was Crying on One Shoulder and Mum on the Other', *Guardian*

Jackson, M. (2010), 'Motherhood: The Third Act', *Maclean's*, 123 (37), 67–9

Juang, L., Park, L., Lau, A., et al. (2018), 'Reactive and Proactive Ethnic–Racial Socialization Practices of Second-generation Asian American Parents', *Asian American Journal of Psychology*, 9 (1), 4–16

Kirke, J. (15 October 2015), 'Total Parenting Control is Futile', *Time*

Lakomy, M., and Kreidl, M. (2015), 'Full-time Versus Part-time Employment: Does It Influence Frequency of Grandparental Childcare?', *European Journal of Ageing*, 12, 321–31

McBain, S. (8 May 2018), 'The New Cult of Perfectionism', *New Statesman*, 147

McGarrigle, C. A., Timonen, V., and Layte, R. (2018), 'Choice and Constraint in the Negotiation of the Grandparent Role: A Mixed-Methods Study', *Gerontology and Geriatric Medicine*, 4, 1–12

McGoldrick, M., (2010), *The Expanded Family Life Cycle* (3rd edn), Pearson, Allyn & Bacon

— interview, https://www.psychotherapy.net/interview/monica-mcgoldrick

Messinger, L., and Walker, K, N. (1981), 'From Marriage Breakdown to Remarriage: Parental Tasks and Therapeutic Guidelines', *American Journal of Orthopsychiatry*, 51 (3), 429–38

Millard C. (1998), 'Later Life Parents Helping Adult Children', *Family Matters*, Winter (50), 38–42

NCT website (2015), 'Dads in Distress: Many New Fathers are Worried about Their Mental Health', https://www.nct.org.uk/about-us/media/news/dads-distress-many-new-fathers-are-worried-about-their-mental-health

Office for National Statistics (2016), 'Why are More Young People Living with Their Parents?', https://www.ons.gov.uk/peoplepopulationandcommunity/birthsdeathsandmarriages/families/articles/whyaremoreyoungpeopleliving withtheirparents/2016-02-22

Oliker, D. M., PhD thesis (2011), 'The Importance of Fathers: Is Father's Day Real?', https://www.psychologytoday.com/intl/blog/the-long-reach-childhood/201106/the-importance-fathers

'Only Children More Likely to Support Parents in Old Age Than Children with Siblings' (12 April 2017), *LSE News*

Osterkamp, L. (1992), *How to Deal with Your Parents When They Still Treat You Like a Child*, New York: Berkley Books

'Parents' Lives Made More Miserable by Boomerang Generation' (March 2018), *LSE News*

Pill, C. (1990), 'Stepfamilies: Redefining the Family', *Family Relations*, 39 (2), 186–93

Rogan, F., Shimed, V., and Barclay, L. (1997) 'Becoming a Mother – Developing a New Theory of Early Motherhood', *Journal of Advanced Nursing*, 25 (5), 877–85

Rosenberg, J., and Bradford Wilcox, W. (2006), 'The Importance of Fathers in the Healthy Development of Children', US Department of Health and Human Services, www.childwelfare.gov/pubs/usermanuals/fatherhood/fatherhood.pdf

Segrin, C., et al. (2012), 'The Association Between Overparenting, Parent-Child Communication, and Entitlement and Adaptive Traits in Adult Children, *Interdisciplinary Journal of Applied Family Science*, 61 (2), 237–52

Stern, J., Fraley, R., Jones, J., Gross, J., Shaver, P., and Cassidy, J. (2018), 'Developmental Processes across the First Two Years of Parenthood: Stability and Change in Adult Attachment Style', *Developmental Psychology*, 54 (5), 975–88

Stone, J., Berrington, A., and Falkingham, J. (2014), 'Gender, Turning Points, and Boomerangs: Returning Home in Young Adulthood in Great Britain', *Demography*, 51, 257, https://doi.org/10.1007/s13524-013-0247-8

Tolstoy, Leo (1887; 1980), *Anna Karenina*, New York: Thomas Y. Cromwell & Co; Oxford: Oxford University Press

Ungar, M. (2005), *I Still Love You*, Toronto: Dundurn Press

Walsh, W. (1992), 'Twenty Major Issues in Remarriage Families', *Journal of Counselling and Development*, 70 (6), 709–15

Zervides, S., and Knowles, A. (2007), 'Generational Changes in Parenting Styles and the Effect of Culture', *E-Journal of Applied Psychology*, 3, 65–7

Love

Barlow, A. (2018), Study: The 10 Questions You Should Ask Your Partner So Your Relationship Can Thrive, University of Exeter Law School

Bates, L. (28 June 2014), 'How to Have A Feminist Wedding', *Guardian*

Bauman, Z. (2000), *Liquid Modernity*, Cambridge: Polity Press

Beall, Anne E., and Sternberg, Robert J. (1995), 'The Social Construction of Love', *Journal of Social and Personal Relationships*, 12 (3), 417–38

Bradford Wilcox, W., and Dew, J. (2010), 'Is Love a Flimsy Foundation? Soulmate Versus Institutional Models of Marriage', *Social Science Research*, 39 (5), 687–99

Bulcroft, K., and O' Connor, M. (1986), 'The Importance of Dating Relationships on Quality of Life for Older Persons', *Family Relations*, 35 (3), 397–401

Calhoun, A. (2017), 'Searching for a Soul Mate is Futile: The Ideal Partner is the One You Create', *Time*, 189 (20), 22

Carolyn, E. C. (2018), 'A Psychological Perspective: Marriage and the Social Provisions of Relationships', *Journal of Marriage and Family*, 4 (4), 992

Coyne, S. M., Stockdale, L., Busby, D., Iverson, B., and Grant, D. M. (2011), ' "I luv u :)!": A Descriptive Study of the Media Use of Individuals in Romantic Relationships', *Family Relations*, 60 (2), 150–62

Cutrona, C. E. (2004), 'A Psychological Perspective: Marriage and the Social Provisions of Relationships', *Journal of Marriage and Family*, 66 (4), 992–9

De Marneffe, D. (2018), *The Rough Patch: Marriage and the Art of Living Together*, New York: Simon & Schuster

Donnelly, A. D., and Burgess, O. (2008), 'The Decision to Remain in an Involuntarily Celibate Relationship', *Journal of Marriage and Family*, 70 (2), 519–35

Ferdman, R. A. (23 March 2016), 'How Well Online Dating Works by Someone Who Has been Studying It for Years', *Washington Post*, https://www.washingtonpost.com/news/wonk/wp/2016/03/23/the-truth-about-online-dating-according-to-someone-who-has-been-studying-it-for-years/?utm_term=.3d402199de0e

Finkel, E. (2017), *The All or Nothing Marriage: How the Best Marriages Work*, New York: Dutton

Fisher, H. (2005), *Why We Love: The Nature and Chemistry of Romantic Love*, Holt McDougal

— (2006), 'Why We Love, Why We Cheat', TED Talk

— (2008), 'The Brain in Love', TED Talk

— (2011), *'Why Him? Why Her?': Finding Real Love by Understanding Your Personality Type*, Oneworld Publications

— (2016), 'Technology Hasn't Changed Love. Here's Why', TED Talk

— (2017), *Anatomy of Love*, New York: W.W. Norton

Gilvarry, C. (2005) *Children of Alcoholics: The UK's Largest Survey*, National Association of Children of Alcoholics

Gottman, J. M. (2013), 'The Four Horsemen: Criticism, Contempt, Defensiveness and Stonewalling', https://www.gottman.com/about/john-julie-gottman/ https://www.gottman.com/blog/the-four-horsemen-recognizing-criticism-contempt-defensiveness-and-stonewalling/

— (1993), 'A Theory of Marital Dissolution and Stability', *Journal of Family Psychology*, 7 , 57–75

—, and Silver, N. (1999), 'The Seven Principles for Making Marriage Work', New York: Three Rivers Press

—, and Gottman, J. S. (2008), 'Gottman Method Couple Therapy', in A. S. Gurman (ed.), *Clinical Handbook of Couple Therapy*, New York: Guilford Publications, 138–64

— (2013), *What Makes Love Last? How to Build Trust and Avoid Betrayal*, Simon & Schuster

Grohl, John M. (December 2005), 'After Divorce, Happiness Levels Decrease and May Never Completely Rebound', Psych Central, www.psychcentral.com

Hobbs, M., Owen, S., and Gerber, L. (2017), 'Liquid love? Dating apps, sex, relationships and the digital transformation of intimacy', *Journal of Sociology*, 53 (2), 271–84

Hudson, T. (2015), 'Finding the One Soulmate', https://www.learning-mind.com/psychology-finally-reveals-the-answer-to-finding-your-soulmate

Huyck, M. (2001), 'Romantic Relationships in Later Life', *Generations*, 25 (2), 9–17

Ilze, S., and Green, S. (2013), 'Types of Domestic Violence Experienced by Women in Abusive Relationships', *Social Work/ Maatskaplike Werk*, 49 (2), 234–47

Jeanfreau, M., Jurich, A., and Mong, M. (2014), 'Risk Factors Associated with Women's Marital Infidelity', *Contemporary Family Therapy: An International Journal*, 36 (3), 327–32

Karney, B., and Bradbury, T. (1997), 'Neuroticism, Marital Interaction and the Trajectory of Marital Satisfaction', *Journal of Personality and Social Psychology*, 72 (25), 1075–92

Katz, J., and Schneider, M. E. (2013), 'Casual Hook-up Sex During the First Year of College: Prospective Associations with Attitudes about Sex and Love Relationships', *Archives of Sexual Behaviour*, 42 (8), 1451–62

Klinenberg, E.(2012), *Going Solo: The Extraordinary Rise and Surprising Appeal of Living Alone*, Penguin

Kopotsha, J. (2018), 'Adam's Behaviour on Love Island is Textbook Gaslighting', *Grazia*,https://graziadaily.co.uk/life/tv-and-film/adam-collard-love-island-gaslighting/

Labrecque, L. T., and Whiskman, M. A. (2017), 'Attitudes Toward and Prevalence of Extramarital Sex and Descriptions of Extramarital Partners in the 21st Century', *Journal of Family Psychology*, 31 (7), 952

Lisitsa, E. (2013), 'The Four Horsemen: Criticism, Contempt, Defensiveness and Stonewalling Blog', https://www.gottman.com/blog/the-four-horsemen-recognizing-criticism-contempt-defensiveness-and-stonewalling/

McCarthy, J. (2011), 'What You Don't Know about Marriage', TED Talk

McNulty, J. K., and Karney, B. R. (2004), 'Positive Expectations in the Early Years of Marriage: Should Couples Expect the Best or Brace for the Worst?', *Journal of Personality and Social Psychology*, 86, 5, 729

Manning, J. C. (2006), 'The Impact of Internet Pornography on Marriage and the Family: A Review of the Research, Sexual Addiction & Compulsivity', *Journal of Treatment and Prevention,* 13 (2–3), 131–65

Mark, K. P. (2018), 'Maintaining Sexual Desire in Long-Term Relationships: A Systematic Review and Conceptual Model', *Journal of Sex Research*, 55(4–5), 563–81

Markman, H. J., Renwick, M. J., Floyd, F. J., Stanley, S. M., and Clements, M. (1993), 'Preventing Marital Distress through Communication and Conflict Management Training: A 4 and 5 Year Follow-up', *Journal of Consulting and Clinical Psychology*, 61 (1), 70–77

Marriage and Men's Health (2010), Harvard Medical Health Watch, Harvard Health Publishing, https://www.health.harvard.edu/newsletter_article/marriage-and-mens-health

The Marriage Foundation (2016), http://marriagefoundation.org.uk/wp-content/uploads/2016/06/pdf-016.pdf

Mauer, D. E. (2018), 'Are Sexless Marriages More Common Than We Think?', *Reader's Digest*, https://www.rd.com/advice/sex/are-sexless-marriages-more-common-than-we-think/

Mills, M. (2019), 'Modern Love – Dating in the Digital Age', Notes from Tortoise Thinking

Murray, C., and Campbell, E. (2015), 'The Pleasure and Perils of Technology in Intimate Relationships', *Journal of Couple and Relationship Therapy*, 14 (2), 116–40

Office for National Statistics (2017), *Families and Households*

— (2017), *Marriage, Cohabitation and Civil Partnerships*

Oloski, K., Pavkov, T., Sweeney, K., and Wetchler, J. (2013), 'The Social Construction of Love Through Intergenerational Processes', *Contemporary Family Therapy; An International Journal*, 35 (4), 773–92

Palmer, B., and Murphy, M. (2013), 'Love', *Encyclopaedia of Health*, New York: Salem Press

Paris, W. (2010), 'Still Doing It', *Psychology Today*, 43 (3), 44

Perel, E. (2007), *Mating in Captivity*, Harper Paperback, NYC

— (2013), 'The Secret to Desire in a Long Term Relationship', TED Talk

— (2015), 'Rethinking Infidelity . . . a Talk for Anyone Who Has Ever Loved', TED Talk

Perry, Samuel L., and Schleifer, C. (2018), 'Till Porn Do Us Part? A Longitudinal Examination of Pornography Use and Divorce', *Journal of Sex Research*, 55 (3), 284–96

The Pleasure Mechanics website and podcast, https://www.pleasuremechanics.com/courses/

Rhoades, G. K., Kamp Dush, C. M., Atkins, D. C., Stanley, S. M., and Markman, H. J. (2011), 'Breaking Up is Hard to Do: The Impact of Unmarried Relationship Dissolution on Mental Health and Life Satisfaction', *Journal of Family Psychology,* 25(3), 366–74

Rosenberg, K. P. (2018), *Infidelity: Why Men and Women Cheat*, Da Capo Press

Ryff, C. D., and Singer, B. (2000), 'Interpersonal Flourishing: A Positive Health Agenda for the New Millennium', *Personality and Social Psychology Review*, 4 (1), 30–44

Scuka, R. (2015), 'A Clinician's Guide to Helping Couples Heal from the Trauma of Infidelity', *Journal of Couple and Relationship Therapy*, 14 (2), 141–68

Seligman, Martin E. P. (2002), *Authentic Happiness*, New York: Simon & Schuster

Smith, M. R., and Patterson, G. T. (1992), paper presented at Adult Children of Alcoholics Support Group, New York

Solomon, A. H. (2017), *Loving Bravely: 20 Lessons of Self-Discovery to Help You Get the Love You Want*, New York: New Harbinger Publications Inc.

Sternberg, R. J. (2004), 'A Triangular Theory of Love', in Reis, H. T., Rusbult, C. E. (eds.), *Close Relationships*, New York: Psychology Press, 258

Timmermans, E., and Bulck, J. van den (2017), 'Casual Sexual Scripts on the Screen: A Quantitative Content Analysis', *Archives of Sexual Behaviour*, 47 (5), 1481–96

Vedantam, S. (2018), 'When Did Marriage Become So Hard?', Hidden Brain Podcast

Vinopal, L. (2017), 'A Year-by-Year Guide to Your Risk of Divorce', https://www.fatherly.com/health-science/twenty-year-guide-divorce-risk/

Waldinger, R. (2015), 'What Makes a Good Life? Lessons from the Longest Study on Happiness', TED Talk

— (2017), '75-year Harvard Study of Happiness', https://news.harvard.edu

Wittenberger, J. F., and Tilson, R. L. (1980), 'The Evolution of Monogamy: Hypotheses and Evidence', *Annual Review of Ecology Systematics*, 11, 197–232

Wolfinger, N. H. (2017), 'American Generation Gap in Extramarital Sex', https://ifstudies.org/blog/number-4-in-2017-americas-generation-gap-in-extra marital-sex

Work

Armstrong, J. (2017), 'Higher Stakes: Generational Differences in Mothers' and Daughters' Feelings about Combining Motherhood with a Career', *Studies in the Maternal*, 9 (1), 3

Arnett, J. J. (2006), *Emerging Adulthood: The Winding Road, the Late Teens through the Twenties*, New York: Oxford University Press

Aron, E. N. (1999), *The Highly Sensitive Person: How to Thrive When the World Overwhelms You*, Thorsons

Barban, N., De Luna, X., Lundholm, E., Svensson, I., and Billari, F. C. (2017), 'Causal Effects of the Timing of Life-course Events: Age at Retirement and Subsequent Health', *Sociological Methods and Research*

Borelli, J. L., Nelson, K. S., River, L. M., Birkin, S. A., and Moss-Racusin, C. (2017), 'Gender Differences in Work-Family Guilt in Parents of Young Children', *Sex Roles*, 76 (5–6), 356–68

Bukodi, E., and Dex, S. (2010), 'Bad Start: Is There a Way Up? Gender Differences in the Effect of Initial Occupation on Early Career Mobility in Britain', *European Sociological Review*, 26 (4), 431–46

Chan, S., and Huff Stevens, A. (2001), 'Job Loss and Employment Patterns of Older Workers', *Journal of Labor Economics*, 19 (2), 484–521

Clance, P. R., and O'Toole, M. A. (1987), 'The Imposter Phenomenon', *Women and Therapy*, 6 (3), 51–64

Damman, M., Henkens, K., and Kalmijn, M. (2015), 'Missing Work After Retirement: The Role of Life Histories in the Retirement Adjustment Process', *Gerontologist*, 55 (5), 802–13

Davey, R., Fearon, C., and McLaughlin, H. (2013), 'Organizational Grief: An Emotional Perspective on Understanding Employee Reactions to Job Redundancy', *Development and Learning in Organizations*, 27 (2), 5–8

Dingemans, E., Henkens, K., and Van Solinge, H. (2016), 'Access to Bridge Employment: Who Finds and Who Does Not Find Work After Retirement?', *Gerontologist*, 56 (4), 630–40

Elder, G. H. (1994), 'Time, Human Agency, and Social Change: Perspectives on the Life Course', *Social Psychology Quarterly*, 57 (1), 4–15

Frey, C. B. and Osborne, Michael A., 'The Future of Employment: How Susceptible are Jobs to Computerization?', https://www.oxfordmartin.ox.ac.uk/downloads/academic/The_Future_of_Employment.pdf

Gergely, E., and Pierog, A. (July 2016), 'Motivation, Values and Career Research among University Students', *Annals of Faculty of Economics*, University of Oradea, Faculty of Economics, 1(1), 933–43

Goldman, Z. W., and Martin, M. M. (2016), 'Millennial Students in the College Classroom: Adjusting to Academic Entitlement', *Communication Education*, 65 (3), 365–7

Hall, D. T., and Chandler, D. E. (2005), 'Psychological Success: When the Career is a Calling', *Journal of Organizational Behavior*, 26, 155–76

Haynie, J. M., and Shepherd, D. (2011), 'Toward a Theory of Discontinuous Career Transition: Investigating Career Transitions Necessitated by Traumatic Life Events', *Journal of Applied Psychology*, 96 (3), 501–24

Heilman, M. E., and Okimoto, T. G. (2008), 'Motherhood: A Potential Source of Bias in Employment Decisions', *Journal of Applied Psychology*, 93 (1), 189–98

Hideg, I., Krstic, A., Trau, R. N. C., and Zarina, T. (October 2013), 'The Unintended Consequences of Maternity Leaves: How Agency Interventions Mitigate the Negative Effects of Longer Legislated Maternity Leaves', *Journal of Applied Psychology*, 103 (10), 1155–64. doi: 10.1037/apl0000327, e-pub 7 June 2018

Howker, E., and Malik, S. (2010), *The Jilted Generation: How Britain Has Bankrupted Its Youth*, Icon

Joseph Rowntree Foundation Report (2018), https://www.jrf.org.uk/report/uk-poverty-2018

Jungmeen E. K., and Moen, P. (2002), 'Retirement Transitions, Gender, and Psychological Well-Being: A Life-Course, Ecological Model', *Journals of Gerontology: Series B*, 57 (3), 212–22

Kets de Vries, M. (2003), 'The Retirement Syndrome: The Psychology of Letting Go', *European Management Journal*, 21, 707–16

Kolligian Jr, J., and Sternberg, R. J. (1991), 'Perceived Fraudulence in Young Adults: Is There an "Imposter Syndrome"?', *Journal of Personality Assessment*, 56 (2), 308

Leonard, G. (1992), *Mastery: The Keys to Success and Long-Term Fulfillment*, New York: Plume

LinkedIn Survey (November 2017), 'Research Shows 75 Per Cent of 25–33 Year Olds Have Experienced Quarter-life Crisis'

Lucking, L, (2018), '50-Plus-Year-Olds Control 75% of Britain's Housing Wealth'

McHugh, P. P. (2016), 'The Impact of Compensation, Supervision and Work Design on Internship Efficacy: Implications for Educators, Employers and Prospective Interns', *Journal of Education and Work*, 30 (4), 367–82

McKinsey Study (2017), 'Jobs Lost, Jobs Gained: Workforce Transitions in a Time of Automation'

McOrmand, T. (2004), *Changes in Working Trends over the Past Decade*, Labour Market Division, Office for National Statistics

Merkel, J. (2015), 'Coworking in the City', *Ephemera*, 15 (1), 121–39

Mitchell, K. E., Levin, A. S., and Krumboltz, J. D. (1999), 'Planned Happenstance: Constructing Unexpected Career Opportunities', *Journal of Counselling and Development*, 77 (2), 115–24

Okay-Somerville, B., and Scholarios, D. (2015), 'Position, Possession or Process? Understanding Objective and Subjective Employability during University-to-work Transitions', *Studies in Higher Education*, 42 (7), 1275–91

Oxford Martin Commission for Future Generations (2013), 'Now for the Long Term', University of Oxford, Oxford Martin School

Perlesz, A., Power, J., Brown, R., McNair, R., Schofield, M., Pitts, M., Barrett, A., and Bickerdike, A. (2010), 'Organizing Work and Home in Same-Sex Parented Families: Findings from the Love Work Play Study', *Australian and New Zealand Journal of Family Therapy*, 31 (4), 374–91

Psych Central (October 2018), '10 Tips to Build Resilience in Teens and Young Adults', American Psychological Association

Reitman, F., and Schneer, J. (2008), 'Enabling the New Careers of the 21st Century', *Organization Management Journal*, 5 (1), 17–28

Riffle, O. M. (2016), thesis, 'Posttraumatic Growth and Career Calling in Undergraduates', Charlotte, North Carolina: University of North Carolina

Robak, E. (2017), 'Generation Y on the Labour Market: Expectations for Shaping the Work–Life Balance', Working Papers 100/2017, Institute of Economic Research

Robinson, O. C. (2015), 'Emerging Adulthood, Early Adulthood and Quarter-life Crisis: Updating Erkison for the 21st Century', in Žukauskiene˙, R. (ed.), *Emerging Adulthood in a European Context*, New York: Routledge, 17–30

— (2018), 'A Longitudinal Mixed-methods Case Study of Quarter-life Crisis During the Post-university Transition: Locked-Out and Locked-In Forms in Combination', https://journals.sagepub.com/doi/abs/10.1177/216769681 8764144

Scott, A., and Gratton, L. (2016), *The 100-Year Life*, Bloomsbury

Sealy, R., and Singh, V. (2006), 'Role Models, Work Identity and Senior Women's Career Progression: Why are Role Models Important?', Academy of Management Annual Meetings Proceedings

Senge, P. M. (1990, 2006), *The Fifth Discipline: The Art and Practice of the Learning Organization*, New York: Random House

Shragai, N. (2017), 'How to Cope with Trauma in Working Life', FT.Com

Smith, J. (2103), '7 Things You Probably Didn't Know About your Job Search', https://www.forbes.com/sites/jacquelynsmith/2013/04/17/7-things-you-probably-didnt-know-about-your-job-search/#65e6c23b3811

Stăiculescu, C., Livinti, R., Stefan, L. R., Todea, S., and Albu, N. (2017), 'Managing the Need for Career Guidance and Counseling for Students Case Study', *Review of International Comparative Management,* 18 (2), 158–70

Sungdoo, K. (2018), 'Managing Millennials' Personal Use of Technology at Work', *Business Horizons,* 61 (2), 261–70

The Percentage of Women in Senior Roles Is Declining Globally (2018), https://www.catalyst.org/research/women-in-management/

Vallerand, R. (2010), 'On the Role of Passion for Work in Burnout: A Process Model', *Journal of Personality,* 8 (1), 289–312

Wiese, B. S., and Freund, A. M. (2011), 'Parents as Role Models: Parental Behavior Affects Adolescent Plans for Work Involvement', *International Journal of Behavioral Development,* 35 (3), 218–24

Willetts, D. (2010), *The Pinch,* Atlantic Books

Women More Likely to Work Part-time (2013), https://www.pewsocialtrends.org/2013/12/11/on-pay-gap-millennial-women-near-parity-for-now/sdt-gender-and-work-12-2013-1-05/

YouGov.co.uk. (2017) 'How Many Brits Like Their Jobs and Their Wages'

Health

Bowling, A., Rowe, G., and McKee, M. (2013), 'Patients' Experiences of Their Healthcare in Relation to Their Expectations and Satisfaction: A Population Survey', *Journal of the Royal Society of Medicine,* 106 (4), 143–9

Brady, G., Lowe, P., and Olin Lauritzen, S. (2015), 'Connecting a Sociology of Childhood Perspective with the Study of Child Health, Illness and Wellbeing: Introduction', *Sociology of Health and Illness,* 37 (2), 173–83

Buettner, D., (2004), 'How to Live to be 100', TED talk

Burstein, H. J., Gelber, S., Guadagnoli, E., et al. (1999), 'Use of Alternative Medicine by Women with Early Stage Breast Cancer', *New England Journal of Medicine,* 340, 1733–9

Campbell, D. (11 October 2017), 'Loneliness as Bad for Health as Long-term Illness, Says GPs' Chief', *Guardian*

— (23 January 2018), 'We'll Live Longer but Suffer More Ill-health by 2035, Says Study', *Guardian*

Chipperfield, J. G., Newall, N. E., Chuchmach, L. P., Swift, A. U., and Haynes, T. L. (2008), 'Differential Determinants of Men's and Women's Everyday Physical Activity in Later Life', *Journals of Gerontology: Series B*, 63 (4), 211–18

Clark, C., Smuk, M., Lain, D., Stansfeld, S. A., Carr, E., Head, J., and Vickerstaff, S. (2017), 'Impact of Childhood and Adulthood Psychological Health on Labour Force Participation and Exit in Later Life', *Psychological Medicine*, 47, 1597–1608

Copeland, W., Angold, A., Shonahan, L., and Costello, E. J. (2014), 'Longitudinal Patterns of Anxiety from Childhood to Adulthood: The Great Smoky Mountains Study', *Journal of the American Academy of Child and Adolescent Psychiatry*, 53 (1), 21–33

Dow, K. H., Ferrell, B. R., Leigh, S., et al. (1996), 'An Evaluation of the Quality of Life among Long-term Survivors of Breast Cancer', *Breast Cancer Research Treatment* 39, 261–73

Godfrey, M., and Townsend, J. (2008), 'Older People in Transition from Illness to Health: Trajectories of Recovery, Qualitative Health Research', 18 (7), 939–51

Golics, C. J., et al. (2013), 'The Impact of Patients' Chronic Disease on Family Quality of Life: An Experience from 26 Specialties', *International Journal of General Medicine*, 6, 787–98, e-pub 18 September 2013, doi: 10.2147/IJGM.S45156

Gostin, L. O., and Garsia, A. (2014), 'Governing for Health as the World Grows Older: Healthy Lifespans in Aging Societies', *Elder Law Journal*, (22), 111–40

Grundy, E., and Read, S. (2015), 'Pathways from Fertility History to Later Life Health: Results from Analyses of the English Longitudinal Study of Ageing', *Demographic Review*, 31 (4), 107–46

Heald, A., Vida, B., Farman, S., and Bhugra, D. (2018), 'The LEAVE Vote and Racial Abuse towards Black and Minority Ethnic Communities across the UK: The Impact on Mental Health', *Journal of the Royal Society of Medicine*, 111 (5), 158–61

Holland, J. (1999), 'Use of Alternative Medicine: A Marker for Distress', *New England Journal of Medicine*, 340, 1758–9

Hurd Clarke, L., and Griffin, M. (2008), 'Failing Bodies: Body Image and Multiple Chronic Conditions in Later Life', *Qualitative Health Research*, 18 (8), 1084–95

Jones, R. (1990), 'Expectations and Delay in Seeking Medical Care', *Journal of Social Issues*, 46 (2), 81–95

Lin, M. C., Guo, H. R., Lu, M. C., Livneh, H., Lai, N. S., and Tsai, T. Y. (2015), 'Increased Risk of Depression in Patients with Rheumatoid Arthritis: A

Seven-year Population-based Cohort Study', *Clinics (São Paulo)*, 70 (2), 91–6, doi:10.6061/clinics/2015(02)04

Ong, A. D., and Löckenhoff, C. E. (2016), 'Bridging the Dynamic Aspects of Personality and Emotion that Influence Health', *Emotion, Aging, and Health*, American Psychological Association

Patel, V. (2018), Acting Early: The Key to Preventing Mental Health Problems', *Journal of the Royal Society of Medicine*, 111 (5), 153–7

Petitte, T., et al. (2015), 'A Systematic Review of Loneliness and Common Chronic Physical Conditions in Adults', doi: 10.2174/1874350101508010113

Rabkin, J. G., Remien, R., Katoff, L., et al. (1993), 'Resilience in Adversity among Long-term Survivors of AIDS', *Hospital Community Psychiatry*, 44, 162–7

Robledo, I. (2016), 'Social-Media Hype about Diseases and Treatments Does Patients No Favors', scientificamerican.com

Schon, U.-K., Denhov, A., and Topor, A. (2009), 'Social Relationships as a Decisive Factor in Recovering from Severe Mental Illness', *International Journal of Social Psychiatry*, 55 (4), 336–47

Short, H. (1 April 2015), 'Let's Talk Menopause Because We are Failing 13 Million Women', *Guardian*, www.theguardian.com

Spiegel, D. (1999), 'Healing Words: Emotional Expression and Disease Outcome', *JAMA* Network (*Journal of the American Medical Association*) 281, 1328

Strauss J. (2013), 'The Baby Boomers Meet Menopause: Fertility, Attractiveness, and Affective Response to the Menopausal Transition', *Sex Roles*, 68 (1–2), 77–90

Thomas, C., Benzeval, M., and Stansfeld, S. (2007), 'Psychological Distress after Employment Transitions: The Role of Subjective Financial Position as a Mediator', *Journal of Epidemiology and Community Health*, 61, 48–52

Timmerman, C., & Uhrenfeldt, L. (2014), 'Room for Caring: Patients' Experiences of Well-being, Relief and Hope during Serious Illness', *Scandinavian Journal of Caring Sciences*, 29 (3), 426–34

Welsh, T. L. (2011), 'Healthism and the Bodies of Women: Pleasure and Discipline in the War against Obesity', *Journal of Feminist Scholarship*, 1, 33–48

Wicks, S. L. (2011), 'An Exploration into Identity Formation in Young People Living with a Chronic Illness', DClinPsych thesis, Canterbury: University of Kent

Wingrove, C., and Rickwood, D. (2017), 'Parents and Carers of Young People with Mental Ill-health: What Factors Mediate the Effect of Burden on Stress?', *Counselling Psychology Quarterly* 32 (1), 121–34, doi: 10.1080/09515070.2017.1384362

Wood, C. (1987), 'Are Happy People Healthier?', discussion paper, *Journal of the Royal Society of Medicine*, 80, 354–6

Identity

Anthias, F. (2009), 'Translocational Belonging, Identity and Generation: Questions and Problems in Migration and Ethnic Studies', *Finnish Journal of Ethnicity and Migration*, 4 (1), 6–15

Arbona, C., et al. (2010), 'Acculturative Stress among Documented and Undocumented Latino Immigrants in the USA', *Hispanic Journal of Behavioural Science*, 32 (3), 362–84, doi:10.1177/0739986310373210

Bromley, C., Curtice, J., and Given, L. (2007), *Attitudes to Discrimination in Scotland: 2006 Scottish Social Attitudes Survey*, Oxford: Blackwell

Burnham, J. (2013), 'Developments in Social GGRRAAACCEEESSS: Visible–Invisible, Voiced–Unvoiced', in I. Krause (ed.), *Cultural Reflexivity*, Karnac

Carothers, B. J., and Reis, H. T. (2013), 'Men and Women Are From Earth: Examining the Latent Structure of Gender', *Journal of Personality and Social Psychology*, 104 (2), 385–407

Cooley, E., Winslow, H., Vojt, A., Shein, J., and Ho, J. (2018), 'Bias at the Intersection of Identity: Conflicting Social Stereotypes of Gender and Race Augment the Perceived Femininity and Interpersonal Warmth of Smiling Black Women', *Journal of Experimental Social Psychology*, 74, 43–9

Crenshaw, K., et al. (1995), *Critical Race Theory: The Key Writings that Formed the Movement*, New York: New Press

Diamond, M. (2002), 'Sex and Gender are Different: Sexual Identity and Gender Identity are Different', *Clinical Child Psychology and Psychiatry*, 7 (3), 320–34

Drescher, J. (2010), 'Transsexualism, Gender Identity Disorder and the DSM', *Journal of Gay and Lesbian Mental Health*, 14 (2), 109–22

Dulin-Keita, A., Hannon, L., Fernandez, J. R., and Cockerham, W. C. (2011), 'The Defining Moment: Children's Conceptualization of Race and Experiences with Racial Discrimination', *Ethnic and Racial Studies*, 34 (4), 662–82

Eddo-Lodge, R. (2017), *Why I'm No Longer Talking to White People About Race*, Bloomsbury

Epstein, R., Blake, J. J., and González, T. (27 June 2017), paper, 'Girlhood Interrupted: The Erasure of Black Girls' Childhood', Washington DC: Georgetown Law Center on Poverty and Inequality, SSRN: https://ssrn.com/abstract=3000695 or http://dx.doi.org/10.2139/ssrn.3000695

Evans, G., and Mellon, J. (2016), 'Social Class: Identity, Awareness and Political Attitudes: Why are We Still Working Class?', *British Social Attitudes*, 33

Galliher, R. V., McLean, K. C., and Syed, M. (2017), 'An Integrated Developmental Model for Studying Identity Content in Context', *Developmental Psychology*, 53 (11), 2011–22

Gibson, M. A. (1997), 'Exploring and Explaining the Variability: The School Performance of Today's Immigrant Students', paper presented at the

Conference on the Second Generation, Jerome Levy Economic Institute, Bard College, http://www.levyinstitute.org/pubs/rpt2_98.pdf

Gillig, T. K., Rosenthal, E. L., Murphy, S. T., and Langrall Folb, K. (2017), 'More Than a Media Moment: The Influence of Televised Storylines on Viewers' Attitudes Toward Transgender People and Policies in Sex Roles', *Journal of Research,* 78 (7–8), 515–27

Glicksman, E. (2013), 'Gender Identity: Biology or Environment?', *American Psychological Association,* 44, 4

Hammack, P. L. (2008), 'Narrative and the Cultural Psychology of Identity', *Personality and Social Psychology Review,* 12 (3), 222–47

Heshmat, S. (2014), 'The Basics of Identity: What Do We Mean by Identity and Why Does Identity Matter?', *Psychology Today,*https://www.psychologytoday.com/gb/blog/science-choice/201412/basics-identity

Iyer, A., and Jetten, J. (2011), 'What's Left Behind: Identity Continuity Moderates the Effect of Nostalgia on Well-Being and Life Choices', *Journal of Personality and Social Psychology,* 101 (1), 94–108

James, P. (2015), 'Despite the Terrors of Typologies: The Importance of Understanding Categories of Difference and Identity', *International Journal of Postcolonial Studies,* 17 (2), 174–95

Kay, A. C., Day, M. V., Zanna, M. P., and Nussbaum, D. A. (2013), 'The Insidious (and Ironic) Effects of Positive Stereotypes', *Journal of Experimental Psychology,* 49 (2), 287–91

Losty, M., and O'Connor, J. (2017), 'Falling Outside of the "Nice Little Binary Box": A Psychoanalytic Exploration of the Non-Binary Gender Identity', *Psychoanalytic Psychotherapy,* 32 (1), 40–60

Morning, A. (2018), 'Kaleidoscope: Contested Identities and New Forms of Race Membership', *Ethnic and Racial Studies,* 41 (6), 1055–73

Norman, H., Elliot, M., and Fagan, C. (2018), 'Does Fathers' Involvement in Childcare and Housework Affect Couples' Relationship Stability?', *Social Science Quarterly,* 99 (5), 1599–1613

Parekh, B. C. (2000), *The Future of Multi-ethnic Britain,* Profile Books.

Song, M. (2018), 'Why We Still Need to Talk About Race', *Ethnic and Racial Studies,* 41 (6), 1131–45

Weedon, C. (2004), 'Identity and Culture: Narratives of Difference and Belonging', *History, Nation and Identity,* Maidenhead: Open University Press

Westrate, N. M., and McClean, K. C. (2010), 'The Rise and Fall of Gay: A Cultural-Historical Approach to Gay Identity Development', *Memory,* 18 (2), 225–40, doi: 10.1080/09658210903153923

Whittle, S., Turner, L., and Al-Alami, M. (2007), 'Engendered Penalties: Transgender and Transsexual People's Experiences of Inequality and Discrimination', *Equalities Review,* Metropolitan University, https://www.

ilga-europe.org/sites/default/files/trans_country_report_-_engenderedpen-alties.pdf

Xiaomei, Z., and Shimin, W. (2014), 'Political Identity: A Perspective from Cultural Identity', *Social Sciences in China*, 35 (2), 155–73

Ziai, R. (2017), 'The Evolutionary Roots of Identity Politics', *Areo* magazine, https://areomagazine.com/2017/08/24/the-evolutionary-roots-of-identity-politics/

Zucker, K. (1999), 'Intersexuality and Gender Identity Differentiation', *Annual Review of Sex Research*, 10 (1), 1–69

The 8 Pillars of Strength

AA World Services (2001), *Alcoholics Anonymous* (4th edn), AA Grapevine, Inc., USA

Action for Happiness , www.actionforhappiness.org

Beattie, G. (2004), *Visible Thoughts: The New Psychology of Body Language*, Routledge

Ben-Shahar, T. (2011), *Happier: Learn the Secrets to Daily Joy and Lasting Fulfillment*, New York: McGraw-Hill

Chatterjee, R. (2017), *The 4 Pillar Plan: How to Relax, Eat, Move and Sleep Your Way to a Longer, Healthier Life*, Penguin

Damasio, A. (1999), *The Feeling of What Happens: Body, Emotion and the Making of Consciousness*, Heinemann

Duggal, N. A., et al. (April 2018), 'Major Features of Immune Senescence, Including Thymic Atrophy are Ameliorated by High Levels of Physical Activity in Adulthood', *Aging Cell*, 17(2); doi:10.1111/acel.12750, e-pub 8 March 2018

Duhigg, C. (2012), *The Power of Habit*, Random House

Hone, L. (2016), *Remembering Abi*, blog:i.stuff.co.nz

Kabat-Zinn, Jon (2012), *Mindfulness for Beginners: Reclaiming the Present Moment and Your Life*, Louisville, Colorado: Sounds True

— (2001), *Full Catastrophe Living: How to Cope with Stress, Pain and Illness Using Mindfulness Meditation*, Doubleday

Lazarus, N. (2019), article commissioned by BBC, *Can Exercise Reverse the Ageing Process?* https://www.bbc.co.uk/news/health-47331544

Mehrabian, A. (1972), *Nonverbal Communication*, Chicago, Illinois: Aldine-Atherton

Mind.org.uk, 'The Mind Guide: Food and Mood'

Mindful research and evidence, https://bemindful.co.uk/evidence-research/

NICE Guidelines (2009, updated 2016), *Treatment for Mild to Moderate Depression*

Pennebaker, James W. (1997), *Opening Up: The Healing Power of Expressing Emotion*, New York: Guilford Press

— (2004), *Writing to Heal: A Guided Journal for Recovering from Trauma and Emotional Upheaval*, Oakland, California: New Harbinger Press

Pollock , R. D., et al. (2018), 'Properties of the Vastus Lateralis Muscle in Relation to Age and Physiological Function in Master Cyclists Aged 55–79 Years', *Aging Cell*, 17(2), doi: 10.1111/acel.12735, e-pub 2018

Schore, A. (2003), *Regulation and the Repair of the Self*, Norton Books

Tedeschi, R. G., and Calhoun, L. G. (2012), *Resilience: The Science of Mastering Life's Greatest Challenges*, Cambridge University Press

Trimboli, A., and Walker, M. (1987), 'Nonverbal Dominance in the Communication of Affect: A Myth?' *Journal of Nonverbal Behavior*, 11 (3), 180–190

Appendix: Lifespan Development

Bridges, W. (1980), *Transitions: Making Sense of Life's Changes*, New York: Addison-Wesley

Havighurst, R. J. (1972), *Developmental Tasks and Education* (3rd edn), New York: David McKay

Hopson, B. (1981), 'Response to the Papers by Schlossberg, Brammer and Abrego', *Counselling Psychologist*, 9, 36–9

Hopson, B., and Adams, J. (1977), *Towards an Understanding of Transition: Defining Some Boundaries of Transitions Dynamics*, Oxford: Pergamon Press

Hopson, B., Adams, J., and Hayes, J. (eds.), *Transition: Understanding and Managing Personal Change*, Martin Robinson

Newman, B., and Newman, P. (1995), *Development through Life: A Psychosocial Approach* (6th edn), Pacific Grove, California: Brooks/Cole

Schlossberg, N. K., Waters, E. B., and Goodman, J. (1995), *Counselling Adults in Transition: Linking Practice with Theory*, New York: Springer

Sugarman, L. (2001), *Lifespan Development: Frameworks, Accounts and Strategies* (2nd edn), Hove: Psychology Press

Generations

Cohe, R. (August 2017), 'Why Generation X Might be Our Last, Best Hope', *Vanity Fair*, https://www.vanityfair.com/style/2017/08/why-generation-x-might-be-our-last-best-hope

Howe, N. (2014), 'The Boom Generation: What a Long Strange Trip', *Forbes Magazine*

Patel, D. (2017), '8 Ways Generation Z Will Differ from Millennials in the Workplace', www.forbes.com/ . . ./8-ways-generation-z-will-differ-from-millennials-in-the-workplace

Petersen, A. H. (2019), 'The Burnout Generation: Millennials and the Mindset of Working All the Time', Buzzfeed

Pew Research Centre, (2018), 'Generations and Age', http://www.pewresearch.org/topics/generations-and-age/

Woodward, A. (2019), 'Millennials and GenZ are Finally Gaining Ground in the Climate Battle: Here are the Signs They're Winning', www.businessinsider.com/signs-millennials-gen-z-turning-tide-climate-change-2019-4?r=US&IR=T

Acknowledgements

Without the open-hearted and courageous generosity of my clients, who have given me permission to disguise but tell their stories or aspects of their lives, during our work together, this book would not exist. To every single one of them I am profoundly grateful for their inspirational honesty and trust in letting me describe their process of change. An overriding preoccupation while writing has been maintaining their confidentiality and anonymity – and to repeat the disclaimer personally, I have made every effort to anonymize people and actual events, while remaining true to the spirit of the work.

My literary agent Felicity Rubinstein has the magical skills of a horse whisperer. I found my absolute conviction that I was capable of writing only one book overturned in the short drive it took to get to the Hay Literary Festival. Before I knew it, I'd written a new book proposal and signed up with Viking Penguin. Thank goodness for such mystical arts. Felicity's wisdom, experience and integrity mean I am lucky enough to have one of the best agents in the business on my side. I am forever indebted to her as my agent and much-valued friend.

My stellar editor Venetia Butterfield has believed in me, encouraged me, edited this book tirelessly and with more patience than I could have mustered. She has brought all her intelligence, knowledge, focus and feistiness to bear and brought the best out of *This Too Shall Pass*. Every meeting, discussion and edit has been imbued with our deep affection, respect and trust. Thank you with all my heart.

I am grateful to Maisy Ash, who worked hard finding hundreds of excellent research articles on each topic, giving me clear notes for them all. Magdalen Howard explored the field of adult development intelligently, and distilled the research, giving me a brilliantly coherent content for the sections on lifespan development and the context and definitions for the different generations, for which I am extremely thankful. Ben Kalin's expert eye for accurate detail meant my referencing and research data is more robust.

I am immensely fortunate to have been able to call on this broad list of fantastic people who have commented on the book: I greatly appreciate the wise and insightful feedback of therapists Geraldine Thomson, Tracy Jarvis, Dr Belinda Giles and Christabel McEwan. Dr Thomas Vann gave me well-informed guidance for the section on Identity. Haydn Williams, CEO of the British Association of Counselling, gave me excellent counsel that is much appreciated. Friends both close and more distant were wonderfully generous with their time, experience and thinking: Rachel Wyndham, Catherine Soames, Juliet Nicolson, Jane Northumberland, James Leigh-Pemberton, Ann Pleshette-Murphy, Cari Rosen, Anya Hindmarch, Clare Asquith, Dr Helen Asquith, Kate Weinberg, Joanna Weinberg, Sue Peart, Cathy Rentzenbrink, Amrita Das, Fiona Golfar, Raqhee Haque, Johan Jensen and Ben Seary. To all of them I am extremely grateful for such a generous act of friendship.

I want to acknowledge the inspiration and ongoing guidance from my years of reading, writing and teaching the great psychotherapy theorists: Sigmund Freud, Carl Rogers, John Bowlby and Fritz Perls, and more recently Esther Perel, Helen Fisher and John Gottman, to name but a few. I have absorbed their ideas and made them my own but recognize the depth of their influence in me and in my writing.

In order to keep the writing flowing, I have not inserted references throughout the text. Instead they can be found in Sources, pages 303–21. Please accept my sincere apologies if there are errors of acknowledgement or omission, for which I take full responsibility.

The team at Viking Penguin have been terrific: I'd like to thank in particular Marianne Tatepo, as well as Isabel Wall,

Julia Murday, Hazel Orme, Corinna Bolino, Emma Brown and Ellie Smith.

My beloved husband, Michael, he of the five marriages, has taught me and fought me, laughed with me, driven me mad but above all loved me and let me love him for decades. His belief in me when I doubt myself, most recently as a writer, is my secret power. Our children, Natasha, Emily, Sophie and Benjamin, and their spouses, Rich, Keenan, Jake and Drusie, have all made insightful suggestions and lovingly supported me while I've been immersed in this project. I am forever thankful to them all.

Index

Page references in *italics* indicate images.

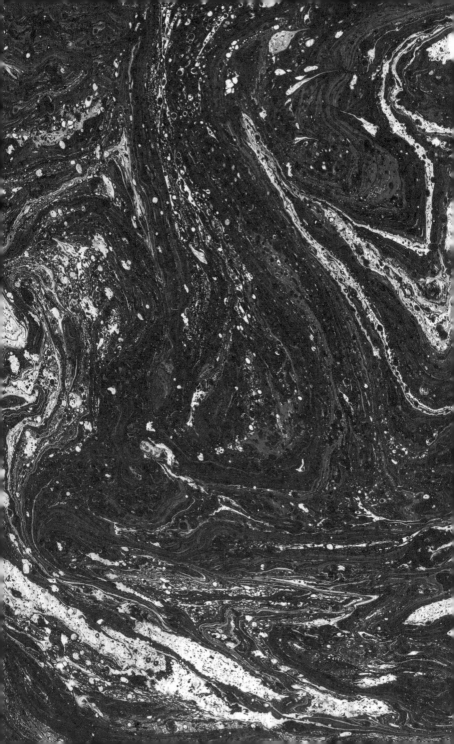